# FOSTERING COMPREHENSION
# IN ENGLISH CLASSES

**SOLVING PROBLEMS IN THE TEACHING OF LITERACY**
Cathy Collins Block, *Series Editor*

*Recent Volumes*

# Fostering Comprehension in English Classes
## Beyond the Basics

RAYMOND PHILIPPOT
MICHAEL F. GRAVES

THE GUILFORD PRESS
New York    London

© 2009 The Guilford Press
A Division of Guilford Publications, Inc.
72 Spring Street, New York, NY 10012
www.guilford.com

Printed in the United States of America

This book is printed on acid-free paper.

Last digit is print number:   9   8   7   6   5   4   3   2   1

**Library of Congress Cataloging-in-Publication Data**

Phillippot, Raymond.
    Fostering comprehension in English classes: beyond the basics / Raymond
Philippot, Michael F. Graves.
        p.   cm. — (Solving problems in teaching of literacy.)
    Includes bibliographical references and index.
    ISBN 978-1-59385-884-1 (hardcover: alk. paper)—ISBN 978-1-59385-883-4
(pbk.: alk. paper)   6 989363
    1. Reading comprehension.   2. Reading (Middle school)   3. Reading
(Secondary)   I. Graves, Michael F.   II. Title.
    LB1050.45.P47 2009
    372.41—dc22

                                                        2008026754

*To Donna, for your perpetual support and love,
and to Mike, for your mentoring
and, more important, your friendship*

—R.P.


*To the many English teachers
who inspired and taught me
as they demonstrated ways of nurturing
their students' comprehension*

—M.F.G.

# About the Authors

**Raymond Philippot, PhD,** is Department Chair and Professor of English at St. Cloud State University, St. Cloud, Minnesota. Dr. Philippot's research interests include whole-class discussions of literature, resources for struggling readers, and reading comprehension at the secondary level. Prior to joining the faculty at St. Cloud State University, he taught high school English in Kansas and Minnesota. For the past several years, he has served as the English Education Chair for the Minnesota Council of Teachers of English.

**Michael F. Graves, PhD,** is Professor Emeritus of Literacy Education at the University of Minnesota and a member of the Reading Hall of Fame. His research, development, and writing focus on vocabulary learning and instruction and comprehension instruction. Dr. Graves has served as the Editor of the *Journal of Reading Behavior* and as the Associate Editor of *Research in the Teaching of English.* He has served or is serving on the editorial review boards for *Reading Research Quarterly, Journal of Reading Behavior, Research in the Teaching of English, National Reading Conference Yearbook,* and *Journal of Reading.* His recent books include *Teaching Reading in the 21st Century* (4th edition, 2007, with Connie Juel and Bonnie Graves), *Reading and Responding in the Middle Grades* (2007, with Lee Galda), and *The Vocabulary Book* (2006). His work has also appeared in a wide range of journals. Dr. Graves currently serves as a consultant on comprehension strategies for Seward Inc.; on vocabulary instruction for SRA/McGraw Hill, the National Assessment of Adult Literacy, WGBH Television Boston, The Electric Company, and an Institute of Educational Sciences grant; and on text difficulty for the World Book.

# Acknowledgments

We wish to thank our excellent and attentive editors at The Guilford Press, Chris Jennison and Craig Thomas. Additionally, we are grateful to our production editor, Louise Farkas, for moving the book along in a timely manner. Also, we appreciate the instructive feedback from reviewers on early drafts of this book.

# Contents

# CHAPTER 1

# Our Take
# on Adolescent Literacy

Literacy development is an ongoing process, and it
requires just as much attention for adolescents as it does
for beginning readers. In today's fast-paced world, literacy
demands are expanding, and they include more reading and
writing tasks than at any other time in history. Adolescents
need high levels of literacy to understand the vast amount of
information available to them, and to fuel their imaginations
as they help create the world of the future.
                    —COMMISSION ON ADOLESCENT LITERACY

This statement, authored by Moore, Bean, Birdyshaw, and Rycik (1999) for the International Reading Association (IRA) in 1999, has been echoed in a growing number of major reports since that time, including the National Council of Teachers of English's (NCTE) *A Call to Action* (2004), the Carnegie Corporation's *Reading Next* (Biancarosa & Snow, 2004), the National Association of State Boards of Education's *Reading at Risk* (2005), the ACT's *Reading between the Lines* (2006), the Center on Instruction's *Interventions for Adolescent Struggling Readers* (2007), and the *Harvard Educational Review's* special issue on Adolescent Literacy (Ippolito, Steele, & Samson, 2008). It reflects, we believe, a widespread if not universal agreement that adolescent literacy is critically important and deserves serious attention.

Unfortunately, over the nearly 10 years that have elapsed since Moore and his colleagues' statement, this widespread agreement seems not to have been accompanied with much action. Scores on the National Assessment of Educational Progress (NAEP), the best national data we have on students' reading proficiency, have remained largely stagnant. Federal support for adolescent literacy continues to be minimal. Last year, for example, the U.S. Department of Education inaugurated with much fanfare the Striving Reading program for underachieving adolescent readers, allocating a total $250 million to the effort. This, however, is a paltry sum compared to the nearly $4 billion the No Child Left Behind (NCLB) program has spent to improve the reading of primary grade students. Furthermore, as we talk to teachers and visit schools, we find relatively little attention to adolescent literacy; and teachers report that they are largely on their own to do—or not do—something to improve their students' literacy.

It is certainly the case that individual teachers can do only a certain amount to increase the literacy skills of secondary students, that ideally schoolwide programs that involve both reading and writing specialists and content teachers in areas such as science, social studies, and health need to be developed. But until more schoolwide programs are developed, it is up to individual teachers, with English teachers unfortunately but not surprisingly shouldering much of the burden. While as an English teacher you are unlikely to have had much training in teaching reading, you have had a good deal of training in teaching literature and writing; you know much more about language than your colleagues in other disciplines; and you are better prepared than other teachers to assist students in becoming stronger readers. The purpose of this book is to give you the knowledge and skills you need to successfully lead all of your students to better comprehend, learn from, and appreciate what they read. We want to emphasize the phrase all of your students. Our goal is to help you lead all of your students— struggling readers, high achievers, and the many students in between these two groups—to achieve the highest level of literacy possible.

In the remainder of this chapter, we briefly describe what we know about U.S. adolescents' reading proficiency, introduce five facets of comprehension that we focus on, and briefly discuss the major theories and instructional considerations that inform the approaches we advocate. We also discuss the centrality of motivation, consider ways of giving struggling readers and English language learners (ELLs) special assistance, and describe the organization and contents of this book.

## Adolescents' Reading Proficiency

It is all too frequently said that U.S. students' literacy skills are "going to pot"—that U.S. students read far less well than they did in the past and far less well than their classmates in other countries. The data do not support these assertions. The NAEP has systematically collected data on students' reading proficiency for the past 35 years. Figure 1.1 shows the results of 11 NAEP tests administered over the past 35 years. While scores have fluctuated a bit, for all practical purposes the average reading proficiency of U.S. students' today is the same as it was in 1971; in fact, for 17-year-olds it is exactly the same. Although international comparisons are difficult to make, the data from such comparisons tell a similarly nondramatic story. U.S. students are certainly not at the top in international comparisons, but neither are they at the bottom. For example, in the most recent international survey for which we have data, the Programme for International Student Assessment (PISA) 2003 (Organisation for Economic Co-operation and Development, 2004), U.S. students ranked 18th among the 40 nations tested.

What is true, and what can be found from both the U.S. data and in the international comparisons, is that U.S. adolescents' reading proficiency is more diverse than that of students in many other countries. There are more students at the bottom and fewer students at the top. Additionally, there are many fewer U.S. students achieving higher levels of proficiency than there need to be. The NAEP, for example, ranks performance as basic (denotes partial mastery of skills necessary), proficient (represents solid academic performance), and advanced (signifies

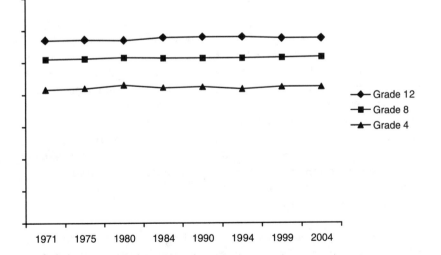

**FIGURE 1.1.** National assessment results, 1971–2004. Data from the National Center for Education Statistics (2005).

superior performance). In the most recent NAEP report (Perie, Grigg, & Donahue, 2006), 29% of U.S. eighth graders scored below the basic level, 42% at the basic level, 26% at the proficient level, and only 3% at the advanced level. Tragically, students of color, students of poverty, and ELLs scored well below these averages. We simply cannot afford to have this many students at or below the basic level, this few students at or above the advanced level, or large differences between the haves and the have-nots in our society. As the authors of the RAND Reading Study Group (2002) note, "The U.S. economy today demands a universally higher level of literacy achievement than at any other time in history, and it is reasonable to believe that the demand for a literate populace will increase in the future." It is not, we would add, just the U.S. economy that demands this higher level of literacy. Negotiating today's world, reaping some reasonable share of the benefits our society has to offer, reading for both pleasure and to better understand the world, and leading a fruitful and rewarding life similarly demands higher levels of literacy.

## Five Facets of Comprehension

The widely publicized report of the National Reading Panel (2000) has identified five components of effective reading programs: phonemic awareness, phonics, fluency, vocabulary, and comprehension. By the time they get to the secondary grades, most students, even struggling readers, have mastered phonemic awareness and phonics and achieved some level of fluency. All secondary students, however, need to continue to build their vocabularies and to bolster their comprehension skills. While helping students build their vocabularies is a significant task, it is a circumscribed one, and we deal with it in a single chapter. The task of helping students bolster their comprehension skills is a much less circumscribed and more challenging one, and it is the major task we address in this book. Specifically, this book is built around a five-facet approach to comprehension instruction. We list and very briefly define each of these five facets below and then deal with each of them in detail in the core chapters of this book.

1. *Fostering learning from text*—Providing students with a combination of prereading, during-reading, and postreading activities that assist them in understanding, learning from, and enjoying each and every text they read.

2. *Teaching for understanding*—Treating important topics in depth so that students thoroughly understand these topics, remember important parts of what they read, and can use the knowledge they gain from reading in school and in their lives outside of school.
3. *Nurturing response to literature*—Recognizing that literature leads to both cognitive and affective outcomes and assisting students in responding to literature in a variety of ways.
4. *Teaching comprehension strategies*—Assisting students in becoming independent readers by ensuring that they master strategies such as predicting, summarizing, and being metacognitive.
5. *Promoting higher-order thinking*—Providing students with both instruction and rich opportunities to engage in analysis, synthesis, evaluation, and other thought-demanding activities.

In many classrooms we have observed and in at least some of the literature on reading and English education, these facets receive very uneven attention. In fact, we find some English classes that are almost solely focused in learning from text and others that are nearly exclusively concerned with response to literature. The preponderance of the attention to comprehension in the literature on reading instruction, on the other hand, is focused on strategies (see, e.g., Pressley, 2006). To ensure that each of these important facets of comprehension gets appropriate attention, we treat each of them in a separate chapter. However, that does not mean that they are unrelated or need be separated from each other in the classroom. They are interrelated in many ways and are often intertwined in classroom activities. For example, when teaching for understanding, multiple texts are often used, and teachers use learning from text activities to assist students with those texts; both response to literature and higher-order thinking are often part of learning from text; and students use comprehension strategies in learning from text, understanding topics deeply, and engaging in critical thinking.

## Theories Informing Our Understanding of Comprehension

A number of theoretical considerations underlie our understanding of comprehension and our suggestions for promoting comprehension. The most important of these come from cognitive psychology, the social-constructivist orientation, and reader-response theory.

## Cognitive Theories

The three concepts emerging from cognitive psychology that have most influenced our approach are schema theory, the interactive model, and metacognition.

### Schema Theory

One of the central theories of cognitive psychology and one of the most important concepts influencing current thinking about reading involve that of schemata (the plural of *schema*). Schemata are units of knowledge that individuals internalize. As Rumelhart (1980) has pointed out, they constitute our knowledge about "objects, situations, events, sequences of events, actions, and sequences of actions." We have schemata for objects, such as cars; for situations, such as being in a restaurant; for events, such as weddings; and for sequences of actions, such as driving to and from work. Schemata constitute our knowledge about the world. We make sense out of what we read by attempting to fit the information we glean from a text to an existing schema. If, for example, we read about a waitperson serving a meal, we immediately evoke our restaurant schema, and evoking that schema provides us with a wealth of information beyond that in the text. We know that customers can order a variety of foods from a menu, that the waitperson will bring their food, and that they will need to pay for it when they are finished.

Among the types of schemata that influence our understanding as we read are general knowledge of the world and its conventions; specific knowledge about various subjects; and linguistic knowledge, which includes the understanding of different patterns of textual organization. Importantly, having appropriate schemata for texts we read is crucial to understanding. As Adams and Bruce (1982) put it, "Without prior knowledge, a complex object such as a text is not just difficult to interpret; strictly speaking, it is meaningless."

### The Interactive Model of Reading

The interactive model of reading, another concept advanced by Rumelhart (1977), complements the concept of schema theory. As described by the interactive model, readers arrive at meaning by simultaneously using information from several knowledge sources. These knowledge sources include letter-level knowledge, word-level knowledge, syntactic knowledge, and various types of world knowledge or schemata. Information moves simultaneously in two directions; the reader's background knowledge and the information that she gleans from the text interact to produce meaning.

Recognizing that reading is an interactive process serves as a caution against overemphasizing the role of readers' schemata in text comprehension. As we noted, readers' schemata are vital to their understanding of texts; however, that does not mean texts are unimportant (Stanovich, 1994). For example, you would not understand much about the scoring of surfing championships unless you knew something about surfing. However, a *Sports Illustrated* article about surfing on the Big Island will convey a very different meaning than a *Teen People* story about the boys who surf near Laguna Beach. Although no text is ever fully explicit, neither are texts vacuous. Texts constrain meaning. Good readers learn to rely appropriately on the text and on prior knowledge, and to adjust their relative reliance on the two for a particular text and a particular situation.

## Metacognition

As applied to reading, metacognition refers to a person's knowledge about her understanding of a text and about what to do when comprehension breaks down. As Garner (1987) has noted, accomplished readers have metacognitive knowledge about themselves, the reading tasks they face, and the strategies they can employ in completing these tasks. For example, on beginning this section a reader might realize that she has no prior knowledge about metacognition (self-knowledge), notice that the section is brief (task knowledge), and decide that the strategy of reading the section through several times would be fruitful (strategy knowledge).

In this example, the reader exhibited metacognitive knowledge prior to beginning reading. However, readers can also make use of metacognitive knowledge as they are reading or after they have completed a text. In fact, active awareness of one's comprehension while reading and the ability to use effective fix-up strategies when comprehension breaks down are essential to becoming an effective reader, and lack of such metacognitive skills is viewed as a particularly debilitating characteristic of poor readers.

Whimby (1975) has given a particularly insightful characterization of a metacognitive reader.

A good reader proceeds smoothly and quickly as long as his understanding of the material is complete. But as soon as he senses that he has missed an idea, that the track has been lost, he brings smooth progress to a grinding halt. Advancing more slowly, he seeks clarification in the subsequent material, examining it for the light it can throw on the earlier trouble spot. If still dissatisfied with his grasp, he returns to the point where the difficulty began and rereads the section more carefully. He probes and analyzes phrases and sentences for their exact meaning; he tries to visualize abstruse descriptions; and through a series of approximations, deductions, and corrections, he translates scientific and technical terms into concrete examples. (p. 91)

Teaching students to be metacognitive is one of the most important and challenging tasks you face, and it is a task we address in detail in Chapter 5.

Good readers, then, bring their schemata to each text they read, and the meaning they gain from the text is influenced by both these schemata and the text itself. They focus on meaning and are metacognitive as they read, noticing if they stop understanding the text. Noticing difficulties allows them to employ various strategies to get them back on the road to meaning. In this view of reading, the reader is actively engaged in constructing knowledge from text. This active construction is an integral part of another theoretical orientation that has shaped our view of teaching and learning, social constructivism.

## The Social-Constructivist Orientation

The social-constructivist orientation has become increasingly influential in education over the past two decades (see Fosnot, 1996; Phelps, 2005) and serves as an excellent complement to cognitive theories. Here, we discuss three aspects of constructivist thinking and its relevance to teaching. First, we discuss the general concept of constructivism; next, we deal specifically with social constructivism; and, finally, we consider the importance the social-constructivist orientation gives to the contexts in which students learn.

### Constructivism

Much of the meaning an individual derives from a situation is constructed by the individual herself. For those who take a strong constructivist position, our knowledge of the world—whether it is knowledge gained from a text or knowledge from any other source—is not the result of phenomena in the real world. It is the result of our interpretation of those phenomena. The meaning we attain is, in fact, constructed by ourselves. Inherent tendencies in the ways we think, categorize, and process information shape the meanings we construct.

## Social Constructivism

Social constructivism begins with acceptance of the basic constructivist position, but then goes beyond this to take the position that it is the social world within which we live—our interactions with our friends, acquaintances, and the larger community—that shapes our understanding of reality. As Gergen (1985) has explained, we understand the world in terms of social considerations, considerations that are themselves the result of interchanges among people. Therefore, the process of understanding is not a direct outcome of viewing the real world; rather, it is influenced greatly by the social world in which we live. Social constructivism is a relativistic notion; because our social backgrounds vary, whether we are interpreting a text or some other phenomena, we do not all see the same thing.

Social-constructivist thinking has significantly influenced educational practice. It is one of the factors motivating the interest in small-group work and rich classroom discussion. If much of what a child learns or understands comes from her social interactions with others, then schools need to provide students with many opportunities for productive social interactions. We certainly agree with this position, and we point out opportunities for cooperative work throughout this book.

## The Significance of Context

Social-constructivist thinking has also led educators to a realization of the importance of the contexts of students' learning. Contexts include the texts students read, the immediate context of the classroom, and the larger context of the place of reading in their world outside of school.

Literacy educators have come to believe that the majority of the texts that students read should be authentic and complete. Authentic texts are those written by authors for the primary purpose of engaging or informing children and adolescents. These are contrasted with contrived texts, those written or modified by educators for the purpose of teaching some sort of reading skills. While the occasional use of contrived texts can be an efficient way to teach a particular skill or strategy, authentic, complete texts ought to be the basic reading fare in any classroom. When contrived texts are used in initial instruction, it is vital that students work with the newly learned material or skill in an authentic context, with authentic texts, as soon as possible. Until students can use what you are teaching in contexts that are meaningful and functional, the skills and material that you teach are, in a very real sense, meaningless.

The broader context in which children read—the literate environment in the classroom and the literate environment in their worlds—is the final context to consider. These contexts have a great influence on students' motivation and engagement. If students cannot see a meaningful reason to engage in the task of becoming fully literate, they are unlikely to put much effort into the task. Creating a supportive and vibrant literate environment in the classroom and helping students understand the uses and power of literacy in their own lives are crucial parts of teaching, particularly for secondary students.

## Reader-Response Theory

Reader-response theory is very consistent with constructivist theories but has different roots and deals specifically with reading, particularly with reading literature. Reader-response theory originated some years ago with the work of I. A. Richards (1929) and Louise Rosenblatt (1938/1995), but was slow to influence classroom instruction. Over the past 30 years, however, it has become a very prominent influence on literature instruction (Beach, 1993; Galda & Graves, 2007; Galda & Guice, 1997). Reader-response theory puts a good deal of emphasis on the reader and on the transaction that takes place between the reader and the text. It stresses that the meaning one gains from text is the result of a transaction between the reader and the text and that readers will have a range of responses to literary works. Readers bring their experience, expectations, knowledge, preferences, attitudes, values, beliefs, and varying degrees of reading proficiency to the act of reading (Rosenblatt, 1938/1995, 1978). Of course, the text itself, the words on the page, serve to guide and shape the meaning that readers create, but when reading complex literary texts students will derive a variety of interpretations. Many literary texts simply do not have a single correct interpretation; and readers should be allowed and encouraged to construct a variety of interpretations—if they can support them.

One important fact to keep in mind when considering reader-response theory is that much of it applies primarily to certain types of texts and certain purposes for reading. As part of explaining when and where reader-response theory applies, Rosenblatt (1978) points out that there are two primary types of reading—efferent or informational reading and aesthetic reading. In efferent reading, the reader's attention is focused primarily on what she will take from the reading—what information will be learned. Much of the reading that both students and adults do is done for the sake of learning new information, answering questions, discovering how to complete a procedure, or gleaning knowledge that can be used in solving a particular problem. Much of the reading done in such subjects as health, science, math, and geography is informational reading. These texts, unlike many literary texts, often constrain meaning substantially, do not invite a variety of interpretations, and should yield quite similar interpretations for various readers (Stanovich, 1994).

The other sort of reading Rosenblatt considers, aesthetic reading, is quite different. In aesthetic reading, the primary concern is not with what students remember about a text after they have read it but with what happens to them as they are reading. The primary purpose when reading aesthetically is not to gain information but to experience the text. Although the aesthetic reader, like the reader whose goal is gaining information, must understand the text, she must "also pay attention to associations, feelings, attitudes, and ideas" (Rosenblatt, 1978) that the text arouses. For the most part, literature is written to provide an aesthetic experience. Most adults read literature for enjoyment; they do not read literature to learn it. And students need to be given opportunities to do the same.

As Galda and Graves (2007) note, regardless of whether students are doing informational reading or aesthetic reading, reader-response theory stresses that reading is a social process. Although we often think of reading as something we do alone, even when we read silently alone in a room, we are part of a "community of readers" (Fish, 1980). While some readers belong to many reading communities, for most secondary students the primary community of readers is made up of their teachers and peers in the classroom. This community generates expectations that influence how we read and how we respond to what we read. We learn ways of approaching texts from the directions for reading that we are given, the assignments that we complete, and the responses of others in that community. What we talk about and how we talk about it are structured by the teacher and others who comprise the classroom community. When individual readers share their personal meanings with others, these meanings become part of a socioculturally constructed interpretation of a text. We test, alter, and enlarge our meaning as we talk about texts with others, or respond through writing, acting, singing, or drawing. As we share our personal meanings with others, their own responses to the text and to our interpretations become part of our experience and thus of our responses. Additionally, other books that we have read influence the meaning that we create.

There is an even broader community at work in shaping how readers read as well as how writers write. Broad cultural expectationsinfluence how we read, and the values, attitudes, and world views that readers bring to any text interact with the values, ideas, and world view of the author who has created that text. When what we read reflects our social and cultural understandings and beliefs, it is difficult to notice how that influences our reading, but when we read books that challenge our assumptions, these assumptions become evident. For example, in reading a story set in San Francisco in which a young boy is awakened by thunder and high wind, calls for his mother and then easily goes back to sleep, a Californian (having grown up in a state where storms are rare and seldom severe) might find little to draw her attention. However, in reading a story set in New Orleans in which a young boy is awakened by thunder and high wind, screams in terror, wails for his mother, and cannot go back to sleep, that same Californian might pause, consider the boy's reaction, and then realize that the boy was probably a victim of Katrina and is likely to be terrified of storms for years to come.

As Galda and Graves (2007) also note, reader-response theory makes it clear that when readers engage with texts they have the opportunity to transform themselves, increase their knowledge, and build values. Reading nonfiction texts transforms the knowledge readers hold as they take in new information and alter concepts. Reading fiction and poetry transforms readers through the creation of virtual experiences that add to their real-world experiences. This increased repertoire of experience offers readers more opportunities for understanding both literature and life. The opportunity to help students shape the way they look at and interact with the world is perhaps the most exciting aspect of teaching literature. The books students read and how they read them will make a difference.

To summarize, our view of the reading process is influenced by cognitive psychology, the social-constructivist orientation, and reader-response theory. According to this view, the reader is an actively engaged member of various social communities who uses various sorts of prior knowledge and information from the text in constructing meaning for what she reads.

# Instructional Considerations

A variety of instructional considerations influence us as we plan comprehension instruction, or for that matter any other instruction. Here are those we find most relevant to comprehension instruction.

## Active Teaching

The term *active teaching* refers to a set of principles and teaching behaviors that teacher effectiveness research has shown to be particularly effective, especially in teaching basic skills. As noted by Brophy (1986) teachers who engage in active teaching are the instructional leaders of their classrooms; they are fully knowledgeable about the content and purposes of the instruction they present and about the instructional goals they wish to accomplish. Active teachers do a lot of teaching. Additionally, although they use a variety of materials as part of their teaching, they do not rely on materials to do the teaching. They directly carry the content to be learned to students in short presentations, discussions, and demonstrations.

## Active Learning

Just as it is vital that the teacher be actively involved in teaching, it is also crucial that the learner be actively involved in learning (Good & Brophy, 2003). The learner must do something with the material she is studying if she is to learn much from it. Thus, following initial instruction, active teachers provide students with rich opportunities for practice, application, and inquiry.

## Scaffolding

We believe that the term *scaffolding* was first used in its educational sense by Wood, Bruner, and Ross (1976), who used it to characterize mothers' verbal interaction when reading to their young children. In these interactions, mothers gently yet supportively guide their children toward successful literacy experiences. Thus, for example, in sharing a picture book with a child and attempting to assist the child in reading the words that label the pictures, a mother might at first simply page through the book familiarizing the child with the pictures and the general content of the book. Then, she might focus on a single picture and ask the child what it is. After this, she might point to the word below the picture, tell the child that the word names the picture, ask the child what the word is, and provide feedback on the correctness of the answer. The important point to focus on is that the mother has neither simply told the child the word nor simply asked the child to say it. Instead, she has built an instructional structure, a scaffold, that assists the student in learning. Scaffolding, as Wood et al. (1976) have aptly put it, is "a process that enables a child or novice to solve a problem, carry out a task, or achieve a goal which would be beyond his [or her] unassisted efforts."

Scaffolding is widely used in the world outside of school, and one particular instance of out-of-school scaffolding—the use of training wheels on children's bicycles—serves as a graphic example of the procedure. Training wheels are supportive; they enable a novice bicycle rider to do something she might not otherwise be able to do—ride a two wheeler. Equally important, training wheels are temporary, and they can be gradually raised so that the budding bicycle rider increasingly assumes the task of riding the two wheeler with less and less support from the scaffold.

Scaffolding is also widely used in schools, and it should be. For example, a teacher is scaffolding students' learning when she cues students to particularly relevant passages to consider in interpreting a challenging short story or explains the organization of a difficult chapter they are about to read. A teacher is also providing scaffolding when she models the thought processes she uses in determining what is particularly important in an informational selection students are about to read, and when she suggests a way to begin an essay they are writing. In each of these cases, the teacher is assisting students in doing something that they might not otherwise be able to do, or not be able to do as well. Chapter 2 describes ways to build supportive scaffolds for the many different types of reading students do.

## The Zone of Proximal Development

The concept of the zone of proximal development (Vygotsky, 1978) places major emphasis on the social nature of learning and emphasizes the fact that learning is very much a social phenomenon. As we have noted, we learn much of what we learn in our social interchanges with others. The notion is therefore very consistent with constructivist theory. At any particular point in time, students have a circumscribed zone of development, a range within which they can learn. At one end of this range are learning tasks that they can complete independently; at the other end are learning tasks that they cannot complete, even with assistance. In between these two extremes is the zone most productive for learning, the range of tasks at which students can achieve *if* they are assisted by some more knowledgeable or more competent other.

If left on their own, for example, many ninth graders might learn very little from the chapter "Documentation: Citing Sources in Text" in the *MLA Handbook for Writers of Research Papers* (Gibaldi, 2003). But, with your assistance in explaining why outside sources are essential in writing a research paper and guiding them through what types of sources are particularly useful, these same students may be able to learn a good deal from the chapter. However, when approaching other topics and other texts—for example, with a chapter on "Kairos and the Rhetorical Situation" in Crowley and Hawhee's (1999) *Ancient Rhetorics for Contemporary Students*—no amount of outside help, at least no reasonable amount of outside help, will foster much learning for most ninth graders. The topic of kairos and rhetorical situations is simply beyond most ninth graders' zone of proximal development.

Outside of school, many people can and do serve as more knowledgeable or more competent others—parents and foster parents, brothers and sisters, relatives, friends, and clergy. You may occasionally be able to bring in outside resources to assist students. More often, however, you will arrange reading situations so that you serve as the more knowledgeable other who assists students in successfully reading selections they could not read on their own. Additionally, in many cases students will be able to pool their resources and assist each other in dealing with reading selections they could not successfully deal with alone.

### The Gradual Release of Responsibility Model

The gradual release of responsibility model depicts a progression in which students gradually assume increased responsibility for their learning. A particularly informative visual representation of the model developed by Pearson and Gallagher (1983) is shown in Figure 1.2. The model depicts a temporal sequence in which students gradually progress from situations in which the teacher takes the majority of the responsibility for their successfully completing a reading task (in other words, does most of the work for them), to situations in which students assume increasing responsibility for reading tasks, and finally

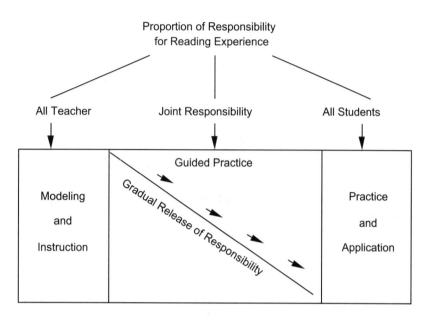

**FIGURE 1.2.** The gradual release of responsibility model.

to situations in which students take total or nearly total responsibility for reading tasks. At this point, you may be thinking that the gradual release model suggests that over the school years the teacher simply gives students increased responsibility, but the situation is somewhat more complex than that. As students progress through school, they certainly assume increased responsibility for their learning, and over time the goal is to gradually dismantle the scaffolds we have built so that students become increasingly independent readers. However, students do not repeatedly read the same sorts of text or face the same tasks over time. Instead, over time, students deal with increasingly challenging texts and with increasingly complex tasks. At any particular point in time, they are likely to be—and should be—dealing with some texts and tasks that are more challenging and some that are less challenging.

Many middle school students will be able to take full responsibility for reading an easy novel such as Pam Munoz Ryan's *Esperanza Rising*. These same students may need you to assume some of the responsibility for their successfully dealing with a more challenging novel such as

Karen Hesse's *Out of the Dust*, and they may require you to assume a great deal of the responsibility for their successfully dealing with Walter Dean Meyers's *Monster*. Many senior high students, however, could deal independently with *Out of the Dust* and would need only a little assistance from you in dealing with *Monster*. But these same senior high students would need considerably more assistance from you in dealing with Maxine Hong Kingston's *The Woman Warrior*. Even graduate students profit from scaffolding with particularly challenging texts or ones they need to understand thoroughly. For example, graduate seminars frequently center on thoroughly understanding a recent text. Thus, the scaffolding that you provide and the extent to which you release responsibility to students is always dependent on the particular texts and tasks that they are working with.

### Cognitive Modeling

Modeling is one very important tool to use as part of active teaching. When teachers model, they actually *do* something rather than just tell students how to do it. A specific sort of modeling, cognitive modeling, is particularly useful in teaching students difficult concepts and strategies. Cognitive modeling consists of teachers using explicit instructional talk to reveal their thought processes in performing the tasks they are asking students to perform. For example, a teacher might model the mental process of considering the symbolism in a poem like Nikki Giovanni's "Ego Tripping."

> "I know from reading lots of poems that titles are very important. When someone mentions ego tripping, they're referring to a person's thinking very highly of himself or herself, so I'll keep that in mind as I go. I notice that in the first stanza alone there are several references to Africa: the Congo, the fertile crescent, a sphinx, and a pyramid. Knowing that the author, Nikki Giovanni, is African American, I think it's possible that she is proud of her African roots and wants to affirm her heritage. One line even reads, 'I walked to the fertile crescent and built the sphinx.' Now, I can't take her literally, so I think I might be on the right path with my idea."

A teacher might also sometimes model very different processes, like how she assesses a website she hasn't used before.

"Okay, I wanted some critical information on Tim O'Brien's *The Things They Carried* so I typed the title into Google and among other things got a URL for BookRags, *www.bookrags.com/notes/tttc/*. The first thing I notice is the .com suffix. Okay, it's a commercial site, so they are probably trying to sell me something. The next thing I consider is the site's name, BookRags, pretty informal. I'm a bit suspicious at this point. But then I look at the content of the review; it's 54 pages and includes such things as an author biography, the context of the work, a plot summary, character descriptions, quotes, ways to track themes like bravery and truth, and chapter summaries. I read the plot summary, and it is well done. I also find a note that explains, 'Our notes contain minimal analysis, so you are free to form your own opinion about the literary work.' I like that. I'm going to give the site a try and see if it is something I want to use from time to time."

Such modeling is a window on the mind and one of the most powerful tools for showing students how to reason as they seek to understand a text.

### Integrated Literacy Instruction

Gavalek, Raphael, Biondo, and Wang (2000) note that integrated literacy instruction is authentic and more efficient compared with instruction that treats the language arts separately. It is more authentic because real-world literacy tasks typically involve several types of literacy, and it is more efficient because working with each of the language arts frequently reinforces students' competency with the others. Thus, while we give the majority of our attention to reading throughout this book, we also emphasize the importance of integrating reading with other language arts, most notably with writing and with discussion.

At one time, reading instruction, at least reading instruction for elementary students, was deliberately separated from writing instruction, which was usually taught during a separate time of day. As virtually all contemporary literacy educators would agree, this was a terrible situation. While most of this book focuses on reading, we want to stress that we see writing as a vital part of the English classroom. In each of the facets of the comprehension curriculum we outline in this book—learning from text, teaching for understanding, responding to literature, working with comprehension strategies, and engaging in higher-order thinking—students need to engage in a good deal of writing.

Discussion is another vitally important tool students need to engage in frequently as they become increasingly sophisticated at comprehending text (Alvermann, 2000). In particular, they need to engage in what Pearson (2005) has called "rich talk about text." Rich talk about text means substantial, well-informed, sophisticated discussions about texts that students have read carefully and are very knowledgeable about. In such discussions, there are no predetermined outcomes. There are real issues at stake; students marshal and support arguments, listen to each other, and come to some conclusions. Sometimes these conclusions will reflect a consensus, but in other cases, members of the group will reach different conclusions and admit that they do not agree with each other. As is the case with writing, students need to engage in rich discussions as part of working with all the facets of comprehension.

### Cooperative Learning

Johnson, Johnson, and Holubec (1994), probably the most prolific researchers and advocates of cooperative learning, define cooperative learning as "the instructional use of small groups so that students work together to maximize their own and each other's learning." As these authors have repeatedly said, "None of us is as smart as all of us." Groups of students working together have the potential to achieve well beyond the achievement of a student working by herself. Importantly, recent theory and research have emphasized that effective groups need to engage in substantive and authentic discussions in which students have significant goals and in Langer's (2001) words "sharpen their understandings with, against, and from each other." Additionally, research has shown that working in cooperative groups can produce multiple benefits. Cooperative learning can improve students' achievement, their effort to succeed, their critical thinking, their attitudes toward the subjects studied, their psychological adjustment, and their self-esteem. Cooperative learning can also foster students' interpersonal relationships, improve their ability to work with others, and build interrelations among diverse racial, ethnic, and social groups.

Cooperative learning is consistent with many constructivist principles we have mentioned. It relies on the belief that the best learning is often social, gives students an opportunity to scaffold each other's work, and puts students in a position to respond to and elaborate on each other's thinking. Because of its great potential, throughout this book we frequently suggest group activities.

## The Centrality of Motivation

Having discussed the theories and instructional considerations that underlie our understanding of comprehension and approaches to promoting comprehension, we turn now to the special case of motivation. Although motivation has not received nearly as much attention as cognition or nearly the attention it deserves, we now understand its huge importance and absolute necessity (see, e.g., Elliot & Dweck, 2005; National Research Council, 2004; Phelps, 2005). Motivation is particularly important for secondary students. Most children arrive at the doors of kindergarten and first grade classes eager and excited about learning to read and confident that they can learn. By fourth grade, however, large numbers of children have lost that motivation and confidence, and by the secondary grades many more students have lost it. This is a tragedy for all students, but as the National Research Council (2004) recently pointed out it is particularly tragic for less-advantaged students, who without motivation are in danger of dropping out of school and facing the many long-term consequences of doing so.

Fortunately, although motivation has not received the attention it deserves, we have still managed to learn a great deal about how to promote it, and what we have learned points to some powerful, straightforward, and widely applicable principles. Here we present these principles as a brief list. We derived the list primarily from the work of Alvermann, Hinchman, Moore, Phelps, and Waff (2006), Brophy (1987), the National Research Council (2004), and Pressley (2006).

- Be respectful of individual students and of their social, cultural, and linguistic backgrounds. Respect, recognize, and celebrate the diversity of today's classrooms.
- Do everything possible to ensure student success. This means finding out what your students can do and then either giving them tasks they are capable of doing independently or scaffolding their efforts at more challenging tasks.
- Present appropriate challenges. Ensuring success does not mean giving students only easy tasks. Grappling with challenging tasks and succeeding at them is a very rewarding experience.
- Scaffold students' learning. We discuss a particular form of scaffolding, scaffolding students' comprehension of individual texts, in Chapter 2. Scaffolding also plays a large role in the other facets of comprehension instruction we describe in this book.

- Support risk taking and help students understand and accept that failures will sometimes occur.
- Encourage students to attribute their successes to their efforts and realize that additional effort can help avoid failures.
- Favor depth of coverage over breadth of coverage. Virtually all topics are interesting once you know something about them.
- Communicate to students that academic tasks often require significant attention and effort.

For more details on these principles, we particularly recommend the National Research Council's *Engaging Schools* (2004) and the chapter on motivation in Galda and Graves's *Reading and Responding in the Middle Grades* (2007).

## Special Considerations for Struggling Readers and ELLs

As we have noted, this book is designed to assist you in improving the comprehension of all of your students—gifted learners, average students, struggling readers, and ELLs. All students need and deserve instruction, support, and varied experiences with all five facets of comprehension we discuss. Thus, for example, gifted learners, and not just struggling readers, will profit from your assistance in learning from difficult texts. Similarly, struggling readers and ELLs, and not just gifted and average students, need and will profit from opportunities to work with higher-level thinking. That said, the range of reading abilities in the secondary grades is enormous, and different students will need different types of assistance. Here we make four recommendations for working with both struggling readers who speak English as their native language and ELLs who struggle with reading.

First, for struggling readers and ELLs who lack basic phonics and other decoding skills, our strong recommendation is that you get help from a reading or ELL specialist. As classroom teachers, you simply do not have the time to devote to these students that they need to succeed. In arranging such outside help, three things seem crucial: (1) you need to seek out the specialist and facilitate the intervention; with the huge load specialists have, they need your help in identifying the students most in need; (2) the aid should come at a time when it does not take the student away from other crucial learning; it seldom makes sense to shorten the time an ELL spends in English class; and (3) you need to coordinate your in-class efforts with the efforts of the specialist, for example, by providing alternate readings that better match your less skilled students' capabilities.

Second, since this book does not deal in depth with struggling readers or ELLs, we would like to suggest some other books that can be particularly helpful. These include *What Really Matters for Struggling Readers* (Allington, 2001), *Making Content Comprehensible for English Language Learners: The SIOP Model* (Echevarria, Vogt, & Short, 2004), *Scaffolding Reading Experiences for English-Language Learners* (Fitzgerald & Graves, 2004), *Success with Struggling Readers: The Benchmark School Approach* (Gaskins, 2005), and *Scaffolding Language, Scaffolding Learning: Teaching Second Language Learners in the Mainstream Classroom* (Gibbons, 2002).

Third, while all facets of comprehension we describe in this book are appropriate for struggling readers and ELLs, the scaffolded reading experience (SRE), which is our main vehicle for fostering learning from text, is particularly appropriate. The SRE is particularly appropriate because it is a flexible framework that can be differentially used with students who need different levels of support. Thus, for example, it is often the case that all students in a class read the same text and receive some scaffolding for doing so, but struggling readers and ELLs receive additional scaffolding, often in the form of more supporting prereading activities. We will expand on this use of SREs in Chapter 2.

Finally, there is a small set of practical and realistic adjustments and accommodations you can make for struggling readers and ELLs that do not require unreasonable amounts of time, unreasonable amounts of preparation time, or your being in two or three places at the same time. Here we list these adjustments and accommodations, with those that are appropriate for all struggling readers listed first and those specifically for ELLs listed next.

- Take particular care to ensure that students have the background knowledge and the vocabulary needed to understand the selections they are reading.
- Give students plenty of time; read parts of selections to them if that seems necessary; summarize parts of selections if need be; and let them read material more than once if that seems appropriate.
- Monitor students' understanding closely; and be prepared to restate major points, paraphrase explanations, use visuals,

reteach important concepts and procedures, and provide any other types of extra supports they may need.

- Pair ELLs with classmates who have strong language and communications skills and show interest and ability in helping others.
- If you have students, aids, or volunteers who are fluent in English and your ELLs' language, use them whenever possible. Don't limit your search for such assistants to your classroom; search throughout your school and beyond it.

## About This Book

This book is divided into eight chapters—this introductory chapter, one chapter focusing on each of the five facets of comprehension we are discussing, a chapter on vocabulary instruction, and a final chapter of classroom vignettes in which we illustrate how the instruction we describe throughout this book plays out in the classroom.

Thus far in Chapter 1 we have expressed our concern about the lack of attention to adolescent literacy, presented data on adolescents' reading proficiency, briefly described the five facets of comprehension we deal with in this book, noted the theories that inform our approaches to comprehension instruction, discussed the major considerations behind our instruction, emphasized the importance of motivation, and suggested some considerations and some resources for working with struggling readers and ELLs. In the remainder of this chapter, we will complete our description of this book and make a few concluding remarks.

Chapter 2, "Fostering Learning from Text," begins by explaining the nature and purpose of fostering learning from text and then describes in detail the SRE, the instructional approach we employ for fostering learning from text. In describing the SRE, we first explain just what an SRE is, present the SRE framework, and describe various types of pre-, during-, and postreading activities that can be used in SREs. Next, we outline possible scaffolded reading experiences for texts of differing complexity and for different genre. Finally, we consider the matter of differentiating SREs to accommodate to the wide range of proficiency found in today's classrooms and the matter of how to incorporate SREs into English classes.

Chapter 3, "Teaching for Understanding," begins by defining what teaching for understanding entails and listing its four attributes. Next, the chapter describes teaching-for-understanding units, the major vehicle we suggest for promoting deep understanding of important topics. In describing teaching-for-understanding units, we elaborate on a process and considerations necessary for developing curricular materials that help achieve deep understanding and outline a sample teaching for understanding unit. In addition, we consider other approaches to fostering understanding, including analytic discussions of literature, knowledge as design, generative learning theory, and jigsaw.

Chapter 4, "Fostering Responses to Literature," describes ways to foster student understanding and appreciation of literature. Using reader-response theory as the guiding theoretical lens, we discuss practical strategies for helping students build interpretations of literature that give appropriate attention to the text and to students' own backgrounds, values, and needs. We also discuss ways to enhance classroom discussions and how literary theory can be used to get students of various abilities to formulate meaningful, well-considered responses to literature. Throughout the chapter, we include numerous ways to use writing as a tool for sharpening students' comprehensions of literary texts.

Chapter 5, "Teaching Comprehension Strategies," consists of three main sections. The first describes the characteristics of comprehension strategies. Next, we describe the eight comprehension strategies that research has shown to be particularly effective. After this, we describe a general procedure for teaching strategies and illustrate the use of this procedure in a 2-day lesson on "Determining What Is Important." The chapter concludes with descriptions of several sequences of comprehension strategies—notice/wonder, tableaux, K-W-L, and reciprocal teaching.

Chapter 6, "Teaching Higher-Order Thinking Skills," describes the importance of higher-order thinking, the types of higher-order thinking, and the nature of higher-order thinking. The chapter then describes an approach to fostering higher-order thinking based primarily on Sternberg's triadic theory (Sternberg & Spear-Swerling, 1996), which includes analytic thinking, creative thinking, and practical thinking. While we believe that the majority of activities to foster higher-order thinking should be embedded in the ongoing authentic reading, writing, and discussion that takes place in English classrooms, we also suggest some direct attention to the matter.

Chapter 7, "Vocabulary Instruction in English Classes," describes a comprehensive, four-part vocabulary program, one broad enough to be of value for 7th- to 12th-grade students with small vocabularies, ELLs, students with typical vocabularies, and those with exceptional vocabularies. The four parts provide rich and varied language experiences, teach individual words, teach word-learning strategies, and promote word consciousness. Students' vocabularies continue to grow throughout high school, and students will profit from our assistance in fostering this growth.

Chapter 8, "Comprehension in Context," shows the various facets of comprehension instruction described in Chapters 2–6 and the recommendations for vocabulary instruction described in Chapter 7 embedded in a month-long unit. In describing this unit, we illustrate how learning from text, teaching for understanding, nurturing response to literature, teaching comprehension strategies, promoting higher-order thinking, and vocabulary instruction are integrated with each other and with other important activities in English classrooms.

## Concluding Remarks

Our goals in the Concluding Remarks sections throughout the book are to briefly summarize the individual chapters and then comment on how you might integrate the ideas presented into your classroom. The section in this chapter, however, will be a little different. Since Chapter 1 presents background information rather than ideas for instruction, we really cannot talk about integrating the ideas into your classroom. Instead, we suggest that you directly engage with this chapter by asking and answering questions such as these: How does your school address the issue of adolescent literacy? Is there a schoolwide program? Are teachers in your school adequately prepared to foster students' literacy? Does the school have reading specialists who work with other teachers and with students most in need of help? How do the results from NAEP and PISA coincide with or differ from the proficiency you have observed in your classroom? Which of the reading theories and instructional principles we outlined are you familiar with? Which are you unfamiliar with? Which do you agree with? Which do you disagree with? What are some specific ways in which you work to motivate students? What additional suggestions do you have for dealing with struggling readers? Taking time to seriously consider these questions, better yet discussing them with a colleague, will leave you with some very useful schemata as you continue reading this book.

## LITERATURE CITED

Crowley, Sharon, & Hawhee, Debra. (1999). *Ancient rhetorics for contemporary students* (2nd ed.). Boston: Allyn & Bacon.

Gibaldi, Joseph. (2003). *MLA handbook for writers of research papers* (3rd ed.). New York: Modern Language Association of America.

Giovanni, Nikki. (1991). Ego tripping. In *Braided lives: An anthology of multicultural American writing* (pp. 207–208). St. Paul: Minnesota Humanities Commission.

Hesse, Karen. (1997). *Out of the dust.* New York: Scholastic.

Kingston, Maxine Hong. (1989*). The woman warrior.* New York: Vintage International.

Myers, Walter Dean. (1999). *Monster.* New York: HarperTempest.

Ryan, Pam Munoz. (2000). *Esperanza rising.* New York: Scholastic.

# CHAPTER 2

# Fostering Learning from Text

> Whether our students are capable readers who arrive at a work with rich expectations or less proficient readers who can barely decode the words or picture a script in their heads, they are helped by activities that invite them to enter the ideas of the text. These invitations can take many forms; but all are designed to activate students' thoughts, experiences, and feelings about something essential in the text that follows or to build background knowledge necessary for reading it.
>
> —JOSEPH AND LUCY MILNER, English educators

As Milner and Milner point out, all students, whatever their level of proficiency, "are helped by activities that invite them to enter the ideas of the text." If there is one key to helping students succeed in becoming able and avid readers—adolescents and later adults who not only can read but who choose to read for the joy, information, and insights that only reading can provide—that key is ensuring that they meet with success in their reading. It is important that students understand what they read, take away from each reading those ideas and insights that they need and want, and realize that they have been successful in their reading. As we noted in Chapter 1, by fostering learning from text our goal is to help each and every student to meet with this sort of success with each and every text he reads. In some cases, the support helps students succeed with a text that would otherwise be beyond their grasp. In other cases, the support helps students more fully and more deeply understand and appreciate a text. In still other cases, we give students differential support, providing those who would otherwise struggle a good deal with a text with a lot of assistance and those who are better able to deal with it less assistance.

The particular form of support we provide for fostering learning from text is termed a Scaffolded Reading Experience, or SRE. In this chapter, we explain just what an SRE is, describe the SRE framework, consider the possible components of SREs, describe several sample SREs, and discuss the possibilities for differentiating SREs to meet the needs of students with varying degrees of proficiency in reading.

## What Is a Scaffolded Reading Experience?

An SRE is a set of prereading, during-reading, and postreading activities specifically designed to assist a particular group of students in successfully reading, understanding, learning from, and enjoying a particular selection. SREs have been described in some detail in two books (Graves & Graves, 2003; Fitzgerald & Graves, 2004) and a number of shorter works (e.g., Clark & Graves, 2005; Fitzgerald & Graves, 2004–2005; Tierney & Readence, 2005). The SRE approach has also been validated in several research studies (Cooke, 2002; Fournier & Graves, 2002; Graves & Liang, 2003; Liang, 2004; Liang, Peterson, & Graves, 2005; Rothenberg & Watts, 1997).

Two closely related concepts are particularly important in understanding the thinking behind SREs—scaffolding and the zone of proximal development. Although we discussed both of these in Chapter 1, we bring them up again here because of their centrality to the SRE and because we want to stress one point about each of them. While the purpose of scaffolding less proficient readers is obvious—we provide scaffolding so they will not fail—the purpose of scaffolding more proficient readers' reading may not be as clear. The purpose of scaffolding more proficient readers is to help them learn more deeply and deal with more sophisticated texts than they could negotiate independently. A recent ACT study (2006) found that working with complex texts was *the* most powerful factor predicting students' success in college.

With respect to the zone of proximal development, we stress that unless we as teachers deliberately choose and structure activities so that they are in students' zone of proximal development, there is a real possibility that we will frequently give less proficient readers tasks they cannot do—resulting in their failing—and frequently give more proficient readers tasks that they are already perfectly capable of doing—resulting in their learning nothing new.

## The SRE Framework

An SRE is a framework for ensuring that students' reading experiences are within their zones of proximal development. It is a very flexible framework that allows you to tailor instruction to specific situations— to particular groups of students, particular texts, and particular purposes. The SRE framework has two parts. The first part, the planning phase, takes into consideration the particular group of students doing the reading, the text they are reading, and their purpose or purposes for reading it. The second phase, the implementation phase, provides a set of prereading, during-reading, and postreading options for those particular students, the selection being read, and the purposes of the reading. The SRE framework is shown in Figure 2.1.

As shown in the figure, the first phase of the SRE is the planning phase, during which you plan and create the entire experience. The second phase is the implementation phase, the activities you and your students engage in as a result of your planning. This two-phase process

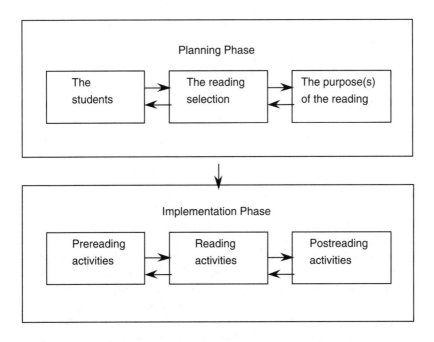

**FIGURE 2.1.** Two phases of an SRE.

is a vital feature of the SRE approach in that the planning phase allows you to tailor each SRE you create to the specific situation you face. Different situations call for different SREs.

Suppose you are working with an advanced communications class of 11th graders, you want them to develop some deep understanding about differences in communication patterns between men and women for an upcoming unit on the psychology of language, and the text you have chosen, Deborah Tannen's *You Just Don't Understand*, is demanding. Or consider a very different situation. Suppose you are working with these same 11th graders, your purpose is to have them read a humorous short story for the pure enjoyment of it, and you have chosen a fairly easy reading selection, perhaps Thurber's "The Night the Ghost Got In."

In both of these situations, your planning leads to the creation of the SRE itself and to your implementing it. As shown in the lower half of Figure 2.1, the components of the implementation phase are prereading, during-reading, and postreading activities. With the Deborah Tannen book, we have already suggested that you want students to develop some deep knowledge about differences in the communication patterns of men and women; you also want them to retain what they learn. This means that your SRE for *You Just Don't Understand* is likely to be a substantial one, with prereading activities that prepare students to read the challenging text, during-reading activities that lead them to interact and grapple with the text in ways that help them understand and learn from it, and postreading activities that give them opportunities to check their understanding of the text, solidify their learning, and consider how what they have learned may be relevant to their lives. Consequently, the class might spend 2 weeks reading selected chapters from the book and completing the learning activities you have assembled.

Conversely, with "The Night the Ghost Got In" and the goal of students simply enjoying the reading experience, your SRE is likely to be minimal. Prereading might consist of a brief motivational activity, students might read the story silently to themselves, and postreading might consist of an optional discussion. Consequently, the class might spend only a day or so reading and responding to this short story.

In addition to recognizing that the SRE framework results in very different SREs for different contexts, it is important to recognize that the components of each phase of the SRE are interrelated. Consider the three components of the planning phase—the students, the text, and your purposes. Once you decide which students you're going to work with, there are only some texts you can use and some purposes you can expect to accomplish. Once you decide which text you are going to use, there are only some students who will be able to read it and some purposes you can hope to achieve with it. And once you decide what your purposes are, there are only some texts you can use to accomplish those purposes and some students who will be able to achieve them. The same sort of interdependency holds with the three components of the implementation phase. For example, if you decide you are going to have some very challenging postreading tasks, you will want to include prereading activities and during-reading activities that thoroughly prepare students to accomplish those challenging tasks.

## Possible Components of an SRE

The possible prereading, during-reading, and postreading components of an SRE are listed in Figure 2.2. Before continuing, however, we want to stress that these are *possible* components of an SRE. No single SRE would include anything like all of these activities.

In the next few pages, we briefly describe each of these prereading, during-reading, and postreading options. Although we deal with each of these kinds of activities separately, as you read about them you will notice overlap among them. For example, a motivating activity may also activate prior knowledge, introduce a new concept, and relate the reading to students' lives. Similarly, a prereading activity targeted at teaching vocabulary may also activate prior knowledge. Such overlap is not a problem. The purpose of listing the various types of activities is to prompt you to think of as many different types of activities as possible, not to categorize activities as being this type or that type.

### Prereading Activities

Prereading activities prepare students to read an upcoming selection. They can serve a number of functions, including getting students interested in reading the selection, reminding students of things they already know that will help them understand and enjoy the selection, and preteaching aspects of the selection that may be difficult. Prereading activities are particularly important because with adequate preparation the experience of reading will be enjoyable, rewarding, and successful. Prereading activities are widely recommended (see, e.g., Aebersold & Field, 1997; Ciborowski, 1992; Fountas & Pinnell, 1996; Marzano, 2004;

**Prereading Activities**
Motivating
Activating and building background knowledge
Providing text-specific knowledge
Relating the reading to students' lives
Preteaching vocabulary
Preteaching concepts
Prequestioning, predicting, and direction setting
Suggesting strategies
Using students' native language
Involving English language learners' communities and families

**During-Reading Activities**
Silent reading
Reading to students
Supported reading
Oral reading by students
Modifying the text

**Postreading Activities**
Questioning
Discussion
Writing
Drama
Artistic, graphic, and nonverbal activities
Application and outreach activities
Building connections
Reteaching

**FIGURE 2.2.** Possible components of an SRE.

Milner & Milner, 2003; Readence, Moore, & Rickelman, 2000; Schoenbach, Greenleaf, Cziko, & Hurwitz, 1999; Yopp & Yopp, 1992), and a number of different types of prereading activities have been suggested. In creating the list of possible prereading activities for SREs, we have attempted to list a relatively small set of categories that suggest a large number of useful activities teachers and students can engage in. As shown in the list of SRE components, we suggest nine types of prereading activities.

*Motivating*, the first category listed under prereading activities, includes any activities designed to interest students in the upcoming selection and entice them to read it. Although a variety of prereading activities can be motivational as well as accomplishing some other purpose, we list motivating as a separate category because we believe that it is perfectly appropriate to do something solely for the purpose of motivating students. Moreover, we believe that motivating activities should be frequently used.

*Relating the reading to students' lives* is so self-evident a category as to leave little to say. We will, however, point out that because showing students how a selection relates to them is such a powerful motivator, it is something we like to do often.

*Activating or building background knowledge* is always important if students are to get the most from what they read. When you activate background knowledge, you prompt students to bring to consciousness already known information that will be helpful in understanding the upcoming text. For example, let us say a group of your seventh graders is researching the plight of migrant workers. Before these students read a story you have recommended from *The Circuit*, Francisco Jiménez's award-winning collection of stories based on his own experiences as a child migrant worker in California, you might encourage them to discuss what they have already learned about migrant workers from their previous reading. In addition to activating background knowledge, it is sometimes necessary to build background knowledge, knowledge that the author has presupposed—probably tacitly—readers already possess. For example, in reading the stories in *The Circuit*, you might find that Jiménez presupposes some specific knowledge of California geography, knowledge that you believe many of your seventh graders lack. In this case, supplying this information would make good sense. As another example of the need to build background knowledge, consider that the author of an American short story set in a movie theater is likely to assume that students are quite familiar with American movies and movie theaters and thus is not likely to explain anything about them in the story itself. For students who were raised in the United States and have been to a lot of movies, the assumption is correct, but you might have to explain quite a bit about movie theaters and related concepts to a Hmong student who had just arrived in the United States.

As contrasted to activating or building background knowledge, *providing text-specific knowledge* gives students information that is contained in the reading selection. Providing students with advance information about the content of a selection—giving students the seven topics discussed in an article on writing personal narratives, for example—may be justified if the selection is difficult or densely packed with information.

As used here, *preteaching vocabulary* refers to preteaching words that are new labels for concepts that students already know. For example, you would be teaching vocabulary—a new label—if you taught eighth graders the word *vermillion,* meaning "bright red." It often makes good sense to take 5 minutes and preteach half a dozen or so new vocabulary words before an upcoming selection.

*Preteaching concepts* is a different matter. Preteaching concepts refers to preteaching new and potentially challenging ideas, not just new labels for ideas students already understand. For example, if you wanted to teach 10th graders the meaning of *transcendentalism,* you would be teaching most of them a new concept. It does not make sense to attempt to preteach half a dozen new and difficult concepts in anything like 5 minutes. Teaching new and difficult concepts takes significant amounts of time and requires powerful instruction.

We have listed *prequestioning, predicting,* and *direction setting* together because we believe that they are similar activities. With any of them, we are focusing students' attention and telling them what is important to look for as they read. Such focusing is often necessary because without it students may not know what to attend to.

In the next prereading activity, *suggesting strategies,* the key word is *suggesting.* SREs are not designed to *teach* strategies. Initially teaching strategies—instructing students in how to do something they could not do previously—focuses students' attention on the strategy rather than on the text itself. For this reason, we have devoted a separate chapter, Chapter 5, to teaching comprehension strategies. However, as part of an SRE, it is often appropriate to suggest that students use strategies they already know. For example, with a book that includes a good deal of information worth remembering, something like Frederick Douglass's *Narrative of the Life of Frederick Douglass, an American Slave,* you might suggest that it would be a good idea for students to summarize key segments of the text. Occasionally, these strategies may be ones that students have learned on their own, but in most cases the strategies will have been deliberately taught in the past.

The final two types of prereading activities are designed for ELLs, who are of course present in many English classrooms in today's schools. The first of these is *using students' native language.* When the going gets tough and when the gulf between students' proficiency in English and the task posed by the reading becomes wide and deep, one extremely helpful alternative is likely to be to use students' native language. You might, for example, present a preview of a challenging book like Sandra Cisneros's *The House on Mango Street* in Spanish. Or you might give your Spanish-speaking students directions for reading the book in Spanish. We have not listed using students' native language in our lists of during-reading or postreading activities in order to avoid redundancy. It is important to remember, however, that employing students' native language is just as viable an option as students are reading a text or after they have read a text as it is before they read. Thus, you might want to give Filipino students a study guide in Tagalog, or you might want to allow Hmong students to sometimes respond to what they read in Hmong.

Another way to bring ELLs' native languages into the classroom is *involving ELLs' communities and families.* In all probability, other students in your class, students in other classes in your school, and people out in the community speak the language or languages spoken by your ELLs. Getting the assistance of these children and adults in your classes has tremendous advantages. The most obvious of these is that they can communicate effectively with your students who are not yet proficient in English. Another advantage is that, by helping your students, your resource people—if their English is not well developed—will improve their own English abilities. Still another advantage is the satisfaction, sense of belonging, and sense of pride that the resource people will get from assisting in your classroom. It is often difficult to convey to parents who are not proficient in English that they are welcome at school and that you really want to work with them to help their children succeed. By bringing parents into the school as resource people, you convey to them that they are not only welcome but needed! It is, to use a phrase that's trite but really does fit here, a "win–win" situation. Again, as is the case with using students' native language, engaging community and family members as resources is just as viable an option while students are reading a text or after they have read a text as it is before they read.

### During-Reading Activities

During-reading activities include things that students themselves do as they are reading and things that you do to assist them as they are reading. Like prereading activities, during-reading activities are frequently recommended (see, e.g., Aebersold & Field, 1997; Bean, Valerio, & Stevens, 1999; Beck, McKeown, Hamilton, & Kucan, 1997; Ciborowski, 1992; Fountas & Pinnell, 1996; Schoenbach et al., 1999; Richardson, 2000; Wood, Lapp, & Flood, 1992; Yopp & Yopp, 1992), although there are probably not as many really different types of during-reading activities. In creating the list of possible during-reading activities for SREs, we have again attempted to list a relatively small set of categories that suggest a large number of useful activities teachers and students can engage in. As shown in Figure 2.2, we suggest five types of during-reading activities, plus the two types of activities for ELLs.

We have deliberately listed *silent reading* first because it is and should be the most frequently used during-reading activity. The central long-term goal of reading instruction is to prepare students to become accomplished lifelong readers; and most of the reading students will do once they leave school—as well as most of the reading they'll do in college or any other sort of post-secondary education—will be silent reading. It is both a basic rule of learning and everyday common sense that one needs to repeatedly practice the skill he is attempting to master. If we choose appropriate selections for students to read and have adequately prepared them to read the selections, then students will often be able to silently read the selections on their own.

*Reading to students* occurs rarely in some secondary schools, and that is unfortunate. Hearing a story or piece of exposition read aloud is a very pleasurable experience for many youngsters and also serves as a model of good oral reading. Reading the first chapter or the first few pages of a piece can help ease students into the material and also serve as an enticement to read the rest of the selection on their own. Reading to students can make difficult material accessible to students who find certain texts difficult, either because of their complex structure or difficult vocabulary. Some students find listening easier than reading; this is certainly the case with many less proficient readers and with some—but by no means all—ELLs. For these students, reading aloud—or playing a commercial tape, CD, or MP3 file—is sometimes very helpful. Still, in most instances students should read silently on their own. One gets good at reading through reading.

*Supported reading* refers to any activity that you use to focus students' attention on particular aspects of a text as they read it. Supported reading often begins as a prereading activity—perhaps with your setting directions for reading—and is then carried out as students are actually reading. For example, in order to help students appreciate the traditions of another culture, you might have them jot down the Chinese traditions that Tom Leong, the protagonist in William Wu's "Black Powder," follows in honoring his father's memory. As another example, if you find that a challenging expository piece on the Harlem Renaissance is actually divided into half a dozen sections but contains no headings or subheadings, you might give students a semantic map that includes titles for the half dozen sections and ask them to complete the map as they are reading. Often, with supported reading activities, a student's goal is to learn something from the reading rather than just reading for enjoyment. Thus, supported reading activities are frequently used with expository material. However, it is also possible to guide students in understanding and responding to narratives, for example, to recognize the major themes in a novel or to empathize with the protagonist of a short story.

Of course, one long-term goal is to motivate and empower students to learn from and respond to selections without your assistance. Thus, with less challenging selections and as students become increasingly competent, your support can and should be less specific and less directive and sometimes consist only of a general suggestion: "After reading the first chapter in Monica Sone's *Nisei Daughter,* I have a suggestion for you. Check with one of your classmates and be sure you have the setting and characters straight. This chapter can be a little confusing, and you want to be certain you are on solid footing as you read the rest of the book." Or, if students are reading a narrative such as Jerry Spinelli's *Star Girl,* you might say, "You'll find that Leo Borlock is quite a character and that he changes a lot during the story. Using a journal to record the changes he undergoes and writing down how you feel about the changes may help you better appreciate what he's going through."

In many secondary classrooms, *oral reading by students,* like oral reading by the teacher, is a relatively infrequent activity. As we previously mentioned, most of the reading students do once they leave school is silent reading, and thus doing a lot of silent reading is important. Nonetheless, oral reading has its place. Certainly, poetry is often best and most effective when read orally. Poignant or particularly well-written passages of prose are often appropriate for oral reading. Students may sometimes enjoy oral reading of poetry or particularly strong prose. Reading orally can also be helpful when the class or a group of students is studying a passage and trying to decide on alternate interpretations or on just what is and is not explicitly stated in the passage. Additionally, students often like to read their own writing orally. And, of course, having individual students read orally can provide you with very valuable diagnostic information. Thus, oral reading is something to include among the many alternatives you offer students. However, two cautions about oral reading are appropriate. First, whenever students are reading in front of the class, they need time for adequate preparation. Poor oral reading is unfortunate for both the reader and the listener. Second, in recommending oral reading, we do not mean to sanction the once popular round-robin reading in which student after student (some good readers and some poor ones) takes turns plotting through a text. As Opitz and Rasinski (1998) and many other educators have noted, this is not an appropriate activity.

Sometimes because of what is either required by the curriculum or what is available, students will be reading selections that present too much of a challenge due to their length or difficulty. In these cases, *modifying the text* is appropriate. The most efficient way to modify a selection is to shorten it. Suppose that you are considering reading Nancy Farmer's *The House of the Scorpion* with an eighth-grade class that includes some struggling readers, and you realize that reading all of this novel just isn't something your struggling readers can or are likely to do. You might therefore briefly summarize the first half of the novel for them and have them read only the second half. Assuming students can and will read the complete novel, will they get as much out of reading part of it? Absolutely not! But, assuming they cannot or will not read all of it, success in reading part of it is certainly preferable to failure in reading all of it.

Another way to make difficult material accessible to students is to tape a selection for students to listen to as they follow along silently in the text. You, or competent students, can make the recordings or you can check out or purchase commercial tapes, CDs, or MP3 files. Recordings can both make material accessible to less skilled readers and provide a model for good oral reading. Additionally, in some cases it may be possible to have a text or a summary of a text available in your ELLs' native languages. Making such tapes would be an excellent opportunity for involving ELLs' communities and family members.

### Postreading Activities

Postreading activities serve a variety of purposes. They provide opportunities for students to synthesize and organize information gleaned from the text so that they can understand and recall important points. They provide opportunities for students to evaluate an author's message, his stance in presenting the message, and the quality of the text itself. They provide opportunities for you and your students to evaluate their understanding of the text. And they provide opportunities for students to respond to a text in a variety of ways—to reflect on the meaning of the text, to compare differing texts and ideas, to imagine themselves as one of the characters in the text, to synthesize information from different sources, to engage in a variety of creative activities, and to apply what they have learned within the classroom walls and in the world beyond the classroom. Not surprisingly given their many functions, postreading activities are also widely recommended (see, e.g., Aebersold & Field, 1997; Alvermann, 2000; Bean et al., 1999; Ciborowski, 1992; Fountas & Pinnell, 1996; Gambrell & Almasi, 1996; Schoenbach et al., 1999; Wood et al., 1992; Yopp & Yopp, 1992), and in most classrooms they are frequently used. In creating the list of possible postreading activities for SREs, we have once again attempted to list a relatively small set of categories that suggest a large number of useful activities. This includes the eight types of activities shown in Figure 2.2, as well as the two types of activities for ELLs.

*Questioning*, either orally or in writing, is a frequently used and frequently warranted activity. Questioning activities give you an opportunity to encourage and promote higher-order thinking—to nudge students to interpret, analyze, and evaluate what they read. Questions can also elicit creative and personal responses—"How did you feel when ... ?" "What do you think the main character would have done if ... ?" Sometimes, of course, it is appropriate for students to read something and not be faced with some sort of accountability afterward. However, in many cases, neither you nor your students will be sure that they gained what they needed to gain from the reading without their answering some questions. Of course, teachers are not the only ones who should be asking questions after reading. Students can and should ask questions of each other, they can and should ask you questions, and they can and should ask questions they plan to answer through further reading, perhaps on the Internet.

Some sort of *discussion*—whether it is discussion in pairs or small groups or discussion involving the entire class—is also frequent and often very appropriate. If there is a chance that some students did not understand as much of a selection as they need to—and there is often this chance—discussion is definitely warranted. Equally importantly, discussion gives students a chance to offer their personal interpretations and responses to a text and to hear those of others. Discussion is also a vehicle for assessing whether reading goals have been achieved, to evaluate what went right with the reading experience, what went wrong, and what might be done differently in the future.

*Writing* is a postreading task that probably ought to be used more frequently than it is. In recent years, there has been a good deal of well-warranted emphasis on the fact that reading and writing are complementary activities and ought often to be dealt with together. We certainly agree. However, we want to stress that writing is often a challenging activity, and it is important to be sure that students are adequately prepared for writing. Among other things, this means that if students are expected to write about a selection, you usually need to be sure they have comprehended the selection well. We say *usually* because sometimes students write to discover what they have comprehended in a selection.

*Drama* offers a range of opportunities for students to get actively involved in responding to what they have read. By drama, we refer to any sort of production involving action and movement. Given this definition, short plays, skits, pantomimes, and Readers' Theatre are among the many possibilities. Wilhelm's *Action Strategies for Deepening Comprehension* (2002) offers helpful suggestions.

*Artistic, graphic, and nonverbal activities* constitute additional possibilities for postreading endeavors. In this broad category, we include visual art, graphics, music, dance, and media productions such as videos, slide shows, audio tapes, and work on the Web, as well as constructive activities that you might not typically think of as artistic. Probably the most frequent activities in this category involve creating graphics—maps, charts, trees, diagrams, schematics, and the like. Other possibilities include constructing models or bringing in artifacts that are somehow responses to the selection read. Artistic and nonverbal activities may be particularly useful because they are enjoyable, are often a little different from typical school tasks, and provide opportunities for students to express themselves in a variety of ways, thus creating situations in which students of varying talents and abilities can excel. This is not to say that such activities are frills or something to be done just to provide variety. In many situations and for many students, artistic and nonverbal activities offer the greatest potential for learning information and for responding to what has been read.

*Application and outreach activities* include both concrete and direct applications—cooking something after reading a recipe—and less direct ones—attempting to change some aspect of student government after reading something about state government that suggests the possibility. Here, we also include activities that extend beyond the campus—planning a drive to collect used coats and sweaters after reading a news article on people in need of winter clothing or taking a field trip to a local art museum after reading about one of the artists represented there. Obviously, there is a great range of application and outreach options.

Although there is some overlap between the next postreading activity we consider, *building connections,* and the one we just discussed, application and outreach activities, we have chosen to list building connections as its own category because it is so important. Only by helping students build connections between the ideas they encounter in reading and other parts of their lives can we ensure that they to come to really value reading, read enough that they become proficient readers, see the relevance of reading, and remember and apply important learnings from their reading. Several sorts of connections are important. First, we want students to connect the wealth of out-of-school experiences they bring to school with their reading, for example, to relate the pride they felt in learning to snowboard with the pride a story character feels when he meets a difficult challenge. Second, we want students to connect what they learn in one subject to what they learn in others, for example, to realize that their understanding of the motives of Doodle's older brother in James Hurst's "The Scarlet Ibis" can help them understand some of the adult behavior they read about in psychology class. Third, we want them to realize that concepts they learned from reading can apply well beyond the classroom, for example, that just as a fictional character's perseverance brought him success, so too might their perseverance at real-life tasks they face bring them success.

The final postreading activity we consider is *reteaching*. When it becomes apparent that students have not achieved their reading goals or the level of understanding you deem necessary, reteaching is often in order; and the best time for reteaching is usually as soon as possible after students first encounter the material. In some cases, reteaching may consist simply of asking students to reread parts of a selection. In other cases, you may want to present a mini-lesson on some part of the text that has caused students problems. And in still other cases, students who have understood a particular aspect of the text may assist other students in achieving similar understanding.

## Some Sample SREs

We have described a fairly lengthy list of possible activities, as we have already noted, far too many to be used with a single selection. Again, however, this is a list of *options*. From this set of possibilities, you choose only those that are appropriate for your particular students reading a particular text for a particular purpose. Suppose, for example, you are doing a joint unit with your eighth-grade social studies colleague and the topic is U.S. history in the late 1700s. As part of that unit, your class is reading the first chapter of the award-winning Newbery nonfiction book *The True and Terrifying Story of the Yellow Fever Epidemic of 1793* by Jim Murphy. Their goals are to learn what yellow fever is, when and where the epidemic began, and how the people of Philadelphia first responded to it. In this situation, you might provide prereading instruction that includes a motivational activity, the preteaching of some difficult vocabulary such as *immunity* and *pestilence*, and a questioning activity—an activity in which students pose *who, when, where, what, how,* and *why* questions they expect to be answered in the chapter, being sure to include questions relevant to their reading goals. Next, for the during-reading portion of the lesson, you might read part of the chapter aloud and then have students read the rest silently, looking for answers to their questions. Finally, after students have finished the chapter, they might break into discussion groups of three or four and answer the questions they posed during prereading. After this, the groups might come together as a class and share their answers. Here is a list of the activities for this SRE for eighth graders reading the first chapter in Murphy's book.

| | |
|---|---|
| Prereading: | Motivating |
| | Preteaching vocabulary |
| | Questioning |
| During Reading: | Reading to students |
| | Silent reading |
| Postreading: | Small-group discussion |
| | Answering questions |
| | Large-group discussion |

There are two characteristics of this example particularly worth recognizing at this point. For one thing, this combination of prereading, during-reading, and postreading activities is only one of a number of combinations you could have selected. For another, you selected the activities you did based on your assessment of the students, the selection they were reading, and their purpose in reading the selection.

We can again highlight the fact that SREs vary considerably by giving another example. Suppose the same eighth graders are reading a simple and straightforward narrative, something like Jack Gantos's *Joey Pigza Swallowed the Key.* Suppose further that their primary purpose for reading the story is simply to enjoy this fast-paced, humorous tale. In this case, prereading instruction might consist of only a brief motivational activity, the during-reading portion might consist entirely of students' reading the novel silently, and the postreading portion might consist of their voluntarily discussing the parts of the story they found most humorous or interesting. Here is the list of activities for this SRE for *Joey Pigza Swallowed the Key.*

| Prereading: | Motivating |
| During Reading: | Silent reading |
| Postreading: | Optional small-group discussion |

It is, as you can see, shorter than the list for *The True and Terrifying Story of the Yellow Fever Epidemic of 1793*. It's short because neither your students, nor the story itself, nor the purpose for reading the story requires a longer and more supportive SRE.

Now here is a much more detailed SRE. This one is for James Baldwin's poignant short story "Sonny's Blues," a text that might be used by 11th and 12th graders. The objectives for this SRE are for students to:

- Develop an understanding of the complexity of Baldwin's prose, particularly understanding the role the setting plays in this story.
- Develop an understanding of the role and power of communication in this story as it shapes the events of the story and defines the brothers' relationship.
- Develop appreciation for characters' point of view in literature.
- Consider the relevance of Sonny's struggle to their own lives.

### DAY 1

*Prereading Activities*

- The teacher provides background knowledge on Baldwin's life and his writing.
- As part of motivating students, the teacher shows a slide show of Harlem in the 1920s and 1930s.
- The teacher reads a fairly meaty preview of the story.

*During-Reading Activity*

- The teacher reads the first several pages aloud.

### DAY 2

*Postreading Activity*

- Students discuss the section read-aloud in small groups and bring up any questions they have in a large-group discussion.

*Prereading Activity*

- The teacher asks students to keep a time line of the events in the story and explains how to do so.

*During-Reading Activity*

- Students read the next several pages of the story silently.

*Postreading Activity*

- Students create the time line as homework.

DAY 3

*Postreading Activities*

- The teacher solicits time line information from the students and creates a large time line for the class as a whole.
- Students note any vocabulary they found unfamiliar and ask for definitions from their classmates.

*Prereading Activity*

- The class brainstorms words associated with light and darkness, and the teacher asks students to look for references to light and darkness as they continue reading.

*During-Reading Activity*

- The students read the next several pages silently, recording references to light and darkness. They may finish this as homework.

DAY 4

*Postreading Activities*

- Students compare two specific references to light and darkness in writing.
- Students discuss their writing, first in small groups and then in a large group.

DAY 5

*Postreading Activity*

- Students update the class time line.

*Prereading Activity*

- Students complete a webbing activity in which they draw relationships between their own lives and the lives of Sonny and his brother and engage in a whole-class discussion about what they found.

*During-Reading Activity*

- Students read the next several pages silently and answer some questions checking their basic understanding of the story and some requiring critical thinking. This may be completed as homework.

DAY 6

*Postreading Activities*

- The class discusses the answers to the factual and critical-thinking questions, and the teacher leads students as they discuss the effects of the setting, point of view, and varying forms of expression used.
- Students update the class time line.

*Prereading Activity*

- The teacher further motivates students and builds their background knowledge by showing a video clip from *Bird*, a movie about jazz great Charlie Parker.

*During-Reading Activity*

- To emphasize the significance of the last section of the story, the teacher reads it aloud.

DAY 7

*Postreading Activities*

- The class discusses the entire story, giving students an opportunity to solidify what they have gained from the story and learned from one another and giving the teacher an opportunity to informally assess students' learning.
- Students are given several options for a culminating activity. They can (1) write a letter from Sonny's mom to the narrator discussing

what she thinks of his handling of Sonny as a character, (2) debate the question of whether Sonny is going to stay clean, (3) reenact a scene from the story, or (4) write a one-page paper about how the setting of the story affects either the narrator or Sonny.

Seven days is, of course, a substantial period of time to spend on a short story. But "Sonny's Blues" is a challenging short story, as well as a text with considerable literary merit and social significance. While you cannot and should not spend a week on every short story, this one is well worth the time.

These three examples illustrate just a few of the myriad forms SREs can take. Each text you use, each group of students you are teaching, and each set of purposes you may have for students reading will result in a different SRE. For a more detailed description of an SRE for "Sonny's Blues," go to *www.onlinereadingresources.com*. At this same website, you will also find detailed SREs for about 50 other texts, including works by Shakespeare, Faulkner, Charlotte Perkins Gilman, Nikolai Gogol, Tim O'Brien, and others.

## Differentiated SREs

Thus far, we have discussed how to foster learning from text using SREs as though classrooms were made up of homogeneous groups of students who needed and would profit from the same type and amount of scaffolding. Clearly, many classrooms are made up of students with diverse interests and proficiency in reading, and in these cases a one-size SRE will not fit all. Two sorts of differentiation are worth considering. On the one hand, you will sometimes want to differentiate SREs based on students' interests. For example, students can read different books while pursuing a common topic or theme. Thus, in exploring the themes of death and grieving, some students might read Sharon Creech's *Walk Two Moons*, others Christopher Paul Curtis's *The Watsons Go to Birmingham*, and others Cynthia Voigt's *Dicey's Song*. Similarly, some students may choose to respond to a reading selection in writing, others with some sort of artwork, others with an oral presentation, and others by going to the library to pursue the topic further. The constraints on differentiation of this type are your time, ingenuity, and ability to orchestrate diverse activities. Additionally, you need to keep in mind that the more different activities students are involved in, the less time you have to assist them with each activity. At the extreme, if

30 students are each involved in a different activity, you can give each of them less than 2 minutes of your time each hour. Thus, there are a number of practical limits on differentiating on the basis of student interest. However, if these limits are kept in mind, differentiation based on interest is very often desirable.

The other sort of differentiation to consider is differentiation based on students' proficiency in reading. Here, the same limits that influence differentiation based on interest apply. That is, constraints include your time, ingenuity, ability to orchestrate diverse activities, and ability to assist students when many activities are going on at once. Beyond these considerations, however, is that of the effect of being repeatedly placed in a group that receives more assistance. Being a member of the group that repeatedly receives more assistance certainly has the potential to weaken students' self-image and motivation to learn. Singling out students for special, essentially remedial, assistance is not something we want to do any more frequently than necessary.

However, these are not the only facts to consider. There is also the fact that success begets success and failure begets failure. Thus, the suggestion that differentiation based on reading proficiency should be infrequent because of the psychological effect it might have must be tempered by the realization that differentiation can make the difference between success and failure. With less skilled readers, it often is important to differentiate instruction to ensure success, even though that differentiation should be no more frequent than is necessary.

Deciding just when differentiation based on reading proficiency is called for is a decision that only you, a classroom teacher with detailed knowledge about your individual students and their strengths, needs to make. We do, however, have four suggestions. First, differentiate only as frequently as is necessary. Second, differentiate only as much as is necessary, that is, don't make large changes when small ones will do. Third, when you do differentiate, try to limit yourself to two levels of support—one for more proficient readers and one for students who would really struggle and quite possibly fail without more support. As much as possible, make one level a set of activities that all students complete and the other level a set of additional supportive activities that only those who need more support complete. The potential negative effects of students repeatedly being in the group receiving more assistance, the amount of time it takes you to create differentiated sets of activities, and your ability to support students when different students are engaged in different activities argue for your seriously considering these suggestions. Finally, when planning differentiated instruction, take into account the recommendations we make in the section on special considerations for struggling readers and ELLs in Chapter 1 and consider in-depth treatments of differentiations like those of Carol Ann Tomlinson in *Fulfilling the Promise of the Differentiated Classroom: Strategies and Tools for Responsive Teaching* (2003) and those of Tomlinson and Cindy A. Strickland in *Differentiation in Practice: A Resource Guide for Differentiating Curriculum, Grades 9–12* (2005).

Shown below is an outline of a two-level SRE that might be used with 11th graders reading Jerome Lawrence's and Robert E. Lee's challenging and insightful play, *The Night Thoreau Spent in Jail*. One asterisk (*) indicates activities all students do, two asterisks (**) indicate activities for more proficient readers, and three asterisks (***) indicate activities for less proficient readers. This SRE is likely to last about a week and a half, although the exact time it takes will vary from classroom to classroom and the schedule given is therefore approximate. A more detailed version of this SRE is available at www.onlinereadingresources.com As we did in outlining the SRE for "Sonny's Blues," we preface this one with a list of objectives:

- To develop an understanding of Thoreau's philosophy, particularly its transcendentalist base.
- To select meaningful passages from the reading and connect them with their own lives and philosophy.
- To express their feelings about a significant philosophy through visual representation or writing.
- To develop an understanding of each person's role in the greater community and universe.
- To consider the relevance of Thoreau's experiences to their own lives.

DAY 1

*Prereading Activity*

- The teacher provides background knowledge about the author and the historical setting.*

*During-Reading Activity*

- The teacher and volunteers read excerpts from Thoreau's writing.*

DAYS 2–5

*During-Reading Activities*

- Students read the play silently.**
- The teacher and volunteers read the play aloud.***
- Students identify intriguing and significant quotes.*

*Postreading Activity*

- Students begin writing explanations and responses to the selected quotes once they have finished reading the play silently.**

DAY 6

*Postreading Activities*

- Students continue writing explanations and responses to the selected quotes.**
- Students discuss explanations and responses to the selected quotes.***
- Each student chooses a quote that best fits his philosophy of life.*

DAY 7

*Postreading Activities*

- Students make posters depicting their favorite quotes.***
- Students write a piece that illustrates, demonstrates, explains, or relates to their favorite quote.**

DAY 8

*Postreading Activity*

- Students share and discuss their posters and writing.*

Note that although in this illustration of differentiated instruction we show the less demanding activities—listening rather than reading, discussing rather than writing, and drawing rather than writing—as being for the less proficient readers, this does not mean that less skilled readers should always get simpler tasks or more skilled readers harder tasks. For example, the above SRE might be modified by having both less skilled and more skilled readers make posters and write about their favorite quotes. Somewhat similarly, students can sometimes be given choices between less demanding and more demanding activities.

## Concluding Remarks

Thus far in this chapter, we have discussed the importance of fostering students' learning from text and described the SRE, our approach to doing so. In describing SREs, we have discussed the purpose of SREs, described the SRE framework, listed and briefly described the possible components of SREs, provided several sample SREs, and discussed creating differentiated SREs. Here, we discuss several considerations you have as you decide how to incorporate SREs into your classroom.

One decision is that of how often to use SREs. Fostering learning from text must compete with the other four facets of a comprehensive approach to comprehension described in this book and with other important English activities for the limited amount of time you have available each day. Moreover, different teachers, different goals, different times of the year, and different grade levels will affect how frequently SREs are used. Still, we believe that they should be quite frequent. SREs provide some of your best opportunities for extending students' zones of proximal development by supporting their efforts, helping them succeed in their reading, and giving them some common experiences to talk about, write about, and know that they share. In this sense, SREs have an intrinsic value that would lead us to use them quite frequently for their own sake—for the stretching, success, and shared experiences they can provide. From another perspective, SREs are useful for the extrinsic reason that they facilitate students learning the content you are teaching. Of course, SREs will generally be less frequent as students progress through the grades and become increasingly independent and self-sufficient. At the same time, older students read increasingly challenging texts and read them for increasingly challenging purposes, so they too will profit from the scaffolding SREs provide.

Another decision to consider is that of how much scaffolding to provide. We have already alluded to the matter, but the topic is worth addressing directly. Our main point is that it is neither a case of the more the merrier, nor one of the less the merrier. The general rule is to provide enough scaffolding for students to be confident and successful in their reading, but not so much that they are not sufficiently challenged, feel that they are being spoonfed, or become bored. In general, then, the suggestion is to provide enough scaffolding but not too much. Further reinforcing the notion that you do not want to do more scaffolding than is needed is the fact that constructing scaffolds takes your valuable time, time that is always at a premium. Still there is no getting away from the fact that in today's classrooms many students need and deserve a significant amount of scaffolding if they are to succeed.

A closely related decision to consider, and the last one we will take up here, is that of how to balance challenging and easy reading. Every student needs and deserves opportunities to read easy material that can be understood and enjoyed without effort and challenging material that he needs to grapple with. Reading easy material cements automaticity, builds confidence, creates interest in reading, and provides students with practice in a task they will face frequently in their everyday lives. Reading challenging materials builds students' knowledge bases, their vocabularies, and their critical thinking skills. Reading challenging materials also provides students with practice in a task they will face frequently in college, in their work outside of school, and in becoming knowledgeable and responsible members of a democratic society. Moreover, reading challenging materials builds students' confidence in their ability to deal with difficult reading selections—if you ensure that they are successful with the challenging material.

The point that needs to be stressed here is that each student— more able, more skilled, and more knowledgeable students as well as less able, less skilled, and less knowledgeable students—needs both challenging and easy reading. This condition cannot be met by providing only material that is of average difficulty for the average student. Assuming classrooms made up of students with varying skills, knowledge, motivation, and reading proficiency—and this description fits most classrooms—routinely providing only reading selections of average difficulty ensures that some students will repeatedly receive material that is difficult for them, others will repeatedly receive material that is of average difficulty for them, and still others will repeatedly receive material that is easy for them. Such a situation is inappropriate for all students. Because the reading tasks we face in the world outside of school vary and because the benefits of reading vary with the difficulty of the reading tasks, all students need frequent opportunities to read materials that vary in the challenges and opportunities they present.

## LITERATURE/FILMS CITED

Baldwin, James. (1995). Sonny's blues. In *Going to meet the man* (pp. 101–142). New York: Vintage International.

Cisneros, Sandra. (1994). *The house on Mango Street.* New York: Random House.

Creech, Sharon. (1995). *Walk two moons.* New York: HarperTrophy.

Curtis, Christopher Paul. (1963). *The Watsons go to Birmingham.* New York: Delacorte Press.

Douglass, Frederick. (1845). *Narrative of the life of Frederick Douglass: An American slave.* Boston: Anti-Slavery Office. Available at *sunsite.berkeley.edu/Literature/Douglass/Autobiography/.*

Eastwood, Clint. (Director). (1988). *Bird* [Film]. Hollywood, CA: Warner Bros. Pictures.

Farmer, Nancy. (2002). *The house of the scorpion.* New York: Atheneum.

Gantos, Jack. (1998). *Joey Pigza swallowed the key.* New York: Farrar, Straus & Giroux.

Hurst, James. (2000). The scarlet ibis. In *Glencoe literature the reader's choice, course 4* (pp. 354–362). Columbus, OH: Glencoe/McGraw-Hill.

Jiménez, Francisco. *The circuit.* New York: Houghton Mifflin.

Lawrence, Jerome, & Lee, Robert E. (1972). *The night Thoreau spent in jail.* New York: Bantam Books.

Murphy, Jim. (2003). *The true and terrifying story of the yellow fever epidemic of 1793.* New York: Clarion Books.

Sone, Monica. (1979). *Nisei daughter.* Seattle: University of Washington Press.

Spinelli, Jerry. (2000). *Star girl.* New York: Knopf.

Tannen, Deborah. (1990). *You just don't understand: Women and men in conversation.* New York: Ballentine Books.

Thurber, James. (1999). The night the ghost got in. In *My life and hard times* (pp. 134–143). New York: Perennial Classics.

Voigt, Cynthia. (1982). *Dicey's song.* New York: Atheneum.

Wu, William. (1993). Black powder. In L. Yep (Ed.), *American dragons: Twenty-five Asian American voices* (pp. 211–234). New York: HarperCollins.

# CHAPTER 3

# Teaching for Understanding

In a phrase, understanding is the ability to think and act
flexibly with what one knows. To put it another way, an
understanding of a topic is a "flexible performance capability"
with emphasis on the flexibility. In keeping with this, learning
for understanding is like learning a flexible performance—
more like learning to improvise jazz or hold a good
conversation or rock climb than learning the multiplication
tables or the dates of the presidents or that F = MA.

—DAVID PERKINS, educational psychologist

In considering learning, Perkins places particular emphasis on two key words—*flexibility* and *understanding*. As teachers, we often begin a unit with certain outcomes in mind, outcomes such as, "Students will read F. Scott Fitzgerald's novel *The Great Gatsby* with an understanding of the social and economic forces that motivate characters' actions," or "Students will develop greater insight into the Roaring '20s as a cultural movement, which is revealed through Fitzgerald's characters." These outcomes are worthwhile and laudable, but they need to be approached somewhat cautiously from a teaching for understanding perspective. We must ask ourselves the following questions: Will students gain knowledge from this unit that extends beyond a particular text? Will their understanding be applicable to other contexts? And will their understanding of central ideas and concepts be retained over time?

As our title indicates, this chapter focuses on teaching for understanding. Fostering understanding requires much more than simply presenting students with information. Three principles emerge from the teaching for understanding perspective: Students will deeply understand the topic of study, meaning they will know its origins and impact in a variety of contexts; students will retain important and essential information; and students will actively apply the knowledge they gain in a variety of situations. Additionally, it is important to recognize from the onset that teaching for understanding demands a significant amount of time, a very precious resource in today's classrooms.

As teachers charged with making valuable use of instructional time, we must ask ourselves, "What is more important—that our students are exposed to a vast array of information or that they are exposed to fewer topics but learn them more deeply and are able to apply that knowledge in a variety of thought-demanding venues?" Certainly, our society has changed dramatically in recent years, and the expectations for what teachers teach and what students learn has changed accordingly. As we noted in Chapter 1, recent NAEP reports indicate that a substantial portion of our students do not possess the necessary skills for fully participating in our ever-changing society. Alarmingly, the 2005 NAEP data (Perie et al., 2006) indicate that 31% of eighth graders and 35% of 12th graders could read at the proficient level. Teaching for understanding is one avenue we ought to pursue in boosting students' performance. We need to move away from learning that results in what Perkins (1992) has termed *inert knowledge, naïve knowledge,* and *ritual knowledge,* striving instead to equip our students with flexible understanding.

Inert knowledge resides in a learner's mind but "doesn't move around or do anything" (Perkins, 1992). When students are assigned to read a text and are later unable to use the information they have gleaned in some meaningful way, the knowledge gained is considered inert. Perkins refers to this as the knowledge equivalent of a couch potato. Another type of surface knowledge is naïve knowledge, as when students are taught a principle or concept such as "local color" but cannot explain or interpret what they have learned. A third type of surface knowledge we seek to avoid is ritual knowledge, a type of performance in which students learn to play the game of school. Ritual knowledge does not enable students to apply newly learned information in dynamic and innovative ways.

How can we avoid the pitfalls noted in the preceding paragraph? By carefully considering our curricular choices and designing meaningful learning opportunities that provide students with deep understandings that are flexible and hence, lasting. Below, we discuss in greater detail what teaching for understanding is.

# Attributes of Teaching for Understanding

As previously noted, one of the basic attributes of teaching for understanding is that it requires significant time (Graves, Juel, & Graves, 2007). Prawat (1989) has delineated three additional attributes:

- It requires focus and coherence.
- It is highly analytic and diagnostic in nature.
- It involves negotiation.

In the following paragraphs, we describe each of these attributes in more detail.

The most basic—and for some teachers, the most problematic—attribute of teaching for understanding is that it cannot occur without learners devoting a significant amount of time to a topic. The knowledge, proficiencies, and attitudes we want students to acquire so that they can learn deeply, retain critical information, and actively use their knowledge are only attained by spending substantial time on the topics under consideration. The cost of spending more time on a particular topic may at first seem too great; that is, if a topic that typically takes 2 weeks to teach requires 4 weeks when teaching for understanding, some of the topics you normally undertake will not fit into the academic year. But it is important to remember that when we do not teach for understanding, students' knowledge is so frail and fleeting as to be useless. We believe the cost-benefit analysis clearly indicates that the time spent on teaching for understanding is well worth it, while time not spent on teaching for understanding is often time wasted.

Since teaching for understanding demands large time commitments, it is only logical that it also demands focus and coherence. If you adopt this approach, choosing to spend more time on a smaller number of topics, you need to make sure you are spending your time wisely. Choosing relevant, engaging topics that are coherent to you and your students is crucial. For instance, if we decide to teach a unit focusing on characterization in short stories, we need to understand—and convey to students—that we are focused on characterization, that we understand what characterization means, and that we have a rationale for studying characterization. Also, characterization as a topic becomes more relevant if regularly brought up in the classroom. Without clarity and coherence, real gains in students' knowledge and proficiency are unlikely.

To ensure coherence and focus, you will often have to negotiate meaning with students. In Chapter 1 we discussed in detail the notion that reading is not a simple act of meaning transferring directly from a text to a reader's mind; it is more constructivist and complicated than that. Readers must think diligently about what they are reading, manipulate ideas, test "passing theories" (Kent, 1993), and work to assemble coherent ideas if they are to understand a text deeply. Often, no two readers will arrive at the exact same interpretation. However, there are instances when you want students to construct a similar meaning from a text, which likely necessitates negotiating meaning. Negotiating may entail rereading a passage or text, followed by a give-and-take class discussion in which each reader's ideas are considered, and eventually a common agreement is made. In the following whole-class discussion, note how Allison, the teacher of an 11th-grade American literature course, adds a more experienced reader's perspective to help students understand stream of consciousness in Tim O'Brien's "On the Rainy River." Prior to Allison's comment, several students expressed confusion about the protagonist's thought process. Allison explained:

> "That technique is called 'stream of consciousness.' It's when a character's ideas are presented in a sort of jumbled way, but it gives us a strong sense of that person's inner reality. The main character, Tim, is confused about whether he should avoid the draft by fleeing to Canada. These seemingly random thoughts show us his internal conflict about whether he's doing the right thing or not."

The final attributes of teaching for understanding are that it is analytic and diagnostic. During a class discussion focused on the importance of narrative setting, for example, we need to analyze students' responses to determine what they are thinking, decide if students are making coherent and logical interpretations, and if they are not, figure out a way to help them construct more lucid understandings. In the following example, the teacher begins the talk about Steinbeck's setting in *Of Mice and Men* with a fairly broad question; as the classroom talk unfolds, note how she focuses more intently on particular words and models the need for a close reading:

TEACHER: How does Steinbeck describe the foothills? What adjectives does he use?

STUDENT: Golden?

TEACHER: He talks about the golden foothills. Now, tell me, what does that mean? How can foothills be golden?

STUDENT: The sun is setting and the light is reflecting off the trees.

TEACHER: The sun was setting and the light is reflecting off the trees. We know that the sun is setting because on the next page we're told it's getting toward evening. And the sun's kind of shining off in the distance making those foothills look golden. Now how about the valley side. The side with the trees. What does he say about the trees? What type of trees are they and how do they look?

STUDENT: They're willows and they're fresh with green and spring.

TEACHER: Okay, he talks about the valley side being lined with willows. With willow trees. And he says they're fresh and green with every spring. And then he says something about the sycamore trees which are also on this one side of the water. Where the trees are. You probably didn't understand this line. But can anybody tell me what the line is?

STUDENT: "With mottled white ... "

TEACHER: The line is actually "the sycamores with mottled, white, recumbent limbs." And branches. Okay. The question is what does that mean? It happens to be a very specific line about what the trees are like but if you don't have a couple of vocabulary words you might have trouble. "The sycamore trees with mottled limbs." Does anyone know what the word "mottled" means?

STUDENT: Spotted, colored, more than one color.

TEACHER: Exactly. More than one color. And then they are "recumbent." Anybody know "recumbent"?

STUDENT: Reclining?

TEACHER: Exactly. I saw an ad over the weekend for a recumbent exercise bike. And I think you can sort of sit back and lie back and pedal. I don't know if it's more relaxing or you work harder. I don't know what the details are. But the word "recumbent" means "reclining, resting." (Marshall, Smagorinsky, & Smith, 1995, pp. 53–54)

Here, the teacher is clearly doing most of the talking, though the questions she poses to the class are analytical in that they encourage students to cue into seemingly minute details that establish the overall importance of setting. Such modeling, if performed with regularity, can serve to teach students how paying attention to small details can result in greater understanding of text.

Thus far, we have focused on what teaching for understanding means, described its primary characteristics, and elaborated on its attributes. We now turn to describing specific approaches you can use to foster deep understanding in your students. In doing so, we first discuss teaching for understanding units, the primary vehicle for teaching for understanding. Following that, we discuss four additional procedures for fostering understanding, approaches that are less time consuming than teaching for understanding units and that can be embedded in many of the reading, writing, and discussion activities that take place in classrooms.

# Teaching for Understanding Units

Several authorities have described and researched teaching for understanding units. These include Perkins and his colleagues (Perkins, 1992, 2004); Wiggins and McTighe (1998); McTighe, Seif, & Wiggins (2004); and Newmann (1996, 2000). Here, we focus on the work of Wiggins and McTighe.

## *Wiggins's and McTighe's Approach*

One approach to teaching for understanding units we find particularly informative is that of Wiggins and McTighe (1998). Central to their approach is the "backward design process." According to Wiggins and McTighe, "many teachers *begin* with textbooks, favored lessons, and time-honored activities rather than deriving those tools from targeted goals or standards." The backward design process encourages planning in the opposite direction—from goals to curriculum. More specifically, backward design suggests that we begin by identifying desired results (goals and/or standards), then determine what sort of evidence would show that students have achieved the goals or standards (student performances), and finally plan learning experiences and instruction (curriculum). Such an approach is neither new nor radical, but it is followed less frequently than it should be. When one of us began his teaching career, for example, he was told what specific books and units had to be covered, although how those books and units dovetailed with districtwide goals—if at all—was never made clear. To gain a clear sense of what Wiggins and McTighe envision by the backward design process, it is necessary to delve into each component more extensively.

The first stage of Wiggins's and McTighe's model involves identifying goals for a particular unit. In choosing goals, you have a number of choices to make. Are your goals consistent with those of your school and district? Will the goals satisfy state standards? Will they meet federal regulations as set forth under NCLB? Will they resonate with NCTE/IRA standards? Will they fulfill other requirements adopted by the local school board? However the goals are chosen, they ought to be articulated within a larger framework understood by interested parties, such as one's colleagues, and eventually to the students themselves. To address the curriculum priorities, Wiggins and McTighe offer a three-step sequence.

Step 1 requires identifying knowledge students should find "worth being familiar with." That is, what do you want students to read, view, or research in a specific unit? In Step 2, the curricular choices become more pointed as you specify important knowledge and skills students should master upon completing the unit. Step 3 consists of choosing enduring understandings for the unit, central ideas that you want to be certain students internalize and retain. When thinking about what constitutes an enduring understanding, the following filters are helpful:

- Filter 1: To what extent does the idea or topic signify a "big idea" that has lasting value outside the classroom?
- Filter 2: To what extent does the idea or topic correspond to central, critical knowledge in the discipline?
- Filter 3: To what extent does the idea or topic require "uncoverage" so that misconceptions can be addressed?
- Filter 4: To what extent does the idea or topic truly engage and interest students?

The second stage of the backward design model—determining acceptable evidence—involves asking ourselves, "How do we know if students learned what we want them to know?" or "How do we know if students met our unit goals?" In the backward design model, you need to "think like an assessor before designing specific units and lessons, and thus ... consider up front how you will determine whether students have attained the desired understandings" (Wiggins & McTighe, 1998). Assessment can, of course, be accomplished in a variety of ways, from informal (e.g., whole-class dialogues about a short story) to formal (e.g., a lengthy written thematic analysis of a novel). We encourage you to use as many forms of assessment as possible throughout a unit to gain as complete a picture as possible of student understanding. If, for example, in the middle of a unit, you note a lack of understanding from several students, reteaching may be necessary.

The third and final stage of the backward design process is the point at which—with enduring understandings and appropriate assessments envisioned—you create instructional activities. Lesson plans and learning activities are the key elements at this stage. Wiggins and McTighe suggest addressing the following questions when developing activities: "What knowledge and skills will students need to perform effectively to achieve desired results? What activities will give students the needed knowledge and skills? What will be taught and how will it be taught given the performance goals? What materials [in the case of English teachers, what texts] are most suitable in achieving the goals?" In summing up their approach to backward design, Wiggins and McTighe note that "Teaching is a means to an end" and observe that "Having a clear goal helps us as educators to focus our planning and guide purposeful action toward the intended results." By beginning with goals, our curricular choices thus become more pointed, lucid, and meaningful.

## A Sample Teaching for Understanding Unit

Having outlined the backward design framework, we now examine what it might look like in practice. Here then is a sample teaching for understanding unit. For this example, we use a 10th-grade class of mixed-ability students as our audience and Harper Lee's *To Kill a Mockingbird* as our primary text. We are using the language arts standards set forth by the Minnesota Department of Education because we are most familiar with these. Standards for most other states have many similarities.

In presenting the example, we first discuss the three stages of the planning process and then outline 4 weeks of instruction.

### Stage 1: Identify Desired Results

Based on the standards for students in grades 9–12, we have chosen the following goals for our unit:

1. The student will read, analyze, and evaluate traditional, classical, and contemporary works of literary merit from American literature.

2. The student will analyze and evaluate the relationship between and among major elements of literature: character, setting, plot, tone, symbolism, rising action, climax, falling action, point of view, theme, and conflict/resolution.
3. The student will engage in a writing process with attention to audience, organization, focus, quality of ideas, and a purpose.

Based on these standards and considering the four filters that help determine what constitutes enduring knowledge, we arrived at the following statement of desired goals: Students will read a narrative work that focuses on racial prejudices. They will learn to identify how stereotypes are formed and why they cloud our judgments of others. And they will gain some understanding of why we use stereotypes and how we can develop resistance to them by learning to evaluate people as individuals rather than as members of groups.

*Stage 2: Determine Acceptable Evidence/*
*Understanding Performances*

In keeping with teaching for understanding principles, we will include several sorts of evidence and understanding performances. These include:

- Frequent discussions centered on the previous day's assigned reading (informal assessment).
- Reading quizzes after every three chapters. While these quizzes test primarily factual information, they function on two levels: First, they prompt students to keep up with the reading schedule; second, they can signal where reteaching may need to occur.
- A reading log where students write down hypotheses, questions, concerns, predictions, and so forth, which will aid them in the final assessment task. Students must respond in their reading logs at least two times per week.
- A three-to-four page reflection/analysis paper that focuses on how the novel's protagonist, Scout, learns from her father's advice that "You never really understand a person until you consider things from his point of view" (*To Kill a Mockingbird*). The reflective component of the paper involves the student writers applying this same advice to their own lives. That is, where in your own life have you misjudged someone, only learning the truth when you heard the other person's story?

*Stage 3: Planning Instruction*

*To Kill a Mockingbird*, Lee's popular and critically acclaimed novel set in Maycomb, Alabama, in the 1930s is a staple in many schools. At the conclusion of this teaching for understanding unit, students will be able to identify the elements of the craft of fiction writing, as well as examine significant social issues still all too relevant today. Also, students will develop essential knowledge of concepts such as *stereotypes, bigotry, racism*, and *perspective taking*. Finally, students will become familiar with the practices of a writer's workshop as they work on their final assessment project, the reflection/analysis paper. The teaching methods used to accomplish the goals of this unit will be varied and include active teaching, cooperative learning, whole-class literature discussions, and various reading activities (silent reading, teacher read-alouds, and student read-alouds).

The 20 days of instruction would proceed roughly as follows, with of course variations in both specific activities and the time devoted to the activities shifting to accommodate the difficulty or ease students experience with the unit.

DAY 1

• Students write a response in their reading log to the prompt, "What is meant by the term *prejudice*, and how do prejudices form?"
• Whole-class discussion of prejudices, stereotypes, and generalizations.

DAY 2

• Introduction to elements of a story: plot, setting, characters, rising action, conflict, resolution, falling action, and symbolism.
• Students read Annette Sanford's "Trip in a Summer Dress" for homework, using it as a means to reinforce their knowledge of the elements of fiction to the story.

DAY 3

• Small-group discussions of how the elements of fiction present themselves in "Trip in a Summer Dress."
• Whole-class debriefing on the small-group work.

DAYS 4 AND 5

- Students conduct Internet research on life in the United States during the 1930s, paying specific attention to the Great Depression and Jim Crow laws. The end result of this project will be that students individually create a text and image poster board to display in the classroom.

DAY 6

- Read-aloud of Chapter 1 of *To Kill a Mockingbird*, pages 1–15.
- Students begin tracking all characters in their reading log: Jem, Scout, Atticus, Dill, Boo Radley.
- Students develop a sociogram indicating the relationships between various characters. They will need to list all the characters mentioned so far in a circular pattern; based on what is revealed in the text, they should draw a squiggly line between characters who have an antagonistic relationship and straight lines to those who share a friendly relationship. Students will update their sociograms throughout their reading of the novel.

DAYS 7–11

- Students continue reading at a pace of roughly 30 pages per day.
- Small- and large-group discussion of the text in relation to the elements of fiction.
- Students respond to reading quizzes every 40–50 pages. Each quiz contains 10 questions and requires both factual information and inferences.

DAY 12

- In small groups, students debate and present their findings on the following enduring knowledge points of inequality, stereotypes, and racial bias: How has racial prejudice manifested itself in the reading so far? Can or does anything like this happen in today's society? If so, what examples can you think of? How much can we rely on legal action (i.e., court cases, law enforcement, etc.) to solve social problems? *Reading log prompt:* "What stereotypes do you notice, if any, in the reading thus far? Provide evidence to support your claims."

DAY 13

- Students watch the film version of the courtroom scene.
- Discuss how the text and film versions are similar and different. Ask students to pay particular attention to determining why Mayella Ewell accused Tom Robinson of raping her. What was her motive for doing so, and what stereotypes do she and her father use in forwarding their case? These observations will help students with their final assessment task.
- Students finish reading the novel, as homework if necessary.

DAY 14

- Wrap-up discussion of how the book concludes.
- Final reading quiz.
- In small groups, students compare their Chapter 1 sociograms to their final sociograms.
- Introduce the final assessment project. We have included a rubric for the reflection/analysis paper (see Figure 3.1).

DAYS 15 AND 16

- Students use the computer lab to draft their reflective/analytic papers.

DAY 17

- Peer revision of final papers.

DAY 18

- Students return to computer lab to finalize papers.

DAYS 19 AND 20

- Students present their reflective portion of their papers to the class.
- Teacher responds to their presentations.
- Teacher begins assessing final papers and will later conference with students concerning their work.

| Category | 4 (surpasses expectations) | 3 (meets expectations) | 2 (below expectations) | 1 (fails to meet expectations) |
|---|---|---|---|---|
| **Content: Analysis of Scout's learning** | Writer clearly focuses on Scout's learning and provides rich, relevant details to support the claim. | Writer focuses on Scout's learning, though supporting details are less vivid and clear. | Writer only somewhat focuses on Scout's learning and gives only vague support to the claim. | Writer does not focus on Scout's learning. Purpose of this paper is not evident. |
| **Organization** | Ideas are logically structured and flow smoothly. Inviting introduction and well-stated conclusion. | Ideas are mostly logical and interrelated. Introduction and conclusion are adequate. | Ideas are disjointed and hard to follow at times. Introduction and conclusion are not entirely aligned. | Little to no sense of where writer is headed. Introduction and conclusion are at odds with each other. |
| **Voice** | Writer is in command of an academic voice. The writing fits the task. | Writer presents a fairly academic voice, but some unevenness exists. | Writer is too informal and casual at times. | Writer does not seem to have considered voice. Very colloquial. |
| **Word choice** | Vivid words and phrases are used, thus creating strong visuals for the reader. | Vivid words and phrases are present, but some choices are inconsistent. | Vivid words are less frequent and little punch or flair exists. | Vivid wording rarely used. Clichés distract from the originality of the writing. |
| **Grammar, usage, and punctuation** | Strong command of grammar and usage present throughout. | Good command of grammar and usage, though some errors exist. | Several errors in grammar and usage detract from the writing. | A profound number of errors severely hinders readability. |
| **Personal reflection** | Writer ties the essay's theme very closely and perceptively to own life. | Writer somewhat ties together the essay's theme to own life. | Writer makes an attempt to tie essay's theme to own life, but not convincingly. | Writer neglects to tie essay's theme to own life. |

**FIGURE 3.1.** Reflection/analysis paper rubric: *To Kill a Mockingbird.*

This teaching for understanding unit is designed to illustrate how deep understandings can be fostered if you use a backward design process for curriculum implementation. Ultimately, we want students to walk away from our classrooms with knowledge that is useful in the world beyond the school walls and that can be applied to everyday situations. After students complete this unit, we would expect they have developed a greater sense of appreciation for people different from themselves, and that they are cautious about using stereotypes. Planning and teaching in this manner can make your teaching more attractive to students, who will be able to make use of the knowledge they gained long after they leave your classroom.

# Additional Approaches to Fostering Understanding

While teaching for understanding units are the major approach to fostering deep and lasting understanding, they are by no means the only approach. Fostering deep understanding is also possible using approaches that are less time consuming and can be used at a variety of points in your classrooms. In the following section, we describe four additional approaches to teaching for understanding: analytic discussions of literature, knowledge as design, generative learning, and jigsaw.

## Analytic Discussions of Literature

Through articulating their ideas about a piece of literature and by listening to peers who may have differing notions, students learn to appreciate and evaluate both a text and an author's craft from multiple perspectives. To encourage analytic discussions of literature, you have several tools on which you can rely. Here, we highlight several of them that have been identified by Eddleston and Philippot (2002):

### Text Selection

The more engaging the reading selection, the more likely students will be to want to discuss the text. However, we must not confuse the idea of engagement with ease of material. Oftentimes, books that are too simplistic lead to discussions that fail to move beyond rehashing a plot. Texts that represent the diversity of students in terms of race, class, sex, religion, and national origin are highly engaging, as are books that challenge students' previously held conceptions and perceptions of the world.

## Writing to Learn

As teachers of literature, we want our students to express the same sort of passion we have for reading, but as classroom realists, we know this does not always occur. All too often we have seen attempts to discuss literature that begin with "So, what did you think about today's reading?" a query that is likely met with silence. Because students are almost always less familiar with a given text than we are and because students in today's diverse classrooms vary greatly in their background knowledge, we need to provide them with thinking time prior to discussion. One way to accomplish this is to assign "short writes" or "quick writes" before beginning a whole-class discussion. A short write requires students to compose a thoughtful response to a teacher-generated prompt; it is typically about three to four sentences long and completed in 5–10 minutes. If a 12th-grade class were reading Khaled Hosseini's *The Kite Runner*, for instance, a compelling short write prompt you might ask after reading the text is, "What factors do you think compelled Sohrab not to speak?" By responding in a short write, every student in class has an idea to contribute to the discussion, thereby alleviating the opening silence that is likely to occur without such preparation.

## Assessment of Discussions

We live in an age of increased teacher accountability. Parents, administrators, and the general public often question the work of teachers. One frequent and very worthwhile activity in our classrooms is discussion. While many of us appreciate the hard work and benefits of a constructivist discussion of literature, others may not, thus assessing discussions is doubly important. One approach to assessing classroom discussion relies on the students themselves. By developing a descriptive, holistic rubric and thoroughly instructing students in how to use it, you can efficiently have students periodically evaluate themselves (see Figure 3.2 for an example). The rubric asks students to reflect carefully on how well their responses to the text illuminate meaning, if they are considerate and attentive to others' ideas, and if they draw in less talkative peers. One of the primary goals of the rubric is to make students highly conscious of their contributions to the discussions so they can strive to become better participants as the class progresses. Additionally, you

## Self-Assessment Discussion Rubric

Name: _____

### 5

This discussant accepts responsibility for making meaning out of literature. He or she consistently demonstrates a careful reading of the text and makes insightful comments that significantly contribute to our understanding of a reading. The discussant refers to specifics from the class text, compares and contrasts that text with related texts, and makes connections with personal experiences and social and cultural issues. A respectful listener who avoids monopolizing the conversation, he or she sometimes pulls together and reflects on ideas that have surfaced in the inquiry discussions and may also ask relevant follow-up questions, thereby pulling other students into the discussion.

### 4

Although speaking less frequently than the discussant described above, this discussant shows growth in willingness to express responses. He or she has the ability to explain ideas clearly and to connect those ideas to others being discussed. This discussant may clarify a specific point being discussed or elaborate on specific examples from the text. Body language and eye contact also indicate substantial involvement in the discussion.

### 3

Speaking occasionally, this discussant may primarily respond on a personal level to the text ("I like it," or "I didn't like it"), perhaps supplying some textual evidence for this point of view. The discussant may speak often but say little that adds significantly to our understanding of a text, and may, in fact, primarily repeat what others have already said or be difficult to follow.

### 2

This class member says little. This discussant's few remarks may be inaccurate, unclear, or too brief to be helpful. Little textual support is offered; there is little evidence that the student has read the text carefully or at all. Or, the student may belittle other speakers' remarks, monopolize the conversation, interrupt other speakers, ignore their remarks when speaking, or talk to those seated nearby rather than to help the whole group.

### 1

The student says nothing and appears uninterested in the class discussions. Or, the student may appear interested in the discussions but, for whatever reason, does not join in.

**FIGURE 3.2.** Self-assessment discussion rubric.

can simply keep track of how often the students contribute to the discussion by tallying their "turns at talking." On a sheet of paper, place checkmarks by students' names whenever they add to the discussion. After collecting and examining the self-assessment rubric, do a rough tally of each individual's turns at talking. You can then return the self-assessment rubric with a comment on whether an individual should work to contribute more or less. Also, you may want to use the terminology on the rubric to help students strengthen their abilities in discussion. For example, say a student rates herself as a "4" on the rubric. You might suggest she focuses on connecting her own ideas to other ideas her peers suggest. Using these two methods in combination will provide a good sense of how well individuals are doing in your classroom.

## Knowledge as Design

As we just noted, discussion can be a very powerful tool in helping students develop meaning from a text. Knowledge as design, a framework created by Perkins (1986), uses discussion in a specific and very powerful way to promote constructivist understandings of literature.

Two basic, yet essential, considerations underlie knowledge as design. The first is that the relationship between a topic's structure and its purpose permits us to talk insightfully and meaningfully about it. The second is that learning is a consequence of thinking, a notion we have alluded to earlier in this chapter. Stated another way, when we can get students to think actively about a particular topic, they are much more apt to learn about the topic. Perkins sets forth four knowledge as design questions that, when discussed in groups, allow students to demonstrate understanding as well as gain new ideas. The four questions are:

- What are the purposes of _____?
- What is the structure (or the components) of _____?
- What are some examples of _____?
- What are some arguments for and against _____?

By structuring a discussion around these four questions, you can determine the level of understanding students have of a topic and discover where gaps in their knowledge exist. Here is a brief example of how a knowledge as design discussion might unfold in an 11th-grade classroom reading of Ray Bradbury's *Fahrenheit 451*. The topic under discussion is censorship.

*Purpose of Censorship*

TEACHER: So let's look first at the purpose of censorship. Why do you suppose people attempt to censor books and ideas?

MARCUS: I guess the reason people want to censor books is to keep students from learning dangerous ideas.

ANNA: But are there dangerous ideas? If so, what sorts of ideas are dangerous?

MARCUS: Well, I think some people look at certain ideas as being taboo or offending personal values and morals. Just look at McCarthyism in the 1950s. People were accused and brought in for questioning because they were suspected of being Communist sympathizers.

*Structure of Censorship*

TEACHER: Now consider how censorship actually happens. What does it look like? How do books get banned from, say, schools or libraries?

MATT: Some parents probably complain a lot.

TEACHER: Who would they complain to?

SARAH: Maybe to the school board and principal. They're the ones who enforce rules about school conduct, right?

*Examples of Censorship*

TEACHER: Can you give some examples of censorship? Have you heard of any books that have been banned in our school or other schools?

JUAN: I'm not sure if it's been banned or not, but I heard *The Color Purple* is disliked because it discusses sexuality. My 10th-grade teacher said it causes a lot of controversy.

*Arguments for and against Censorship*

TEACHER: Now, what are some of the arguments for and against censorship? Is it ever okay to censor books?

MARCUS: Sure it is. In schools we shouldn't have books that use tons of swear words and include detailed discussions of sex. That's not right.

ALLEN: I disagree. You might not want to teach a book like that, but it should be available. Remember the Constitution? It gives us the right to freedom of expression and information. As long as no one forces you to read it, it's fine to have it on a bookshelf.

This of course is only one of myriad knowledge as design discussions that might take place in an English class and each one will vary somewhat in its form as well as in its content. For example, sometimes you will need to step in to ask probing questions more frequently than this teacher did, and other times you will need to redirect the discussion when the talk seems only tangential. To be sure, not every topic will fit within the knowledge as design framework and not every discussion should be a design discussion. Still, the knowledge as design approach provides a useful and widely applicable framework that can be used with many topics and in many classrooms.

### Generative Learning

While many of the instructional procedures we discuss in this book are particularly appropriate for narratives, the concept of *generative learning* applies primarily to expository texts. According to Wittrock (1974, 1991), generative learning is fostered when students themselves generate meaningful relationships among the ideas within a text and between the ideas within a text and their existing knowledge or schemata. Some of these possible relationships are shown below:

| *Activities involving ideas in the text* | *Activities relating ideas in the text to prior knowledge* |
|---|---|
| Composing titles | Giving personal examples |
| Composing heading | Creating new examples |
| Writing questions | Drawing pictures or other |
| Paraphrasing | artwork |
| Writing summaries | Giving demonstrations |
| Making charts and graphs | Making comparisons |
| Articulating main ideas | Drawing inferences |
| Reflecting on ideas | Making predictions |
| Solving problems | |
| Creative writing | |

The central task in promoting generative learning is designing situations in which such generations can take place. In addition to designing situations in which generations can occur, we need to be mindful of three other considerations—motivating students, directing their attention, and understanding their existing schemata. Motivating students can often be difficult, but it is well worth the effort. Explaining to students that generative learning actually helps them remember what they read and will help them learn material in less time will go far in terms of motivating them. Directing students' attention requires helping them determine which ideas in a text are particularly important and require links to other ideas. Finally, to facilitate generative learning, we need to have a good sense of students' prior knowledge about a specific topic and be ready to fill in gaps where necessary. For instance, when introducing Shakespeare, often in ninth grade, we need to attend to Elizabethan language issues so that students understand some of the conventions.

An example of how generative learning theory can function illustrates its powerful effects on students' deep understanding. If a ninth-grade teacher developed a semester-long literature course with a theme of "The Literature of War" and introduced Rena Kornreich Gelisson's Holocaust memoir *Rena's Promise* as the initial text, a good deal of pre-teaching would probably occur. Likely topics that students can and should link to include:

- The causes of World War II.
- The countries involved in the war.
- The Nazi party's rise to power.
- The Nazis' persecutions of Jews.
- The nature and functions of concentration camps.

Calling up their knowledge of these topics and linking what they learn as they read *Rena's Promise* will significantly increase students' understanding and appreciation of the text. With much of the groundwork laid in terms of getting students to comprehend how in times of war, one power (e.g., Nazis) often subjugates another (e.g., Jews), a foundation exists for understanding the more general concepts of war and oppression. As the semester progresses, the teacher may then begin to explore the U.S. involvement in war and oppression.

Once they completed *Rena's Promise*, the class might examine a website devoted to the Japanese internment camps, such as the one found at *library.thinkquest.org/TQ0312008/Enter.html*. Because the students already will have had experience with similar concepts, such as concentration camps and racial/ethnic generalizations, connections will be more easily made and understood and their schema will enable them to comprehend more rapidly how wartime often results in unfair persecution of people. According to Wittrock (1991), "Generation includes the process of relating individual events and ideas presented in class and relating instruction to knowledge and experience." To help extend the generative learning process, you could ask students if there are any modern-day equivalents to either the Holocaust or the Japanese internment camps. Using their existing knowledge of war, oppression, and persecution students will need to revise their models of thinking about these topics to generate connections across time and locations.

## Jigsaw

Jigsaw is yet another approach for fostering deep understanding. This cooperative learning technique was developed and researched by Aronson and his colleagues (Aronson & Patnoe, 1997; Aronson, Blaney, Stephan, Sikos, & Snapp, 1978). Jigsaw requires the students themselves to become experts on a subtopic of a larger topic, then teach that subtopic to others in the class. The key to a successful jigsaw is that the topic under study contains subparts capable of being isolated for teaching purposes. In a classroom of 30 students, a typical jigsaw involves the following five steps:

1. Five heterogeneous groups comprised of six students each are formed, with each group member responsible for one aspect of the material being studied. With an 11th-grade class beginning a unit on poetry, for example, one student in each group will become an "expert" on free verse, another on haiku, another on sonnets, another on rhyming couplets, another on concrete poetry, and the sixth member on found poetry.

2. Once an individual has studied her subtopic, say sonnets, she gathers with the other four sonnet experts from the remaining four groups.

3. The five experts on sonnets discuss their individual findings, working to refine and build their knowledge.

4. The experts, after refining and augmenting their topics, return to teach their original group members. Thus, the sonnet expert teaches her peers about sonnets, the haiku expert teaches about haiku, and so on. Since the student experts are the only ones who have gained a deep knowledge of their topics, their peers are motivated to learn from them, and they are motivated to teach well.

5. Once each group member takes a turn at teaching, resulting in six subtopics covered, the teacher checks to ensure that all the material has been learned correctly, not just some of it. Should a significant lack of understanding be evident in students' demonstration of learning, the teacher will need to address problem areas.

While studies have repeatedly shown the positive effects of a variety of approaches to cooperative learning (Johnson et al., 1994; Slavin, 1987; Tierney & Readence, 2005), this does not mean that teachers have no role to play in preparing students to engage in and succeed at these activities. We recommend teaching students the four types of cooperative skills to ensure successful group functioning (Johnson et al., 1994).

The first type, *forming skills*, centers on the bottom-line skills needed to establish functioning groups. These include knowing how to assemble in groups in a quick and orderly fashion and using quiet voices so as to not disturb the work of others. *Functioning skills*, the second type, are aimed at managing group efforts to finish tasks and maintain positive working relations among members. You will want to teach students how to set time limits for project completion, as well as how to clarify misunderstandings regarding what needs to be done. The third type is comprised of *formulating skills*. These involve the mental processes required to build deeper understanding of the material being learned. With formulating skills, it is helpful to assign group roles to students. Examples of the roles include summarizer, corrector, elaborator, information seeker, memory helper, and understanding checker. By assigning individual roles to students, each person in the group performs an important function and thus every member is a valuable asset. Finally, the fourth type revolves around *fermenting skills*, which allow students to engage in academic controversies, rather than merely accepting easy answers to complex issues. Students will need to learn how to criticize ideas, not the people who forward the ideas. Another fermenting skill involves asking members to justify a conclusion. Once students understand and can use these four types of skills, they are far likelier to engage in fruitful, dynamic group-learning activities.

Almost all classrooms present myriad opportunities for jigsaw. For example, using jigsaw to establish peer review sessions of student writing could work extremely well, particularly for editing. One student will become an expert at comma usage, another at pronoun–antecedent agreement, another at fragments, and so forth, but it is unlikely that students will become self-taught experts. You will need to play a very active role in assisting the students in refining their knowledge of grammar and usage.

## Concluding Remarks

We have covered a range of issues related to teaching for understanding in this chapter, all of which are geared toward teachers presenting material in such a way that students develop deep understanding of essential knowledge. We began by defining teaching for understanding and listing its four attributes, and then described teaching for understanding units, described a process and considerations necessary for developing curriculum that helps achieve deep understanding, and outlined a sample teaching for understanding unit. In addition, we covered other ways for fostering understanding, including using analytic discussions of literature, knowledge as design, generative learning theory, and jigsaw.

Upon first glancing at the table of contents of this book, or perhaps upon reaching the first page of this chapter, you may have thought, "Well, yes, everything I do as a teacher promotes understanding." And you are quite correct. We all have understanding as one of our primary goals; if not, we would likely be a part of some other profession. As a colleague once put it, "As teachers, we do not set out with the goal of teaching for *misunderstanding*." With each passing semester and each passing year, we seek to help our students achieve active minds filled with useful, flexible understandings. Unfortunately, though, many students fail to develop deep understanding of important topics. Thus, there is a real need to be very careful and deliberate in fostering deep understanding.

Not every unit should, or can, go through a rigorous teaching for understanding makeover. Most unfortunately, we simply do not have time to lead students to deep understanding of everything they study. Therefore, we encourage you to be selective when deciding just what topics to teach for understanding. If what you teach has potential for a learner to use throughout her lifetime, then it should be considered essential knowledge and ought to be covered in depth.

Finally, we want to consider the relationship between this facet of comprehension—teaching for understanding—and the previous one—using SREs to foster learning from text. SREs deal with a single text. Teaching for understanding typically deals with multiple texts. Often, teaching for understanding units include one or more SREs. And equally often, SREs include one or more of the less time-consuming teaching for understanding activities such as analytic discussions of literature or jigsaw.

## LITERATURE CITED

Bradbury, Ray. (1993). *Fahrenheit 451*. New York: Simon & Schuster.

Fitzgerald, F. Scott. (1925/1995). *The great Gatsby*. New York: Scribner.

Gelisson, Rena Kornreich. (1996). *Rena's promise*. Boston: Beacon Press.

Hosseini, Khaled. (2003). *The kite runner*. New York: Riverhead Books.

Japanese internment camps and their effects. (n.d.). Retrieved August 19, 2007, from *library.thinkquest.org/TQ0312008/Enter.html*.

Lee, Harper. (1960). *To kill a mockingbird*. New York: Warner Books.

O'Brien, Tim. (1990). On the rainy river. In *The things they carried* (pp. 41–63). New York: Broadway Books.

Sanford, Annette. (1997). Trip in a summer dress. In H. Rochman & D. Z. McCambell (Eds.), *Leaving home* (pp. 119–131). New York: HarperCollins.

Steinbeck, John. (1981). *Of mice and men*. New York: Bantam Books.

Walker, Alice. (2003). *The color purple*. New York: Harvest.

## ᪥ CHAPTER 4 ᪥

# Fostering Responses
# to Literature

Rooms, corridors, bookcases, shelves, filing cards, and
computerized catalogues assume that the subjects on which
our thoughts dwell are actual entities, and through this
assumption a certain book may be lent a particular tone and
value. Filed under Fiction, Jonathon Swift's *Gulliver's Travels*
is a humorous novel of adventure; under Sociology, a satirical
study of England in the eighteenth century; under Children's
Literature, an entertaining fable about dwarfs and giants and
talking horses; under Fantasy, a precursor of science fiction;
under Travel, an imaginary voyage; under Classics, a part of
the Western literary canon. Categories are exclusive; reading
is not—or should not be. Whatever classifications have been
chosen, every library tyrannizes the act of reading, and forces
the reader—the curious reader, the alert reader—to rescue the
book from the category to which it has been condemned.

—ALBERTO MANGUEL, historian

$A$s teachers of literature, we must ask ourselves—and certainly our
students—why is literature important and how do we derive meaning
from a text? Should we, as Manguel suggests, encourage students to
disregard a book's classification, opting instead to view a given text in
a multiplicity of ways? Many of us have sat in a high school or college
English classroom where the instructor told us the "true" meaning of an
author's intent, with special attention paid to unraveling the symbolic
structures and metaphoric allusions. But what of the students who fail
to read a book on that level? Unfortunately, they become lost in the
English classroom, or they attempt to determine what they think the
instructor wants to know, resulting in parroting a response to literature
that is void of both original thought and personal engagement.

Our aims in this chapter are to discuss four theoretical positions—transactional theory, Marxist theory, feminist theory, and deconstruction theory—underpinning our approach to responding to literature, and then provide numerous examples of informal and formal writing activities to help students achieve deeper, more thoughtful considerations of literary texts. We are certainly aware that writing about literature is not the only way for students to respond to fiction. In fact, discussing literature often results in students contemplating multiple interpretations. We have chosen to focus on written responses in this chapter for several reasons, including the strong relation between writing and thinking and the fact that writing is one of the most important academic skills students will need to exhibit throughout their lives. Additionally, in Chapter 3 we present a good deal of information about using discussions in the classroom.

## Using Multiple Theories to Respond to Literature

Literary criticism is often considered the domain of the "ivory tower," where esoteric theories meet complex narratives (think postcolonial theory and Conrad's *Heart of Darkness*). However, secondary teachers can use a range of critical theories in the classroom. Appleman (2000) refers to each theory (reader response, Marxism, feminism, poststructuralism, deconstruction, etc.) as a critical lens capable of giving students "a way of reading their world; the lenses provide a way of 'seeing' differently and analytically that can help them read the culture of school as well as popular culture." In the following pages, we will focus on describing four of these lenses and provide examples of how each can be used to explore students' understanding of literature and everyday life.

### Rosenblatt and the Transactional Theory of Reading

The situation we described above, in which the instructor tells a class what a book's "hidden" meanings are, has its roots in a literary movement known as New Criticism (Ransom, 1941). In its simplest form, when New Criticism is used in a classroom, a teacher instructs and students listen. Essentially, New Critics examine literature as a self-contained work of art; that is, the book itself holds the "answers" and you, the reader, need to read carefully to find them. A New Critic shuns the author's background as well as the historical context of when the book was written. Applebee (1993) contends that the majority of literary instruction in secondary schools is approached in keeping with the tenets of New Criticism. Problems arise with this method largely because one correct reading—and only one—is thought to exist. Should a student reading Arthur Miller's *The Crucible* determine its most salient theme something such as "humanity needs to be open to religious difference," would miss the mark from a New Critic's perspective because this interpretation, while present within the text, does not entirely adhere to Miller's reasons for writing the play.

Recognizing the limitations of New Criticism, Rosenblatt posited that reading entails more than just finding the answer held within the text. In her most influential works, *Literature as Exploration* (1938/1995) and *The Reader, the Text, the Poem* (1978), Rosenblatt offers an alternative and lasting vision for literary response that gives equal weight to the text and the reader, a radical notion for most scholars of the time. She describes the necessity of placing the reader on level ground with, or perhaps even above, the text. A piece of literature, she notes, does not contain all the answers. It is what the reader brings to the text that ultimately results in "how a book means."

Although Rosenblatt's theory for responding to literature first appeared in the late 1930s, it failed to gain traction in secondary schools until the 1970s. With its emergence came a retooling of the theory and a new title—reader-response theory; however, the core of Rosenblatt's notion remained, namely that the reader needs to bring his experiences to bear on the text. In the decades subsequent to the 1970s, scores of preservice English teachers were taught to engage their students in the literary experience by asking, "Have you ever experienced [fill in the blank] before?" This query serves to place the reader's life along side the text as a way to bridge the gap between lived experience and literary experience, a practice Pirie (1997) has described as the "doctrine of individualism."

According to Christenbury (2000), reader-response classrooms display five characteristics:

1. *Teachers encourage students to talk at length about ideas presented in literature.* To achieve a great deal of student talk about literature, you should avoid what Cazden (1988) has termed the I–R–E pattern of classroom discourse whereby the teacher Initiates a question, a student Responds, and then the teacher Evaluates the response. Instead, urge students to puzzle through a poem's meaning, have them converse

about a character's motivation, and generally invite them to talk at length about any piece of literature. Sometimes, students will disagree with one another, resulting in civil arguments about a text's meaning. Such disagreements do not indicate that students are uncivil, rather they are a sign of true engagment.

2. *Teachers aid students in making a community of meaning.* In any given classroom, individual students bring a range of life experiences, which often results in very diverse responses to literature. At times, factual misunderstandings will occur, but by creating a community of meaning, students themselves clarify misinformation and strive to build solid interpretations together. You will want to be mindful of not jumping into the mix to correct mistakes, while at the same time, you may want to teach students about respecting differences and helping one another out.

3. *Teachers ask far more often than they tell.* True reader-centered classrooms are identified by teachers who are not at the front of the room doing most of the talking. Students, in reader-centered classrooms, are the ones struggling to make sense of a text. This is not to say you should be completely reticent. If students struggle to make sense of a particular passage, for instance, rather than tell them what it might mean, a reader-response teacher will give students a prompt or two in an effort to help make sense of their reading.

4. *Teachers encourage students to make personal connections to the texts they read.* One of the central tenets of reader-response theory is that the reader brings a wealth of lived experience to a text, and the meeting of the two results in a high level of engagement. However, it is crucial that the reader's experience is used to "buttress their points" (Christenbury, 2000). So long as students use their personal backgrounds to shed new light on the text, it is worth asking them to bring up such experiences.

5. *Teachers affirm student responses.* Probably the most obvious way to affirm student responses is to give them overt praise (e.g., "That's a very insightful comment") or to agree with them (e.g., "I, too, see it that way, Mark"). Going beyond overt praise, Christenbury recommends that you refer to student comments throughout a class period by asking other students to respond to a peer. Doing so lets students know that their voices do matter in class, and it validates their perceptions and insights about literature.

While we embrace reader-response criticism as a refreshing antidote to the inflexibility of New Criticism, which did little to engage adolescents or engender more reading, we also must consider some of the shortfalls of a reader-centered classroom. Perhaps most obvious is that if a teacher only asks students to make personal connections to a text, several deficiencies become apparent. First, only asking students to make personal connections discourages a close reading of a text, resulting in what will most likely be a superficial understanding. If you are teaching Barbara Kingsolver's novel *The Bean Trees*, and your central goal is to have students somehow relate to Taylor, the protagonist, then they miss out on the larger issues presented in the text. Another significant problem with reader-centered classrooms is what happens to the reader who fails to find any personal connections with a particular text. More likely than not, such a reader will turn away from the text, claiming, "If I don't see my life in the text, it's not worth reading."

Finally, and maybe most important, we need to be mindful of why we teach literature in the first place. In methods courses, we often ask preservice teachers, "Why are literature courses such an integral part of the secondary school curriculum? What is the value of teaching literature?" Invariably, students respond by saying literature provides us with insight about the human condition; it allows us to explore different perspectives and different cultures that we might not otherwise have an opportunity to see. Should we accept these reasons as plausible, then we must address a question posed by Appleman (2000) regarding the place of a reader-centered classroom: "How can literature foster a knowledge of others when we focus so relentlessly on ourselves and our own experiences?" (p. 29). In short, it may not, and so we must consider other theories for fostering response to literature.

We advocate the use of reader-response theory, although we do so with a few caveats. First, we encourage you to use it as a springboard to engage students. By connecting students' personal background to the text about to be read, you are far more likely to encourage students to want to read the selection. Also, teach your students to ground their opinions in text-specific examples. For instance, when they are reading Margaret Atwood's *The Handmaid's Tale* and you ask what the book's theme is, they ought to say more than simply, "It's about the mistreatment women suffer at the hands of men." You might encourage them to cite examples such as the appellations of the handmaids (e.g., Offred, Ofglen), the significance of Offred's repeating the phrase "Nolite te bastardes carborundum," and the general jobs occupied by women throughout. Remember that reader response is but one of many ways we can elicit responses to literature. Below we discuss three more theories.

### *Marxist Literary Theory*

If you were to watch a variety of television programs for days on end, you would undoubtedly be subjected to a skewed sense of reality for the majority of U.S. residents. Middle and upper-middle class values are the norm, and people seldom seem to work. Situation comedies tend to portray nuclear families whose problems are easily and quickly resolved. Home improvement shows highlight renovation projects costing several thousand dollars. Is that an accurate picture for most of us? Probably not. This is where a Marxist analysis can help illuminate social and power struggles in society.

Marxist literary theory is largely concerned with the political and historical contexts shaping a piece of literature, as well as "the ways in which literary texts and the reading audiences for those texts—including themselves, their classmates, and their teachers—are socially constructed" (Appleman, 2000). That is to say, a piece of literature is written by a person at a certain point in time with a particular set of beliefs. A Marxist critique allows a reader to question who did the writing, what is the writing doing, and how is it doing it? Reality, at least from a social-constructivist's viewpoint, is subjective, and therefore, it is open to criticism.

To demonstrate how we can use a Marxist lens to critique fiction, let us return to our earlier allusion to television. One of the most popular sitcoms in recent years was *Friends*, a series that follows the lives of six 20-something characters, 3 of whom are female and 3 of whom are male. The setting for the show is New York City generally, and a coffee shop and apartment specifically. The apartment where much of the action takes place is enormous by New York City standards, leading the viewer to wonder how dwellers pay the rent, given their itinerant jobs. Also, we know that New York City is among the most racially diverse cities in the United States. So why is it that we rarely see any one other than people of European descent populating the settings? We must conclude that the writers of the show are privileging a particular ideological viewpoint, one that features only attractive characters who have few financial concerns, plenty of free time, and who are racially segregated in a setting that is anything but homogenous.

Examining *Friends* from a Marxist frame of reference—which necessarily includes issues of power, race, class, and ideology—raises all sorts of questions. What does *Friends* say about its creators? What does the huge appeal of the show say about the audience? What financial issues does the show tackle or ignore? What class/socioeconomic factors are presented? What socioeconomic realities are ignored? Which characters exude power and in what ways is it manifested? What ideologies operate in the show? As you begin to unpack some responses to these questions, you will no doubt notice that *Friends* represents a certain kind of worldview, one that privileges white, middle-class values, where leisure time dominates and the everyday struggles many of us face are absent.

Moving from a television series to literature, a Marxist critical lens operates in much the same manner. Patricia McCormick's powerful young adult novel *Sold*, centers on Lakshmi, a young Nepali girl whose stepfather sells her to someone under the guise that she will become a maid for a wealthy family and will thus send her earnings back home to her impoverished family. The sad reality, however, is that she is sold to a brothel in India. Told in lyrical-prose style, *Sold* boldly illuminates the underbelly of the sex slave industry in a way that both saddens and infuriates its readers.

Prior to reading *Sold*, you will most likely need to spend some prereading time building students' prior knowledge regarding the economic and political forces in Nepal. Once you have done so, your class may enter the world of the text through the lens of a Marxist critique. Below are questions you and your students can explore:

- In the United States, what, if any, rules or regulations exist to protect children from unfair labor practices? What about in Nepal and India?
- Create a table with two columns. On the left-hand column, use the heading "Holds Significant Power," and on the right-hand column, use the heading, "Holds Little or No Power." Students should place each character from the text in one of the two columns. Then, in an effort to ensure a close reading, ask them to cite text-specific examples of why they placed the character in the column they did.
- An ideology is a prevailing set of beliefs about the world. What are some examples of ideologies that operate in *Sold*? Always try to use specific examples to support your claim.
- Even within the brothel there are social stratifications. What do you think these different levels of "access to privilege" suggest about humanity as a whole?

We offer the above examples of Marxist critique knowing that some administrators, teachers, and certainly parents will blanch at the mere mention of the term *Marxism,* associating it with "the practice or indoctrination of communism" (Appleman, 2000). However, Marxism as political doctrine should not be equated with a Marxist literary critique, the finer points of which you can discuss with your students and concerned individuals. In sum, a Marxist reading of a text asks students to interrogate an author's reason(s) for writing a text, the beliefs he is promoting in a text, and how race, class, and power privilege certain characters while others are disadvantaged by such social factors.

## Feminist Literary Theory

As illustrated by the Marxist example, studying a piece of literature with a particular theoretical perspective in mind allows us to highlight and view the story in a certain way. Feminist literary criticism, not surprisingly, allows us to examine a text in terms of how women and girls are represented, explicitly and implicitly. For students and teachers new to feminist criticism, it is helpful to "examine the ways in which literary texts reinforce patriarchy because the ability to see when and how patriarchal ideology operates is crucial to our ability to resist it in our own lives" (Tyson, 1999). Feminist theory, however, extends far beyond analyzing the events of the text itself. As feminist readers—and this is applicable to males and females—we are urged to question which authors are included on a school's reading list and why; we are to note how male and female writers employ different styles; and we are to note the subtleties of how different writers—male and female—portray different characters (again, male and female).

The utility of learning about feminist critique is not limited to literary texts. As a means to engage students in this theoretical perspective in a manner they may not initially view as entirely academic, we suggest the following activity. Bring in to your classroom several contemporary magazines students find either appealing or that are targeted to their specific age group. For girls, some titles may include *Glamour, Teen People,* and *Seventeen,* while for boys, some titles may include *Sports Illustrated, Hot Rods,* and *Vibe.* Place the girls in small groups of four and the boys in small groups of four, giving each group a small stack of magazines intended for their counterparts. That is, the female groups receive magazines intended for boys, and the male groups receive magazines intended for girls. Based on the magazines' story contents and advertisements, each group should generate a list of 8–10 statements describing what they believe the editors are saying about girls and boys. For example, a female group might list rugged, athletic, technological, and beer-obsessed as some primary characteristics about males. Each statement should be supported using magazine-specific advertisements and stories.

After the groups have assembled their lists and gathered their support, each group presents its findings. As a whole class, you can determine similarities across same-sex groups, discussing what these findings say about perceived gender differences. On a large scale, then, what are magazine publishers saying about females and males? Are they reinforcing ways that girls ought to act? Are they reifying activities in which boys ought to participate if they are to be considered "masculine"? And by exclusion of certain images and ideas, what are we to make of those girls and boys who do not act, think, and behave in the ways societal forces say they should? Do phrases such as "act like a lady," or "be a man" still matter today, and if so, what do they mean and how should the sexes act?

The activity above serves as instructional scaffolding for introducing feminist literary theory, in addition to helping students see that this theory can serve them in the real world, too. Moving to literature, students can apply similar sorts of questions to any number of texts. For instance, in an 11th-grade advanced literature class, you may be reading Jean Rhys's alternative vision of Charlotte Brontë's *Jane Eyre*, titled *Wide Sargasso Sea*. This text would work best after you have already studied *Jane Eyre*; having read *Jane Eyre* first will allow students to grasp more fully the connection between the texts. Here are examples of questions to guide students in a feminist analysis of *Wide Sargasso Sea*:

- Compare the time when Charlotte Brontë published *Jane Eyre* (1847) to when Rhys published *Wide Sargasso Sea* (1966). What changes have occurred in women's sex-role expectations?
- Why is Rochester's name never overtly used in the text?
- What effect does Rochester's use of the name Bertha (in reference to Antoinette) have on Antoinette?
- Using evidence from the text, cite examples of Antoinette flexing her power.
- Using evidence from the text, cite examples of Rochester flexing his power.
- At the novel's conclusion, who emerges more powerfully, Antoinette or Rochester?

The use of feminist theory serves to provide students not with a definitive way to examine a text (or other cultural object), but rather it gives them an alternative way to look at the powers that shape our worldviews. This is not to say feminist theory encourages "man-hating." What it does is force us to look at how women have been historically closed off to many of the avenues of power and equality.

### Deconstruction

Arguably, no other school of literary criticism inspires more confusion or misunderstanding than deconstruction. Even a simple, workable definition can prove to be elusive. J. O. Milner and L. F. M. Milner (2003) offer a telling analogy to explain deconstruction's philosophical underpinning: "A seasoned umpire was behind home plate and a young hitter was at bat. The tension was high for the young player. He was sweating with every pitch. After a fastball whizzed over the plate, the umpire paused in his calling of balls and strikes. The hitter, puzzled, turned and said, 'Well, what was it? A ball or a strike?' The umpire gazed directly at him and slowly said, 'Sonny, it ain't nothin' till I call it.'" And so it is with a literary interpretation: It ain't nothing' till a reader makes it something. For our purposes, deconstruction is a process by which readers examine language for its fluid and shifting nature, as opposed to the assumption that language is static and fixed.

A deconstructive reading of a text seeks to show how language itself is highly unstable, and how an astute reader can demonstrate the inherent contradictions in a narrative. As most of us know, the transmission of words rarely occurs in an unambiguous, neutral vacuum; rather, we hear and read words, then attach a multitude of subtexts to a message, which helps explain why we have disagreements with others. For example, let's say you offered a friend a glass of red wine, and he responds, "No thanks, I'm not interested." You could interpret the rejection in a number of ways: Is he not interested in red wine because he only drinks chardonnay? Is he not interested in taking the time to consume a glass of wine with you? Is he not interested in wine generally? A deconstructionist will attempt to piece together the ambiguities and multiple contradictions in a language to show that many interpretations are possible, not one fixed reading, as the New Critics would have it.

When teaching deconstruction to students, we need to be mindful of some pitfalls (Moore, 1997). Moore warns us to be cautious of allowing students to view the process as an "anything goes" destruction of a text. "As a way of reading, it does not aim to obliterate the meaning of a text but to open up a text so that meaning multiplies indefinitely through a process in which we resist complacency in our readings." Furthermore, a deconstructionist encourages us to guide students away from dualistic thinking, a hallmark of adolescent cognition. While deconstructionists value thinking about texts in imaginative, multivariate ways, teens often think in terms of black or white, good or evil, or sanity or insanity. Coaxing them toward a more flexible way of thinking helps young readers "to see more readily the ways in which our experience is determined by ideologies of which we are unaware because they are built into our language" (Tyson, 1999).

Because deconstruction is rather ephemeral and difficult to describe, Appleman (2000) suggests starting students with the deconstruction of metaphors rather than whole texts. As we mentioned earlier, deconstructionist literary interrogation rests on the notion that meaning in language is always in flux, and thus, too, is an author's work. Show students the following metaphor: Love is a rose. Ask them to provide what they consider the *intended* meaning of this metaphor. Responses may include, "Love is delicate and beautiful, just like a flower," or perhaps, "Love is fragile, like rose petals, but is also capable of pain, like a rose thorn." Once you have established intended meanings, you can ask them to deconstruct the metaphor by discussing unintended meanings. Sample responses here may include, "Love always withers and dies, just like a rose," or, "Love requires too much pruning, like a rose bush." This example begins to illustrate that despite an author's best intentions, language can always be deconstructed to reveal various interpretations.

From deconstructing metaphors, students can move on to poems, short stories, and novels using the framework below for guidance:

- Students select a text they think might have multiple meanings.
- Students read the text very carefully, noting specifically where it opens itself to various ways of meaning.
- Students write responses to the following questions: "What do I think is the author's intended meaning of the work under consideration? In other words, what do I believe the author wanted me to take away from the text?"
- Finally, students cite a few examples of text-specific language where the intentional or obvious meaning breaks down because the author's ideas can be interpreted in a variety of ways.

We noted at the onset of the section on deconstruction that this theory is often misunderstood and difficult to understand, for teachers and students alike. That said, we do see its value in the secondary classroom, particularly so because it forces students to think in very divergent ways about language, authorial intent, and the very nature of reality. With your guided practice, you will see that your students are capable of this very sophisticated, intellectual form of literary interrogation.

### A Final Word about Literary Theory

In writing this chapter, we felt it important to include a section on literary theory because it is not only a worthwhile intellectual pursuit, but also useful in "reading" everyday events. However, we touched upon but a few of the many literary theories available to you. Should you find yourself compelled to learn about other possibilities, we recommend you research the following schools of criticism: moral/philosophical, historical/biographical, formalist, rhetorical, Freudian, archetypal, new historicism, structuralism, poststructuralism, postcolonial, and postmodernism. Regardless of which theories you choose to use in your classroom, you will find that students can grasp the concepts and will be able to look at texts from various vantage points.

# Writing about Literature

Many English classrooms are dominated by two principle activities—reading and writing. Typically, a teacher assigns a text (poem, short story, play, or novel), students read it, and then the teacher asks students to respond to the reading through any number of writing tasks. What we are most concerned with is giving you a sense of what sorts of writing tasks result in intellectual and creative thought that will engage your students. As we have noted in Chapter 3, merely asking students to respond to factual questions on a study guide will not result in enduring understanding; more likely than not, such information will be lost shortly after the text has been read.

In this section of the chapter, we focus on two types of writing about literature—informal and formal. For the sake of discussion, we separate these two kinds of writing, although we recognize that in a classroom context, informal writing often leads into formal writing. In our own teaching, we frequently ask students to do impromptu writing from which they then develop more formal essays. As we stress throughout this book, making all learning tasks engaging, meaningful, and interconnected is crucial; and writing is certainly no different.

### Informal Writing

Prior to the late 1960s, a majority of English teachers enacted a "product approach" to writing instruction, meaning they would assign a topic, ask students to complete it on their own, grade it, and return it to the students with little, if any, follow-up instruction (Fulkerson, 1979). Such papers tended to be exposition, and a great deal of attention was paid to grammatical correctness. Writing to think or generate ideas was rarely done.

Writing instruction changed dramatically in the late 1960s and early 1970s when individuals such as Donald Murray, Ken McCrorie, Janet Emig, and Peter Elbow began advocating a "process approach" to writing whereby the task of composing was viewed as evolutionary, with the writer being granted time to rethink and rework his ideas. Writers were encouraged to generate ideas, draft, revise, workshop their pieces, and edit. It is from this movement that we can trace the origins of informal writing. Anson and Beach (1995) posit that informal writing differs markedly from more formal writing in that it tends to be expressive, tentative, subjective, and exploratory.

*Journaling* is one of the most widely used modes of expression to write about literature in the contemporary classroom. A literature journal allows students to explore potential interpretations of a text, to pose questions about confounding aspects of a story, or to respond to open-ended prompts from the teacher (Beach, Appleman, Hynds, & Wilhelm, 2006). Students who are more introverted, and thus are reluctant participants in classroom discussions, often appreciate the opportunity to "talk" about a text through journals.

In addition to having students respond in a journal as described in the preceding paragraph, you can develop a host of ways to encourage literary thought. One of us asks students to use T-charts in their journals. On a word processing document or a blank sheet of paper, students draw a horizontal line across the top of the page and a vertical line down the middle. Atop the left-hand column, they should write, "What I Wonder" and atop the right-hand column, they should write, "What I Think." As students work their way through a text, they respond on the T-chart in a highly speculative and tentative manner. For example, if they are reading August Wilson's *Fences*, a story of a father and son at odds about the latter accepting an athletic scholarship, a student may write under the "What I Wonder" column, "I remember talking earlier this semester about the significance of titles. Last year we read a Robert Frost poem where he said something about fences serving to wall things in or wall things out. I'm curious to see what the two main characters in this play, Cory and Troy, are walling in or out." Because this entry would likely be written at the beginning of the play, the student writer may not have a very well developed sense of the importance of his wondering, so he can leave the "What I Think" side blank, returning to it once he enters the text and finds a reasonable answer to his question. Encourage your students to add to their T-charts throughout the reading of a text. Also, students should feel free to add to or change their responses based on newly gained information.

Another form of journal writing is the dialogue journal. Anson and Beach (1995) encourage its use between students. For instance, in a 10th-grade literature course, you assign Amy Tan's intergenerational novel *The Joy Luck Club*. Students can either choose their own partners or you can assign the pairs. Each day, one of the partners writes about the text, including questions and possible interpretations and passes his response to the partner, who responds to the initial reaction and adds new thoughts. Given our ubiquitous access to email, exchanges can be easily transmitted electronically.

In addition to the student-paired journal described above, Atwell (1998) advocates using a dialogue journal between the student and the teacher. One primary difference in the two modes of dialoguing is that student and teacher exchanges will occur far less frequently. Obviously, a teacher with five or six sections of eighth-grade English cannot respond with any regularity to 150 students. That said, one of the great benefits of Atwell's dialogue journal is that you gain tremendous insight about a student's level of understanding and effort, whereas you may not have such access in the between-student dialogue journals until you collect and read them. Regardless of which mode you choose, we strongly encourage you to model what is expected of students in their dialogue journals. Merely telling your class to dialogue journal is not enough; explaining to them why you are asking them to partake in the activity and showing them what kinds of responses are valuable will result in the kinds of thinking about literature you want to encourage.

*Free writing* is a mode of informal writing used to generate ideas on a general topic related to a piece of literature or specific portion of a text. Usually timed at roughly 5–10 minutes, free writing enables students to write down thoughts without concern for completeness of expression, grammatical conventions, and the absolute viability of an idea. Perhaps most importantly, students should never censor or block their ideas during free writing. According to Elbow (1973), "Don't stop for anything. Go quickly without rushing. Never stop to look back, to cross something out, to wonder how to spell something, to wonder what word or thought to use, or to think about what you are doing." The impetus for free writing is to give students permission to free themselves from thinking in definitive, absolutist ways. Allowing students to write without concern for getting it perfect often results in producing divergent ways of interpreting a story.

Free-writes can serve to focus students' attention at the beginning of a class period. One effective way to begin class is to provide students with a prompt that relates to an overall goal you might have for the day. Assume you are to begin reading Tim O'Brien's, "On the Rainy River," which chronicles a young man's moral dilemma regarding whether to cross the U.S. border into Canada to avoid fighting in the Vietnam War. By giving students the following prompt, you not only focus their attention on the story, but also you activate their schema so they can anticipate what they will soon encounter in the story: "What thoughts and emotions might you have if you received a letter from the local draft board stating that you had to report for war duty? Would you entertain the idea of refusing to serve? Why or why not?"

This free-writing prompt can also be an excellent aid for discussion. With the best of intentions, we often begin class by trying to engage our students in classroom talk, yet students are sometimes reluctant speakers because we fail to provide them with adequate thinking time (Eddleston & Philippot, 2002). Having students spend 5–10 minutes on a free-write creates a classroom context where everyone is focused on a similar topic, and everyone can, in turn, add to the discussion.

*Clustering* (variously referred to as mind-mapping, semantic-mapping, or simply mapping) is the last informal writing technique we discuss. The key idea behind clustering is that students graphically represent main ideas or characters and their attending relationships. Visual learners and ELLs find clustering a particularly useful tool in understanding the connections within a text (Dornan, Rosen, & Wilson, 2003; Galda & Graves, 2007).

In its simplest form, a cluster begins with the writer placing the main character or idea in the center of a piece of paper. From there, the writer lists all the ideas or related characters on the periphery, with lines extending outward from the main circle. Figure 4.1 shows an example of a cluster based on Alice Walker's "Everyday Use."

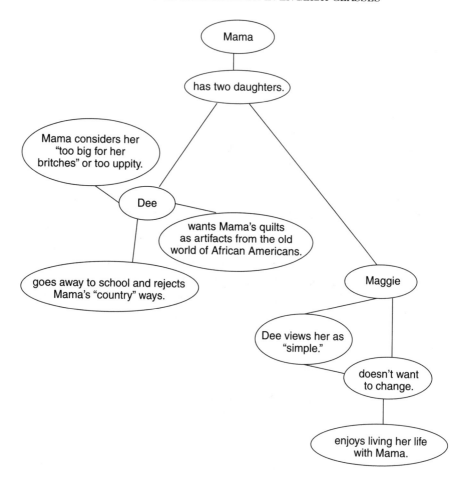

**FIGURE 4.1.** Cluster map for Alice Walker's "Everyday Use."

A variation on the cluster map that encourages a close reading of a narrative is a sociogram. Like a cluster map, the main character of a story is placed in the center of the paper; all other characters in the story are placed on the periphery. Students need to use the author's descriptions and dialogue to determine the relationships between and among the characters. Whereas in a cluster map, students simply draw a straight line to another character or idea, in a sociogram, the type of relationship is revealed through different types of lines. For instance, referring back to "Everyday Use," Mama's relationship with her daughter Dee is strained, so a student might represent that tension with a dashed line.

Dee's sister, Maggie, has strong feelings of affection for Mama, so this line might be wavy. Each student will need to develop a "legend" that describes what the various lines indicate about a relationship. In short, a sociogram demands that students use story-specific understandings to determine how the characters view one another.

## Assessing Informal Writing about Literature

As educators, we live in an age of increasing accountability, especially in terms of measuring our students' progress. Even though journaling, free writing, and clustering are meant as springboards for fostering deeper understandings of literature, they can and ought to be assessed. Because of the nature of how these writing activities are implemented— typically, they are done quickly, with a greater emphasis on generating ideas, often at the expense of organization and thoroughness—we do not recommend weighing them heavily in terms of overall importance to a final grade, nor do we suggest you grade them as you would a more formal piece of writing. Also, we have yet to meet an English teacher who begs for more papers on which to write copious feedback. Consequently, we offer some ways to assess informal writing that is both instructive and less time consuming.

The *check system* is an easy, quick way to acknowledge students' writing without laboring over commentary. Prior to grading reading journals, for example, you should establish in writing criteria for excellent work, satisfactory work, and below expectations work. If you asked students to write in their reading journals three times per week, with each entry a minimum of one page, you already have a starting point for your criteria. Beyond those elements, excellent work may involve original ideas or interpretations, thoughtful questions posed about the literature, and the use of text-specific information to support ideas. An excellent journal will receive a check-plus, a satisfactory journal will receive a check, and a below expectations journal will receive a check-minus. Below is an example of a general rubric for grading reading journals:

### ✓+ (Excellent)

The student engaged in the literature we are currently studying at a high level of sophistication and understanding. The student posed questions that reflect a complexity of thinking regarding the text. Original interpretations and musings were forwarded using text-specific details for support.

✓ (Satisfactory)

The student adequately addressed issues presented in the literature; ideas and interpretations were brought forth, although often superficially. At times, the student merely summarized the plot rather than raise potential interpretations and questions.

✓– (Doesn't meet expectations)

The student only minimally addressed issues in the literature. It appears that the student was merely going through the motions of the assignment, which is manifested in a lack of critical engagement. Also, the entries were short and seemingly had little to do with the actual text.

One big advantage of using the check system is that it allows you to assess students' writing fairly quickly. Though you are not providing students with individualized, personal commentary, you can underline sentences and phrases you find particularly compelling or interesting, making sure to tell students that the underlines represent ideas you found highly insightful and compelling.

Another informal writing assessment strategy we find useful is *student self-assessment*. It is one technique that if used properly can aid students in better understanding their own strengths and weaknesses. According to Milner and Milner (2003), "Because schooling has traditionally located evaluation outside of the student—in the teacher, the parent, the school, and the school district—students have learned to depend on others for identification of their weaknesses or confirmation of their achievements." At some point in students' lives—and we hope it is sooner rather than later—they need to know how to look inward to gauge their own progress, then make decisions based on their self-evaluation.

Prior to asking students to perform self-evaluations, it is important that you explain why you are doing so. Daniels (2002) suggests using the self-evaluation instrument with literature circles shown in Figure 4.2.

This self-assessment tool, coupled with a teacher observation chart shown in Figure 4.3, will give you a well-rounded picture of how an individual performs on this particular activity.

If the student self-assessment does not match up with the teacher observation chart, then you will need to confer with the student regarding your different perspectives. Our experience in using self-

**Student Self-Evaluation of Performance in Literature Circles**

For each question below, rate yourself on a scale of 1 to 5, with 1 being the lowest and 5 the highest.

Text: _____    Date: _____

Student name: _____

I arrived at class having read the assigned material:        _____

I listened to what others had to say about the text:        _____

I prepared questions and insights ahead of time:        _____

I encouraged others to participate in the discussion:        _____

I contributed positively to our discussion:        _____

TOTAL: _____/25

**FIGURE 4.2.** Student self-evaluation of performance in literature circles.

assessments is that students are, for the most part, honest about their efforts and work quality.

The literature circle self-assessment just described requires little time on the part of the students, but is nevertheless revealing. A more time-consuming and self-reflective form of self-assessment can be applied to writing assignments. Earlier in the chapter, we discussed journal writing or reading logs. Prior to handing in their journals, students can be instructed to review the musings, tentative interpretations, and questions they wrote during a unit focused on a specific text. Next, you can provide them with a list of potential issues to address in their self-assessment, which should probably be a minimum of one page. A partial list of questions follows:

- To what extent do your responses go beyond merely summarizing the plot? Use a specific example to illustrate each point.
- In what ways did your interpretations change over time? Again, be specific.
- How, if at all, did your thoughts about any of the characters change over time?
- What do you perceive as the strengths of your reading log?
- What do you perceive as the weaknesses of your log?

**Teacher Observation Sheet for Assessing Literature Circle Performance**

Group: _____     Date: _____

| Student | Prepared (Y/N) | Participated (Y/N) | Thinking Skills | Social Skills |
|---|---|---|---|---|
| 1. | | | | |
| 2. | | | | |
| 3. | | | | |
| 4. | | | | |
| 5. | | | | |

**FIGURE 4.3.** Teacher observation sheet for assessing literature circle performance.

- Describe one or two entries that you are particularly proud of. What makes them stand out for you?
- If you were to assign a check-plus, check, or check-minus to your log, which would it be and why?
- Do you think keeping a reading log is a valuable activity? Explain your response.
- Do you prefer writing entries about anything that strikes you as interesting in the text, or would you rather write in response to a prompt I assign?

The last two questions in particular can serve to help you refine the reading log for future use. Based on the feedback you receive, you may want to scale back the number of entries students write, or perhaps you learned that students enjoy responding to prompts. In short, you and your students you can learn a great deal from self-evaluations.

Regardless of the kinds of informal writing you ask students to engage in, we cannot stress enough its importance. As many scholars have pointed out, writing promotes and clarifies thinking (e.g., Langer, 1986; Langer & Applebee, 1987; Smith, 1990), so the more of it you ask students to do, the more intellectually nimble they will become. By using the assessment techniques we describe, as well as others you may already know about, you will have greater insight about your students' thinking. However, we all know that informal writing should not be the only composing students do in the English classroom. In the following section, we discuss formal writing about literature.

## Formal Writing about Literature

When writing informally about literature, students tend to engage in the process with less apprehension than they would a more formal essay, knowing that the stakes are usually much lower. Their papers will not be returned with every comma splice and incomplete thought marked in red ink, which is often the case with formal writing. Formal writing, though often difficult for students to do well and time consuming for you to teach and assess, is relevant and necessary. Formal writing helps students understand the importance of sustained intellectual effort, it promotes close reading, and it sharpens their attention to formal linguistic structures.

We fully recognize that formal writing about literature takes many shapes and forms, and for this section of the chapter, we have decided to focus on writing literary analysis papers, primarily because it is a pervasive genre in schools. So that your students do not come to resent writing formal literary analysis papers, we will discuss how to design engaging assignments, along with certain skills and techniques you will want to impart to them to ensure success. Merely telling your students to write a three-page paper on the theme of Hemingway's *The Old Man and the Sea* will surely elicit groans. Finally, we conclude this section with a brief discussion on how to evaluate formal writing, which extends beyond simply attaching a grade to a composition.

Many of us can recall being assigned a thematic analysis paper. We were told to compose the essay outside of class with very little in the way of directions or models. Essentially, we either knew how this genre of writing was supposed to unfold, or we did not. The simple fact is, as a literature teacher, you are almost certainly expected to teach students to write formal literary analysis papers. To aid you in doing so, we offer several suggestions.

### Developing an Assignment

Formal writing about literature should not be assigned without context. Much of what you do and talk about in class should help prepare students for writing the literary analysis paper. In addition to whole-class and small-group discussions of literature that serve to scaffold students' ability to write this paper, you can have them use the informal writing discussed earlier in this chapter as a springboard for potential ideas. In short, ask students to do lots of prewriting, which helps "prime the pump."

John Steinbeck's "Johnny Bear" provides several opportunities for prewriting. To encourage student thinking about certain aspects that play a significant role in the story, you could have students prewrite informally on the following topics that you generated: Why are humans so attracted to gossip, especially when its truthfulness is questionable? Do a Google search for the term *idiot savant*. Take note on what you find. Recall certain movie genres you have seen, such as crime films or horror films. To what extent has setting played a role in establishing the tone of what occurs in such films? Television programs (such as *Entertainment Tonight*) and magazines (such as *People*) chronicle the lives of celebrities. What is it about celebrities—be they movie stars, athletes, politicians, or business leaders—that fascinates us so much? How do community norms and mores become entrenched? Of course, you need not have students respond to all prompts, but we wanted to provide a sample of the kind of prewriting that helps students. Also, the list of topics for prewriting can certainly be extended beyond what we have included.

Over the course of time, your class will have read "Johnny Bear," discussed it, and participated in prewriting exercises. Next, you will need to lay the groundwork for the formal writing assignment. Most literary analysis essays are structured as arguments, whereby the writer seeks to prove a certain point. Without going into too much detail, you should teach your students the basics of argumentation: claim (thesis statement), evidence (supporting details from the story), and conclusion. We recommend you show models of this arrangement to students, paying special attention to the importance of using quotations from the text to uphold the thesis statement.

One obvious yet crucial aspect of assigning formal writing that is sometimes overlooked is the usefulness of giving students a handout detailing all the required elements of the paper. If you have a website, you can post it there. On the assignment sheet, provide students with an overall purpose and the parameters of the paper. For instance, in a paper for "Johnny Bear," your purpose statement might read, "Reading literature does more than entertain us; it provides us insight into ourselves and to the world around us. In your essay draw parallels between the issues or themes in 'Johnny Bear' and contemporary life. How do the themes in Steinbeck's story mirror life events generally, or your life specifically? Your paper should be three to four pages, double-spaced using a word processing program, and it must conform to the conventions of argumentation we discussed in class (claim, support, conclusion). Be certain to use specific textual information in drawing your parallels between the story and real life. Finally, consult your prewriting assignments to help you generate ideas."

Setting time lines for first, second, and final copies is important so that students can workshop their papers. Let's say you give students a week to complete draft one. On the day the draft is due, each student should bring two copies of the paper to class. At the beginning of class, place students in groups of three and have them give each other feedback. You may want to provide students with a specific peer review question to attend to while responding. For example, you may ask, "What, specifically, is the writer's claim? If you cannot detect it, perhaps you might suggest one." Questions such as this help guide the reviewer so that he is focused on required elements of the paper. Giving students multiple opportunities to revise their essays allows them to refine their ideas to the extent that they can take pride knowing they have worked hard at a sustained intellectual task.

*Evaluating Formal Writing*

Regardless of how hard we try to examine students' writing in an objective manner, the process of grading their work will always be somewhat subjective. Some teachers tend to view good student writing as being free of mechanical and usage errors, while others look for well-developed ideas, ignoring such matters as verb-tense and pronoun–antecedent problems. One of the most effective ways we have found to grade student writing is to use well-developed rubrics, which enable us to assess writing as the sum of several parts, not just one particular aspect.

A very popular and well-regarded way to examine writing is through the use of the six-traits writing rubric (Spandel, 2004). The six traits are ideas, organization, voice, sentence fluency, word choice, and conventions. Ideas, or the content of the essay, refer to what the writer is focusing on in his paper. Organization deals with the order in which the writer presents his ideas. Voice focuses on the manner in which the writer conveys his content (serious, humorous, informal, formal, etc.). Sentence fluency concerns the variability of sentence types (simple, compound, complex, compound–complex) and the flow of the overall work. Word choice looks at whether word usage matches a particular writing task and audience for the writing. Finally, conventions deal with grammar and usage matters.

One of the most useful aspects of the six-traits writing rubric from our vantage point is that it can be flexibly used in evaluating student work. Spandel's (2004) book contains dozens of sample rubrics that can be adapted to fit virtually any writing task you develop.

*Other Formal Writing Tasks*

As an English teacher, you have an unlimited number of topics on which to have students write using a variety of genres. The formal writing about literature we have described has been solely limited to literary analysis; however, other options exist. Below we briefly describe three additional writing tasks focused on literature.

A *multigenre assignment* (Romano, 2000) allows students to choose a singular theme, topic, or text, and through various genres developed by the student, that theme is cast in multiple ways. For example, if you are studying the poetry of Langston Hughes, your students can represent a specific aspect of Hughes's poetry—such as their conceptions of "Harlem"—by using advertisements, journal writing, original poems, news stories from the 1920s, and pictures, along with any other text connected to the theme. So that students are highly deliberate about the choices they make in developing their multigenre paper, you might require some sort of "framing essay" in which they discuss what they are representing and how their supporting texts contribute to a unified whole. Given many of our students' technological sophistication, they could develop a multimedia presentation and post it on a classroom website or perhaps submit it to the NCTE's annual student writing contest (see *www.ncte.org* for more details).

*Creative writing in response to literature* is another activity that students find engaging. Almost every English teacher has heard students voice their disappointment with a story's ending, so challenge them to rewrite a story's conclusion in a more satisfying way. Or have them write a newspaper article based on a story. In an effort to examine a text from a different viewpoint, ask students to tell the story from a different character's perspective. Visual learners might relish the idea of taking a scene from a novel and drafting a movie script. There are endless possibilities when it comes to writing creatively about literature. What we really appreciate about this kind of writing is that it gives students freedom to be creative, while at the same time it requires their deep understanding of the text.

Finally, *inquiry papers* (Eddleston, 1998) position the students as "textual investigators" who determine what is interesting or confusing about certain elements of a text. By posing a question about an aspect of a text they want to know more about, they become responsible for creating meaning. Inquiry papers can vary in length, but the key component is that students ask a question and offer a potential answer. Sharon Eddleston set aside time during class for students to share their inquiry papers with their peers, who then had the opportunity to respond to the initial inquirer. For instance, a student reading Arthur Miller's *Death of a Salesman* might ask, "Does Willy Loman really believe he's a success as a husband and businessman, or does he know deep down he's a fraud?" Using textual support, the student seeks answers to his inquiry. The use of inquiry papers necessitates a significant amount of teaching and modeling on your part, but it does give students the power to determine what they want to know about a piece of literature. Because the student chooses the area of a text to explore in detail—in opposition to the teacher determining the topic—greater interest will likely follow. And as we know, the more students are interested in their work, the more mental energy they will devote to it.

# Concluding Remarks

Much of the work an English teacher does revolves around having students respond to literature in one way or another. Many of the preservice teachers with whom we work cite their own love of literature as the primary reason for wanting to become teachers. Thus, we believe responding to literature deserves a central role in this book.

We opened the chapter by examining the importance of introducing students to a range of response theories, beginning with Rosenblatt's (1938/1995) transactional theory of reading, which posits that a reader brings unique experiences and beliefs to bear on a text, resulting in an individualized sense of a text's meaning. From there we looked at additional lenses with which to critique literature, including Marxist theory, feminist theory, and deconstruction theory. Each lens allows students a unique opportunity with which to engage in literature. The remainder of this chapter attended to informal and formal writing about literature, along with ways to assess it.

Critical to the success of most of the activities we discuss here is the need to be explicit in teaching your students how to go about responding to literature. It would be wonderful if all 10th graders knew the elements of literature and automatically pick up on them when reading a short story, but this is not the case. Modeling how you make meaning from a text is a tremendously powerful vehicle for communicating with students. Yes, it is a messy process, but students need to see that you, too, need to work hard when reading. Doing so will demystify the process of response.

Additionally, we need to stress that variety is truly the spice of life in an English classroom. Expose your students to a variety of texts, from the classics to contemporary works to young adult literature. Ask them to read plays, short stories, poems, and new media works found on the web. Give your students multiple opportunities to develop their responses to literature over time. Have them write about literature in ways that explore tentative interpretations that will not heavily affect their grade, and at times, ask them to produce a formal academic paper requiring lots of time and effort. Ultimately, we want students to become critical, independent thinkers who enjoy delving into literature, so give them the tools to do so and the authority to make meaning for themselves.

## LITERATURE/FILMS CITED

Atwood, Margaret. (1985). *The handmaid's tale*. New York: Fawcett Crest.

Brontë, Charlotte. (1847/1997). *Jane Eyre*. New York: Signet Classics.

Conrad, Joseph. (1902/1999). *Heart of darkness*. New York: Penguin.

Crane, David, & Kauffman, Marta. (Creators). (1994–2004). *Friends* [Television series]. New York: NBC Television.

Hemmingway, Ernest. (1952). *The old man and the sea*. New York: Scribner.

Hughes, Langston. (1951)."Harlem." In *Montage of a dream* (p. 71). New York: Holt.

Kingsolver, Barbara. (1988). *The bean trees*. New York: Harper Perennial.

McCormick, Patricia. (2006). *Sold*. New York: Hyperion.

Miller, Arthur. (1949/1998). *Death of a salesman*. New York: Penguin.

Miller, Arthur. (1952/1995). *The crucible*. New York: Penguin.

O'Brien, Tim. (1990) On the rainy river. In *The things they carried* (pp. 41–63). New York: Broadway Books.

Rhys, Jean. (1966/2001). *Wide Sargasso sea*. New York: Penguin.

Steinbeck, John. (1939). Johnny bear. In *The long valley* (pp. 145–168). New York: Viking Press.

Tan, Amy. (1989). *The joy luck club*. New York: Ivy Books.

Walker, Alice. (1973). Everyday use. In *In Love and trouble: Stories of Black women* (pp. 7–59). New York: Harcourt Brace Jovanovich.

Wilson, August. (1986). *Fences*. New York: Penguin.

# CHAPTER 5

# Teaching
# Comprehension Strategies

We don't read a novel the same way that we read a menu or
a newspaper. But how does our reading differ across genre
or from author to author? What about a memoir or a novel
like Willa Cather's *My Antonia*: Do we read these differently
than we do a novel like Fitzgerald's *The Great Gatsby*?
And if we don't read them the same way, how do we read
them? Narratives, along with all other texts, conform to a
continuum of complexity that depends on both the feature
of the particular text and the capacities of the reader.
—JIM BURKE, English teacher and writer

In Samantha Peters's English education program, she was required
to take only one course focused exclusively on reading instruction. As
she began her first teaching position in an economically and culturally
diverse high school, Samantha's lack of know-how quickly became evident. Students who struggled to understand their texts fell further and
further behind as the semester progressed, not because she failed to
notice their lack of comprehension, but rather because she lacked anything like a systematic approach to helping them improve their level of
understanding—a shortcoming we fear is far too common among newly
certified teachers. The methods courses Samantha took focused primarily on reader response to literature, but as Jim Burke astutely points out
in the quotation above, not all books require the same approach.

Unfortunately, comprehension strategies, which Pearson and his
colleagues (Pearson, Roehler, Dole, & Duffy, 1992) defined as "conscious and flexible plans that readers apply and adopt to a variety of

texts and tasks," receive little if any attention at the secondary level, largely because they are commonly considered the purview of elementary teachers. Certainly we agree that it is of utmost importance that younger students be explicitly taught comprehension strategies, but we also realize that more and more secondary students lack some of these necessary skills. Ideally, the teaching of comprehension strategies should occur in upper elementary or middle school grades, but if for some reason it does not, it needs to happen later. This is particularly true for struggling readers. However, better readers will also benefit from reviewing and practicing the strategies presented herein.

In the pages that follow, we describe the characteristics of comprehension strategies, list and define eight individual strategies, provide a 2-day, partial instructional plan for teaching a strategy, and consider four sequences of strategies that students can use across a range of different texts.

# Characteristics of Comprehension Strategies

Referring back to Pearson and his colleagues' definition of comprehension strategies, it is important to keep in mind that all strategies ought to be taught as tools to be used flexibly. A particular strategy that works for one student with a given text may very well prove ineffective with a different student reading another text. Pressley (2000) has noted that proficient readers possess a vast array of reading strategies that best fit each text they read. Our hope is that all readers, including ELLs and those with learning disabilities, learn how to use strategies flexibly so that they can become independent learners who enjoy reading. In the following pages, we focus on commonly agreed upon characteristics of comprehension strategies, using brief examples that illustrate each of them.

## Comprehension Strategies Are Conscious Efforts

As we read, we need to deliberately employ strategies that help us understand what we read. For example, many students—certainly those who are adept readers—automatically use inferences to make meaning of a text. However, for those who are less proficient readers, you will want to be explicit in terms of teaching them what an inference entails and how to make them. Then, as the class reads a section out loud, for instance, you may want to pause so they know they need to make an inference. With time and practice, these overtly conscious efforts become habitual and automatic, thus decreasing the need for direct attention. However, it is important to recognize that even well-learned strategies can be brought to consciousness and placed under the control of the reader. When your students are fully aware of why and when they use certain comprehension strategies, they will be better equipped to draw upon them when encountering new and challenging texts.

### Comprehension Strategies Are Flexible

Flexibility and adaptability are hallmarks of strategies. Teaching students that a given strategy can be used in a variety of ways depending on the text and their purpose for reading it is essential. For example, one of our former students, John Erlman, teaches a class entitled World Literature. One of the books he regularly teaches and enjoys using is Homer's *The Odyssey*. Because the narrative is not told in a strictly linear manner, students often struggle to understand the chronology of events. To help untangle the epic, John asks students to create a time line from when Odysseus originally left Ithaca for the Trojan War to when he returned home to his one true love, Penelope. As they read each chapter, students place the events on the continuum. John does this so readers can visualize Odysseus's journey sequentially, and thus they better understand the entire structure of the narrative. Students could do this same activity with other nonlinear texts, or with narratives that have numerous characters and settings.

### Comprehension Strategies Should Be Applied Only When Appropriate

An important aspect of teaching strategies involves helping students determine when a strategy is useful and appropriate, and, conversely, when it is not. If, for instance, you have taught students that rereading is beneficial to grasping key concepts, and you ask them to reread a selection they thoroughly understood because of its simplicity—or if you simply want them to gain a general idea of the piece—then rereading is not an appropriate strategy. However, if you are teaching students how to become better test takers, then you would want to stress the importance of rereading directions and test passages.

### Comprehension Strategies Are Widely Applicable

Most strategies can be applied across a wide range of ages, abilities, and reading material. It is important that an eighth grader can summarize key events in *Freaky Green Eyes* by Joyce Carol Oates. It is important that an 11th grader can summarize Chinua Achebe's anticolonialist epic *Things Fall Apart*. And it is important that preservice English teachers can summarize key concepts in this text.

### Comprehension Strategies Can Be Overt or Covert

Some strategies involve readers in creating some sort of observable product, while others involve mental operations that cannot be directly seen. If you ask students to summarize a short story in writing, for example, a physical manifestation of that strategy exists, and thus it is overt. On the other hand, determining what is important in a text is a strategy that is largely done in the reader's head, and therefore we cannot observe it being performed. We suggest that when initially teaching strategies, you focus on students producing an observable artifact so you know they understand the strategy in question. Over time, however, most strategies become unobservable mental processes.

## Essential Comprehension Strategies

Although there exist a tremendous variety of comprehension strategies, researchers agree on a handful of several key strategies that have proven most beneficial (see e.g., National Reading Panel, 2000; Pressley, 2006). Below we highlight eight of these strategies, define them, and provide examples of how to teach them. Keep in mind that the strategies we discuss do not necessarily exist independent of one another; rather, the mental processes needed to enact one strategy, such as summarizing, often require the reader to rely on another strategy, such as making inferences. Since readers actively construct meaning as they work their way through a text, it is important that they have at their disposal all of the strategies we describe, not just one or two of them.

### Using Prior Knowledge

As the name of this strategy suggests, a reader needs to draw upon her schema of a particular topic prior to reading so that she may be better prepared to integrate the new information she will encounter with her existing knowledge. For instance, let us say you are teaching a 10th-grade general English class, and you are about to begin reading Walter Dean Meyers's *Fallen Angels*, the setting for which is the Vietnam War. Students without much information about the political upheaval of the 1960s in the United States may struggle with the text. Furthermore, if they specifically lack knowledge about the Vietnam War and why it was such a polarizing event for citizens and soldiers alike, they may very well misunderstand the motives and feelings of Perry, the main character. Rather than look to the past, you might ask students what they know about more recent wars, such as the war in Iraq or Afghanistan. Students may have vague ideas about these military efforts that they have encountered from watching the news or from reading online news sites such as *cnn.com*. Although students might not possess deep understandings of war, they will be much more apt to comprehend what they read because they have called to the forefront of their thoughts ideas of what recent war times are like and how military efforts impact soldiers and the general population.

Should students have little or no prior knowledge about a given topic, it is important that you provide them with at least a basic framework for understanding whatever topic they are going to encounter. So, prior to beginning a book such as *Fallen Angels*, ask students what they know about the Vietnam War. When did it begin and end? Why did the United States become involved? You might even use selected scenes from the film *Apocalypse Now* to help students visualize the setting. Anything you can do to help them tap into their existing knowledge of the topic under study will help them understand more of what they will soon encounter in the text you assign.

We all use prior knowledge in a host of ways each and every day—from determining what products to buy at the grocery store to deciding on where to live. Of course, using prior knowledge is no guarantee that we will always make the right choice, just as it does not guarantee that we will always completely understand everything we read, but it certainly does enable us to anticipate potential issues we are likely to face.

### Asking and Answering Questions

When using this strategy, a reader asks questions both prior to and while reading a selection; then she attempts to address the questions as she progresses through the text. Throughout this book, we have made repeated references to the fact that good reading must be an active process, and asking and answering questions about a text, if done properly, virtually ensures it. By asking a series of questions related to a text, a reader will be far more attentive to the information that will help answer her questions.

Consider a ninth-grade class about to begin reading Pete Hautman's novel *Godless*, a story of a high school boy's struggle with religion, friendship, and authority. More likely than not, students will find the protagonist's invented religion, Chutengodianism, odd. Students' questions may range from the elementary (Why does Jason's mother seem to think he's always ill?) to the more sophisticated (Why do virtually all cultures have some form of religion?). Students' questions are likely to fall across a wide spectrum. More advanced students will probably ask different kinds of questions than struggling readers. But, as the cliché states, no question is a dumb question because individuals have varying degrees of background knowledge, literary experiences, and life experiences.

### Determining What Is Important

This strategy entails having readers understand what they have read and forming judgments about what is and is not crucial information. Most texts contain far too much information for the average student to focus on and learn (Chambliss & Calfee, 1998). Therefore, determining essential information is an important and frequently used strategy. If you were to ask your students to summarize a text, for instance, you would necessarily want them focusing on the most significant aspects of what they read, not minor details or extraneous points.

In many texts—more so with exposition than with narratives—the authors provide direct cues to what is important, such as overviews, headings, subheadings, words in bold, and the like. This is not always the case, though, and in some instances students will need to rely upon their existing schema to infer what is important. When reading Maya Angelou's autobiography *I Know Why the Caged Bird Sings*, a 10th-grade student may note the following ideas and persons as important:

- As young children, Maya and her brother Bailey are sent by their separated parents, who live in California, to live with their paternal grandmother and uncle in Stamps, Arkansas.
- Maya's grandmother and uncle operated the only African American mercantile store in Stamps, which is the setting for a good portion of the book.

- Racial prejudices divided the town of Stamps and significantly impacted Maya's worldview.
- A year after arriving in Stamps, Maya's father visits them from California, then takes the children to visit their mother in St. Louis, where they stayed for 1 year.
- Maya's mother's boyfriend, Mr. Freeman, sexually molests Maya; he is arrested for the crime, found guilty, and sentenced to 1 year in jail. After being released early, he is killed, presumably by Maya's uncles.
- As a result of lying to the judge about prior sexual assaults Mr. Freeman perpetrated on Maya, she takes a vow of silence; Maya and Bailey are sent back to Arkansas.
- Mrs. Flowers, a dignified woman in Stamps, encourages Maya to immerse herself in books.
- After both Bailey and Maya graduate from eighth grade, Bailey sees some white men kill and bury a black man. Their grandmother decides to take them away from Stamps to California.
- At age 14, Maya was given a scholarship to attend the California Labor School, a college for adults.
- While visiting her father in Los Angeles, Maya becomes involved in a fight with Dolores, her father's fiancée. Maya runs away and lives with a group of young homeless people for 1 month. Afterwards, she returns to San Francisco to be with her mother.
- Maya becomes pregnant at the age of 16 and gives birth to a boy.

In this example, the student distilled a 246-page book down to 11 important events. Obviously, she left out numerous details, focusing instead on those points that she saw as most significant to the overall text.

### Summarizing

Summarizing is best described as focusing on the primary idea or compelling reason why an author has chosen to write on a particular topic. Students who are asked to summarize must first determine what is important in the selection, then condense those ideas into a coherent structure using their own words. Brown and Day (1983) recommend the following steps for summarizing, to which we have made slight modifications:

- Deleting trivial or irrelevant information
- Deleting redundant information

- Providing a superordinate term for members of a category
- Finding and using generalizations the author has made
- Creating your own generalizations when the author has not provided them

The previous list of important ideas in Angelou's autobiography constitutes a fairly complete summary of Maya's story. By focusing only on the most relevant and important events of her life, students can determine the significance of the author's point in relating her life story. An even briefer summary, centered on a single theme, demonstrates the power of summarizing:

Maya Angelou grew up under difficult circumstances. She was raised, at various times, by her grandmother, uncle, mother, and father, in different parts of the United States. Despite her itinerant life, she managed to learn how to cope with racial intolerance and developed a love for learning. In short, each encounter with different people and new locales proved valuable in her development as an African American woman of letters.

## Making Inferences

When students use this strategy, they infer meanings by using information from the text and their existing schemata to fill in information that is not explicitly stated in the text. No text is entirely explicit, so readers must constantly make inferences to construct the full meaning of what they are reading.

Suppose that you are reading Charlotte Perkins Gillman's "The Yellow Wallpaper" with a group of 12th graders, and one student begins to question why the main character feels trapped in her room. When she uses her existing knowledge of the lack of educational and occupational opportunities for women at the time that Gillman wrote the story, she may then infer that the protagonist is attempting to break away from the tyranny of society's view of what women really can and ought to do with their lives.

## Dealing with Graphic Information

For this strategy—which is rarely used with fiction because narratives seldom contain illustrations, graphs, maps, or diagrams, though it is often crucially important with exposition—readers give special attention to the visual information supplied by the author. The graphic representations listed above often provide key points that students can use to help reinforce what they have just read.

An eighth- or ninth-grade class reading Alfred Lansing's *Endurance: Shackleton's Incredible Voyage,* has an excellent opportunity to use this particular strategy. Briefly stated, Lansing details Ernest Shackleton's crew's adventures as they attempt to sail from England to the antarctic, with many perilous circumstances along the way. Because the territory they traverse is somewhat exotic, the author includes a map tracing Shackleton's journey on the very first page. Students can refer to the map throughout their reading to gain a better sense of where the action takes place. Additionally, students can explore the website *www.pbs.org/wgbh/nova/shackleton,* which contains maps of the antarctic and video clips of the various islands Shackleton and his crew encountered. Throughout their reading, students can go to the website to reinforce and enhance their understanding of what a dangerous landscape Shackleton's men encountered.

### Imaging

When imaging, readers create mental pictures of the text they are reading, or they can graphically represent the relationships among elements of a text. Students use the former type of imaging by visualizing the characters, settings, and events of a narrative. For instance, as you begin reading Gina Berriault's "The Stone Boy," a story of a boy who accidentally shoots his brother while hunting, tell students to picture what Arnold and Eugie, the brothers, look like; ask them to form images of the landscape where the story takes place. For those of us who are more proficient readers, the use of imaging occurs automatically; we envision a character's looks and the settings where the action occurs. Students do not necessarily do this, so prompting them to do it will help them visualize what they read.

Another form of imaging consists of graphically organizing key ideas in text in a way that displays their relationships, which is much more likely to happen with exposition, though not exclusively. One example is the use of semantic maps, whereby students note relationships among categories of ideas or objects. Figure 5.1 is an example of a semantic map related to Malcolm X's thoughts on education, which he formulated while in prison, developed from *The Autobiography of Malcolm X.*

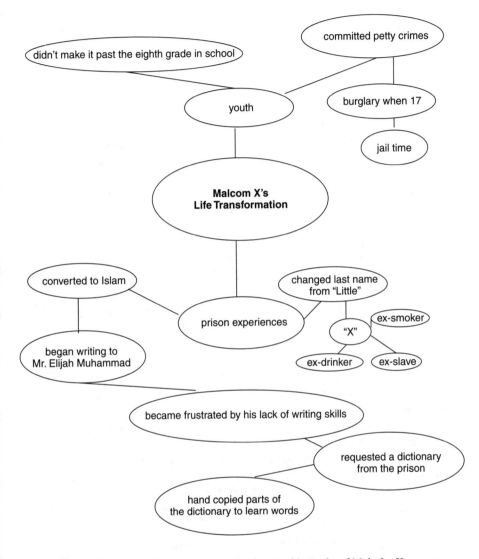

**FIGURE 5.1.** Semantic map for *The Autobiography of Malcolm X.*

One final note regarding imaging: ELLs may find this strategy particularly useful because their graphic skills are oftentimes more advanced than their (English) language skills.

## Monitoring Comprehension

Metacognition, the ability to monitor one's comprehension, is a definitive characteristic of proficient readers. Of the strategies discussed thus far, monitoring comprehension is the most general. When employing this strategy, readers carefully consider what they desire to gain from a text and their understanding—or lack thereof—of the text as they read. Should the reader sense a lack of comprehension, she will use whatever strategy is most relevant to improve understanding. Readers monitoring their comprehension ask questions of themselves such as, "Am I understanding what the author is saying? If I don't understand something I am reading, what can or should I do? What can I do to help me better remember the materials I am reading?"

As a sophisticated reader, you probably understand perfectly well a good deal of the texts you encounter. However, there are times when all of us struggle with certain material. In those instances, we need to ask ourselves, "What can I do to increase my understanding?" Oftentimes, we simply need to reread the paragraphs that caused us difficulty in order to build meaning. If during rereading we discovered some of the vocabulary was foreign to us, we may choose to use a dictionary to define the words in question. Should the author include graphics, we may pause to study them. We may also consciously check our existing knowledge of the topic to see how it meshes with the new material. In sum, we will readily access any number of strategies to help us comprehend the text because we are proficient readers. It is this same course of action that we can help our students do to achieve greater understanding in their reading.

Having described eight strategies—using prior knowledge, asking and answering questions, determining what is important, summarizing, making inferences, dealing with graphic information, imaging, and monitoring comprehension—we wish to stress that students will understand, appreciate, and learn more from their reading when they use these with regularity. However, we also want to stress that students will learn these strategies at different rates. With sufficient time spent teaching the strategies, coupled with scaffolding so students gradually adopt these practices independently, all students can grow into independent readers who have at their disposal a wealth of practices to enhance their understanding of texts.

At the beginning of this chapter we remarked on students' varying degrees of familiarity with and adeptness at employing these comprehension strategies. To reiterate, some of your students who are proficient readers may not know at a conscious level that they use the strategies frequently, yet they do. For such students, a brief review is perhaps all that is necessary. On the other hand, a recent report claims that up to 70% of all older readers require some form of remediation (Biancarosa & Snow, 2004). Consequently, we recommend that you check students' proficiency in using the strategies prior to teaching them in an effort to see which ones are already known and which are not. Using an expository text from a weekly news magazine such as *Time* or *Newsweek* and an age-appropriate short story, you can ask students to use inference, determine important facts, summarize, and the like. Based on what you find regarding their use of the strategies, you can then determine those areas where you need to provide instruction.

In the next section, we describe an approach to teaching a strategy, determining what is important. We then outline the first 2 days of instruction for the strategy so that you gain a better understanding of the instructional activities and time needed.

# Teaching a Comprehension Strategy

In this section, we describe two class periods of instruction devoted to helping students determine what is important. Because this strategy demands that students distinguish between highly relevant, important ideas and less relevant, supporting ideas, it will require a significant amount of time and practice. The 2 days presented below will likely be a significant part of the instruction needed by more capable readers, while not nearly enough for struggling readers. Our intention here is to provide you with a framework for thinking about how to approach teaching a specific strategy that you can adapt to your particular students.

### Day 1

The instruction below is intended for a 10th-grade class of mixed ability students who, based upon the assessment suggested above, require some explicit teaching in how to determine what is important in expository text. Of course, the students may have been exposed to this strategy in their upper elementary and middle school classes, but it is apparent that many still struggle to extract the most important ideas, as evidenced by the frequent inclusion of supporting details. This first day of instruction consists of four parts: motivation and interest building, teacher explanation, teacher modeling, and whole-class student participation. The text we use in teaching this strategy is Maya Angelou's *I Know Why the Caged Bird Sings*.

## Motivation and Interest Building (15 Minutes)

Almasi (2003) and Pressley (2006) have noted that motivation is essential when undertaking strategies instruction because learning and using these strategies is difficult, demanding work for students. If students are to engage in this hard work, they need to see some benefit of their labor. What that benefit is will vary from student to student; it may be simply understanding a new text, feeling confident in approaching a difficult text, or getting a better grade on a test.

To foster motivation and interest in reading *I Know Why the Caged Bird Sings*, begin by asking each student to jot down three or four events from their lives that have had a significant impact on them. Let them know beforehand that you will be asking for volunteers to share some of their ideas (you may want to model the activity by creating and reading your own list first). As individual students share their events (e.g., a trip, summer camp, first job, death of a loved one, etc.), write their responses on an overhead, LCD, or on the board.

After noting several responses, ask the class to determine if they can come to some unanimity regarding what makes the amalgamated list significant; that is, what commonalities unite the entire class' list? Students may struggle with this concept, replying that the only unifying theme is that each person's response is unique to that individual. Regardless of what unfolds in this discussion, you can use it as a lead-in to a teacher explanation of what autobiography is and ways to determine the most significant aspects of it.

## Teacher Explanation (10 Minutes)

Explain that autobiographies are first-person accounts of an individual's life often written in a chronological order, which is the case with Maya Angelou's text. You will want to stress that autobiographers often include minute detail to convey the significance of certain episodes, but since you are focusing on determining what is important, it is the "bigger picture" with which you are most concerned.

Now that you have described the characteristics of autobiographies, explain the strategy you are using—determining what is important. Inform students that the book is well over 200 pages, and that even the best readers cannot be expected to remember each and every detail the writer presents. Furthermore, tell them that this strategy, while certainly demanding of their time and energy, will help them improve their understanding of not only this particular book, but also books in other areas, such as history, science, health, and psychology, to name a few.

*Teacher Modeling (10 Minutes)*

If you were to simply tell students to make sure they determine what is important while they read, chances are they will not approach their reading any differently than they had in the past. It is usually important to model what this strategy entails. Begin by conducting a think-aloud using the first two short paragraphs from Chapter One of Angelou's text. Putting these two paragraphs on an overhead or PowerPoint slide allows all students to see the text you are referencing:

> When I was three and Bailey four, we had arrived in the musty little town, wearing tags on our wrists which instructed—"To Whom It May Concern"—that we were Marguerite and Bailey Johnson Jr., from Long Beach, California, en route to Stamps, Arkansas, c/o Mrs. Annie Henderson.
>
> Our parents had decided to put an end to their calamitous marriage, and Father shipped us home to his mother. A porter had been charged with our welfare—he got off the train the next day in Arizona—and our tickets were pinned to my brother's inside coat pocket.

Read these words aloud, pausing frequently to model the thought processes you undertake in determining the most important information. It might look something like this:

> "I'm trying to figure out what the most important ideas are in the first paragraph. The author seems to want me to jump into her story at the point when she and her brother are sent to live in Stamps, Arkansas. But why are they wearing tags on their wrists? And who

is Mrs. Annie Henderson? Where are the parents? [Underline the names Marguerite, Bailey Johnson Jr., and Mrs. Annie Henderson.] I think the idea that they are being sent to live somewhere else without their parents is the most important idea; the other points are not as significant. In the second paragraph, I learn that the kids' parents are divorced and their father sent them to live with his mother (the kids' grandmother). [Underline Father shipped us home to his mother.] Is Mrs. Henderson their grandmother? I suspect she might be because (c/o) means 'care of.' But what kind of parents send their 3- and 4-year-old children on a train from California to Arkansas? Maybe I can infer that the parents are poor and can't look after their kids. At any rate, it seems the most important idea in the second paragraph is that Marguerite and Bailey are sent to live with their grandmother because their parents' marriage dissolved. The information about the porter doesn't seem very relevant. [Cross out the information about the porter.]"

Having modeled the strategy, ask students if they understood why you made the decisions you did. If there still seems to be some misunderstanding or confusion, repeat this activity using two or three new paragraphs so students begin to understand the thought processes of a successful reader.

### Whole-Class Participation with Teacher Guidance (10–15 Minutes)

Now that you have shown the class how you mentally maneuver through text to determine what is important, it is time students joined in. The third and fourth paragraphs from Chapter One of Angelou's text contain several significant ideas that students are likely to identify as important:

> I don't remember much of the trip, but after we reached the segregated southern part of the journey, things must have looked up. Negro passengers, who always traveled with loaded lunch boxes, felt sorry for "the poor little motherless darlings" and plied us with cold fried chicken and potato salad.
>
> Years later I discovered that the United States had been crossed thousands of times by frightened Black children traveling alone to their newly affluent parents in Northern cities, or back to grandmothers in Southern towns when the urban North reneged on its economic promises.

Begin by asking students to describe briefly what these two paragraphs are generally about (Maya did not fully remember her journey across the country, but later in life she learned that many African American children traveled great distances to live with relatives). Then, ask them how they went about making such a determination (focus on the words *Negro, journey, Black children, crossed*, etc.). To fully unpack all the ideas Angelou expresses in these two paragraphs, some background information on the African American diaspora after the Civil War may be necessary, which you can discuss with them. For example, in post-slavery United States, many African Americans moved to northern cities—such as Chicago and New York—in an effort to secure better employment and to escape the horrors of slavery associated with the South.

After the class has determined the general idea of the text provided—namely, that African American children were regularly uprooted for a variety of reasons—ask students if they can distill the paragraph down to one primary idea. Using a quick-write, have them write down the most important idea using exactly three sentences and in no more than 5 minutes. Once completed, ask several volunteers to read their quick-writes, noting how accurately they identified the most important idea.

One additional form of assistance may be necessary in completing this task. Depending on the verbal acuity of your students, some of the words in the paragraphs may be unknown, and thus their ability to determine what is important falls by the wayside. In particular, the words *plied* and *affluent* are key in figuring out the idea, so you will want to determine if students know these words, and if not, briefly teach them.

## Day 2

The second day's instruction for working on the strategy determining what is important consists of three components—reviewing with teacher modeling, whole-class guided practice, and pair-share.

### Reviewing with Teacher Modeling (10 Minutes)

The first day of instruction was largely spent explaining the strategy and showing students how to determine what is important. Begin today's class by briefly reviewing. Students using this strategy are to focus on the most important information while allowing less important details to fade into the background. By using the overhead (or PowerPoint) from the first day's instruction, you can quickly model your thought processes to show how you begin determining essential information. You may also want to motivate students by stressing that using this strategy will actually reduce the amount they need to learn and remember.

### Whole-Class Guided Practice (15 Minutes)

Select another paragraph or two from the first chapter, place it on the overhead, and ask your students to verbalize the most important idea(s). As students articulate their answers, ask them to provide the reasons behind their responses. That is, ask them, "How did you come to that conclusion?" "What specific words and phrases are most important?" "Why did you not include the information she provides about X?" As students give specific words and phrases, write them on the board, then discuss as a class why those particular words and phrases capture the passage's most important idea. If it is clear to you that students have a fairly firm grasp of how to use this strategy, move on to the next activity, pair-share. If they do not understand the strategy, you will need to further explain and model the steps outlined earlier.

### Pair-Share (20–25 Minutes)

Place students in pairs, distribute copies of *I Know Why the Caged Bird Sings*, and ask students to turn to a page in Chapter One that they have not read. Clearly indicate the two or three paragraphs on which you are asking students to focus their attention. Have each partner read the paragraphs silently, jotting down the key words and phrases that aid in determining the most important idea. Once the individuals have completed this task, they should write down what they believe is the most important idea.

Thus far, each person in a pairing should have written down key words and phrases and the most important idea of the paragraphs. Next, the partners share with each other their findings, providing reasoning for why they chose the words they did and how they determined the important information. Doing so makes using this strategy a conscious effort, which is one of the hallmarks of comprehension strategies mentioned earlier in this chapter. As the partners share information, they negotiate and refine their ideas in preparation for explaining to the whole class what they discovered. While the pairs share with the class what they view as the most important information, listen intently for miscues; when necessary, help off-track pairs by guiding them toward more accurate information.

A few reminders are in order regarding teaching comprehension strategies. First, determine by means of an informal assessment what strategies your students already know and use proficiently and which ones they do not. Second, while the 2-day instructional plan we have outlined is likely to be a significant part of the instruction needed by proficient readers, less skilled readers are likely to require significantly more work with the strategy. All readers need reviews, prompts, and frequent opportunities to use the strategy with a variety of texts. Finally, note that your task is to give all students enough instruction and review that they will fully master and internalize a strategy without extending instruction to the point that you bore them.

Up to this point, we have focused our attention on how you teach a single strategy. Proficient readers typically rely on the use of multiple strategies when encountering new texts. In the last section of this chapter, we describe several sequences of comprehension strategies.

## Teaching Sequences of Strategies

There are many sequences of comprehension strategies that have proved beneficial. The remainder of this chapter is devoted to describing four such sequences: The K–W–L procedure, notice and wonder, reciprocal teaching, and tableaux.

### The K–W–L Procedure

Originally developed by Donna Ogle (1986), the K–W–L strategy is especially useful with exposition. The three-part process involves students identifying What I *Know* (about the forthcoming topic), What I *Want* to Learn (about the topic), and What I Did *Learn* (about the topic). The first two steps are prereading activities, while the third step is a postreading activity.

The first step—what I know—includes two stages. Prior to reading a selection, you provide students with the topic, in this case Japanese internment camps; they think about it; and then they write down what they already know about it. You might begin the class by stating, "Today we'll begin studying Japanese internment camps. Take a few moments to think of all the information you currently know about that topic." Next, ask students to write down what they know about Japanese internment camps. The primary text you are studying is *Only What We Could Carry: The Japanese Internment Experience,* an anthology edited by Lawson Fusao Inada. One student might list the following:

- It occurred during World War II.
- It happened after Japan bombed Pearl Harbor.
- It involved the U.S. government placing Japanese Americans in remote concentration camps.
- It was brought about by Executive Order 9066.
- It stripped Japanese Americans of their dignity.
- It confused and outraged Japanese Americans because many of them were born in the United States.

Once students have created their lists, ask them to develop categories for their responses, which is the second stage of this step. For instance, in the example above, one category might be "How Japanese Americans felt about what happened." Yet another category could revolve around "historical dates." When planning for this procedure, you may want to place students in cooperative groups for the listing portion, with each group reporting what they already know. As they list their responses, you should record them on an overhead or the board for all to see. As a whole class, students can then generate categories as you help them negotiate the generalizations.

The second step—what I want to learn—flows directly from the first. Using the lists and categories generated, students identify areas about which they want to uncover more information. Because individual students will have varying degrees of existing knowledge about any given topic, you should encourage personalized lists, as different students will want to know different aspects of a topic. Continuing with the sample topic of Japanese American internment camps, a student may have the following questions about which she wants to know more:

- How did the U.S. government go about displacing Japanese Americans?
- How long were detainees held in the camps?
- Where were the camps located? Were all camps alike?
- Did non-Japanese Americans think this action was justified?

- What were the living conditions like in the camps?
- What happened to Japanese Americans after the Executive Order was lifted?

The third and final step—what I did learn—asks students to describe, usually in written form, what they learned after completion of the reading. For instance, the student who wanted to know how non-Japanese Americans reacted to the internment discovered that many Americans bought in to the idea that Japanese Americans were potentially dangerous, and thus they supported the internment. It is also important to encourage students at this stage to describe what they sought to learn but did not from the particular selection so that they can pursue additional reading on their own. If the student did not receive an adequate response to what life was like in different internment camps, she can go online and further her knowledge by searching Google, or reading any number of texts on the topic.

At this point you have demonstrated your use of the strategy and led students through using it with a particular text, *Only What We Could Carry*. One crucial step remains: teaching students how to use the strategy independently. This will take some time, and that time will be spent using instruction similar to what we described for teaching students the strategy of determining what is important. That is, in a well-crafted instructional unit and in follow-up work, you (1) motivate students and build their interest in the strategy, (2) thoroughly explain the strategy, (3) model the strategy, (4) involve the class as a whole in using the strategy with teacher guidance, (5) have students work with the strategy in a pair-share activity, (6) give students frequent opportunities to use the strategy, prompt them to use it, and review it, and (7) further teach its use if that proves to be necessary.

Taught in this way, the K–W–L strategy permits students to self-regulate what they want to learn from a selection. Some students may have a wealth of information on a particular topic, so they may need your assistance in guiding them toward more advanced material, while others have little knowledge. The K–W–L strategy can act as a self-controlled curriculum differentiator in the sense that individuals determine what they want to discover about a topic and what kinds of resources will help them discover new information. Additionally, teachers benefit greatly by using K–W–L because it provides relatively direct feedback concerning what students actually did learn. Using this feedback, you may need to revisit certain topics if you see students who have incorrect or incomplete knowledge of a particular topic.

### Notice and Wonder

In the K–W–L procedure, we noted that the first two steps are prereading activities, while the third step is a postreading activity. The notice and wonder activity occurs entirely during reading and is particularly useful with narrative texts. This strategy consists of the teacher asking students to key in to a particular element or motif in a selection while they are reading, noting the context in which that element is used. With each encounter of the element or motif, students write down the page on which it appeared and the exact words the author used in the reference on the left-hand side of a piece of paper. On the right-hand side of the page, students write a question about what those words make them wonder.

| Notice | Wonder |
| --- | --- |
|  |  |

For example, a seventh-grade class is set to begin reading Sharon Creech's Newbery Award-winning *Walk Two Moons*. The novel is a bit of a mystery, with the main character, Salamanca, serving as the narrative voice. Only brief allusions are made to her mother, but they appear frequently throughout the text. Since the mother has an important role in Salamanca's journey, and you do not want students to overlook the fleeting references to her, you will need to tell students—prior to beginning reading—to cue in to mentions of her. Notice and wonder begins as a teacher-led strategy, and gradually it becomes a student-led strategy. Rather than the teacher asking students to read a chapter or the entire text and then go back to notice the references, students themselves become responsible for cueing in to the allusion, making predictions about the importance of the reference, and heightening awareness about what has happened to Salamanca's mother. For example, on page three of the text, a student would notice, and subsequently write down the following reference: "My father started chipping away at a plaster wall in the living room of our house in Bybanks shortly after my mother left us one April morning." Beneath the wonder column, she might then write, "I wonder why Sal's mother left the family. Maybe she wasn't happy in her marriage, so she left to start a new life." At the conclusion of the text, students can go through their entire notice and wonder chart to see how accurate their predictions and hunches were or simply to reflect on the importance of author clues in the text once answers to the questions have been revealed.

Adept readers, whether they are conscious of it or not, constantly question why an author includes certain details and facts. The notice and wonder activity simply makes the act of picking up on small, yet very important, details more overt. For struggling readers, this overt process creates a structure that will help them to eventually make the act of questioning more automatic. Regardless of ability levels, by looking for important context clues, which are brought to light by the teacher before reading, students attend to a close reading, contemplate the significance of a particular element or motif, and begin forming literary interpretations.

### Reciprocal Teaching

Reciprocal teaching is a small-group activity initially developed by Palincsar and Brown (1984) in which students collaborate to construct meaning from informational texts, although it certainly can be used with narratives as well. It consists of four strategies: generating questions, clarifying issues, summarizing, and making predictions. You begin by serving as the group leader, carrying out the strategies and modeling them for the others, but over time, you hand over more and more responsibility to students. Ultimately, reciprocal teaching's goal is for all students to become actively engaged in using the strategies without the help of the teacher. To begin, a reading selection is divided into short segments, perhaps two paragraphs or so, and the leader reads the first segment out loud to the remaining group members. Below we briefly describe each of the four strategies involved.

### Generating Questions

Upon completing the reading of the segment, group members develop questions raised by the passage and collaborate to answer the questions. Let us say a class of 10th-grade students is reading from the first chapter of Luis Alberto Urrea's *By the Lake of Sleeping Children: The Secret Life of the Mexican Border*, a collection of investigative portraits of the hardscrabble life led by many on the United States–Mexico border. Once the leader completes reading the first two paragraphs, group members ask, and try to answer, the following questions:

- What do *colonia* and *barrio* mean?
- Why does the author use the word *dreaded* when referring to his father working for the federal judicial branch of Mexican law enforcement?
- Why would the author's mother, a socialite from Manhattan, choose to marry a Mexican man who clearly couldn't maintain the lifestyle to which she had become accustomed?

### Clarifying Issues

If any question remains unanswered, or if the passage produces significant misunderstandings, the leader of the group, in consultation with others, works to clarify matters. This step may involve the use of outside material to address the question at hand. For instance, in addressing the first question concerning the use of the word *colonia*, students are given some context about places where the author lived ("I … grew up in a mix of colonia, barrio, ghetto, and suburb … "), so they may need to search an online source to determine the exact meaning of the term.

### Summarizing

Once the questions are answered and any misunderstandings are clarified, the leader or other group members summarize the segment under consideration. Someone from the group may say, "The opening two paragraphs provide us with the author's background, with most of the description centered on how his Mexican father met and married his American mother. It really seems as though Urrea wants us to see how these two very different worlds came together to produce a son who straddled both worlds."

### Predicting

Based on the segment just read, any preceding segments, and the discussion thus far, group members form predictions about the upcoming segment. Students might predict that the author will grow up having difficulties negotiating these two worlds, or perhaps that he will feel more connected to one parent rather than the other. The sequence of reading, generating questions, clarifying issues, summarizing, and predicting is then repeated with subsequent segments.

Reciprocal teaching is particularly appropriate with texts that are complex or contain ideas that are, for the most part, new to students. Burke (2003) suggests using this activity in pairs. Students alternate reading aloud, and the listener can ask clarifying questions at any time. Furthermore, Burke encourages students to ask two types of questions—surface questions, which revolve around facts, and deep questions, which seek to uncover larger issues in a text. A surface question for *The Odyssey* might be, "Can you remember the name of Odysseus's son?" A deep question, Burke writes, is one such as, "Why does Penelope remain loyal to Odysseus for so many years?" In short, reciprocal teaching encourages students to collaboratively question a text closely so as to understand its meaning deeply.

## Tableaux

According to Wilhelm (2002), tableaux "help students visualize and explore both the text and the subtext of a narrative, including settings, scenes, situations, characters, relationships, and meanings. They can represent vocabulary, create mental models of complex concepts and procedures, or visually translate a host of themes and ideas." This strategy capitalizes on students' visual and kinesthetic intelligences through "freezing" a scene and representing its theme to the class through acting. Tableaux consists of five steps:

1. Choose a text that is worth visually depicting.
2. Identify central concepts or events in the selection that are significant to the overall understanding of the text.
3. Review important details and ideas that an audience must know about the concept or event.
4. Collaborate with a group about how to represent the scene in such a way that the audience will see its significance.
5. Ensure the audience understands the importance of the representation.

### Choose the Text

Any novel, short story, or play with strong characters and weighty themes will work. An eighth-grade class, for example, is reading Alfred

Uhry's play *Driving Miss Daisy*, a story about a wealthy Jewish woman and her African American driver, Hoke. It spans several decades and explores issues of race, class, religion, and friendship. One group feels this play has several scenes worthy of tableaux.

### Identify Important Events

The group in question feels that the scene where Hoke and Miss Daisy are in her car outside her synagogue that has just been bombed underscores the theme of intolerance.

### Review Important Details

The students in the group have identified three key details necessary to conveying the emotionality of this scene. They are Daisy's initial disbelief that such a thing would happen to her temple, Hoke's discussion of the lynching of his friend's father, and Daisy's denial that the lynching had anything in common with her temple's bombing.

### Collaborate to Represent the Scene/Event

The students want to convey that suddenly, for the first time in the play, Miss Daisy is forced to recognize that hatred cuts across skin color and affects all people. The group's challenge will be to focus on this idea.

### Ensure the Audience Understands the Scene

To convey their point, the group decides that all but one of the members will wear red shirts; the outlying student will wear a blue shirt, and will be shunned and ill-treated by the others, similar to what occurs in the educational exercise brown eyes, blue eyes. This exercise was originally developed in 1970 by Riceville, Iowa, teacher June Elliott, who sought to show her elementary students the ill effects of prejudicial behavior. She designated blue-eyed students as superior to brown-eyed students, with the former receiving preferential treatment to the latter (Center for the Humanities, 1970).

Wilhelm (2002) also notes that acting is but one of many ways to create a tableaux; they can also be done through drawings, collages, technology, and a variety of fine art media.

Tableaux, like the K–W–L strategy, notice and wonder, and reciprocal teaching, puts students in charge of determining the most significant ideas in a text. Unlike the other activities in this section, though, tableaux combines the cognitive aspects of sequencing comprehension strategies with kinesthetic aspects. We strongly support tapping in to students' multiple intelligences whenever possible, and tableaux certainly does so.

# Concluding Remarks

In this chapter, we have discussed the characteristics of comprehension strategies, described eight individual strategies, provided the first 2 days of instruction for teaching a strategy, and discussed instruction for four strategy sequences. For students who already have some proficiency with the strategies discussed, we recommend overtly teaching the strategies followed by a good deal of guided practice. However, for those students who are significantly deficient in their reading, we recognize that you probably do not have the time to sufficiently do all that needs to be done to fully instruct students in using strategies. In such a circumstance, you may need the help of a teacher whose primary role is to aid struggling readers.

## LITERATURE/FILMS CITED

Achebe, Chinua. (1994/1959). *Things fall apart*. New York: Anchor Books.

Angelou, Maya. (1969). *I know why the caged bird sings*. New York: Bantam.

Berriault, Gina. (1995). The stone boy. In J. Moffet & K. McElheny (Eds.), *Points of view: An anthology of short stories* (pp. 383–395). New York: New American Library.

Coppola, Francis Ford. (Director). (1979). *Apocalypse now* [Film]. United States: United Artists.

Creech, Sharon. (1996). *Walk two moons*. New York: HarperTrophy.

Gillman, Charlotte Perkins. (1899/1989). The yellow wallpaper. In *The yellow wallpaper and other writings* (pp. 1–20). New York: Bantam.

Hautman, Pete. (2004). *Godless*. New York: Simon & Schuster.

Homer. *The Odyssey* (R. Fagles, Trans.). New York: Penguin.

Inada, Lawson Fusao (Ed.). (2000). *Only what we could carry: The Japanese internment experience*. Berkeley: California Historical Society and Heyday Books.

Lansing, Alfred. (1999). *Endurance: Schackleton's incredible voyage.* New York: Carrol & Graf.

Malcolm X. (1973). *The autobiography of Malcolm X.* New York: Penguin.

Meyers, Walter Dean. (1988). *Fallen angels.* New York: Scholastic.

Oates, Joyce Carol. (2003). *Freaky green eyes.* New York: HarperTempest.

Uhry, Alfred. (1986). *Driving Miss Daisy.* New York: Theatre Communications Group.

Urrea, Luis Alberto. (1996). *By the lake of sleeping children: The secret life of the Mexican border.* New York: Anchor Books.

# Teaching Higher-Order Thinking Skills

What is important in teaching is balance: Students should be given
opportunities to learn via analytical, creative, and practical thinking
as well as via memory. There is no one right way to teach or learn that
works for all students. By balancing types of instruction and assessment,
you reach all students, not just some of them.
—ROBERT STERNBERG AND LOUISE SPEAR-SWERLING, educational psychologists

As Sternberg and Spear-Swerling (1996) suggest, we need a balanced
approach to reading instruction that promotes higher-order thinking
skills as well as more literal comprehension. If your secondary school
experience was anything like ours, perhaps you can recall reading a
novel, such as Ernest Hemingway's *The Old Man and the Sea*, silently,
and then answering questions on a study guide. Many of those questions asked for basic recall of information. "What baseball legend did
the old man dream of taking fishing? How long did the battle between
the man and the fish last? What was the outcome?" While such questions serve an important role in determining whether students understand the novel's plot, they do little in terms of encouraging complex
reasoning, a skill virtually all adults need to possess in our society.

In working with preservice and inservice teachers, neither of us
has ever heard a teacher say, "I wish my students weren't such complex, analytic readers because it makes my job too difficult." As you
undoubtedly know, just the opposite is true. Virtually all teachers want
students to possess and apply sophisticated thinking skills essential to
making sense of complex material, be it fiction or exposition, print, or
some other media. You most likely are committed to asking students
to engage in such skills. Our purpose in this chapter is to bring these

higher-order thinking skills to the forefront of your thinking. In today's world, they are crucial.

We begin by exploring what we mean by higher-order thinking, and then present a recent taxonomy of thinking skills (Anderson & Krathwohl, 2001). Next, we discuss the triachic theory of intelligence (Sternberg & Spear-Swerling, 1996), which exhorts educators to rethink traditional notions of learning. In addition to describing how to promote higher-order thinking with novels and other print materials, we recommend activities for applying these skills to films and electronic media, both of which have become pervasive in today's classrooms.

## Characteristics of Higher-Order Thinking

To define higher-order thinking is difficult. Philosophers, cognitive psychologists, developmental psychologists, and educators all invoke the notion using different terminology and understanding. For the sake of this chapter, we use the terms *higher-order thinking* and *critical thinking* interchangeably, defining this sort of thinking as "the intellectually disciplined process of actively and skillfully conceptualizing, applying, analyzing, synthesizing, and/or evaluating information from, or generated by, observation, experience, reflections, reasoning, or communication, as a guide to belief and action" (Scriven & Paul, n.d.). Resnick (1987) has gone beyond a definition to delineate key features of the concept:

- Higher-order thinking is nonalgorithmic. That is, the path of action is not fully specified in advance.
- Higher-order thinking tends to be complex. The total path is not "visible" (mentally speaking) from any single vantage point.
- Higher-order thinking often yields multiple solutions, each with costs and benefits, rather than unique solutions.
- Higher-order thinking involves nuanced judgment and interpretation.
- Higher-order thinking involves the application of multiple criteria, which sometimes conflict with one another.
- Higher-order thinking often involves uncertainty. Not everything that bears on the task at hand is known.
- Higher-order thinking involves self-regulation of the thinking process. We do not recognize higher-order thinking in an individual when someone else "calls the plays" at every step.

- Higher-order thinking involves imposing meaning and finding structure in apparent disorder.
- Higher-order thinking is effortful. There is considerable mental work involved in the kinds of elaborations and judgments required.

In a ninth-grade English class, the characteristics above become manifested in many ways. Suppose students have completed a 2-week unit focused on advertising and its effects on adolescents. You read Alice Walker's poem "Without Commercials," along with some expository pieces describing pervasive advertising techniques such as bandwagon, glittering generalities, and celebrity endorsement (see *www.adbusters.org* for examples). Additionally, you spent considerable time examining actual ads found in magazines, on the web, and on television, paying close attention to the rhetorical tools employed to persuade consumers. To wrap up the unit, you asked students to develop, in pairs or small groups, an advertisement satire using multimedia for a product their age group is interested in purchasing. One of the central precepts of satire is that a person must have a thorough grasp of the concept before he can actually mock it. With this topic, students rely on their creativity, knowledge of rhetorical elements, and insight of the adolescent market to develop a satire of an advertisement that is for teens by teens. For instance, computer software such as iMovie allows amateurs to edit film and overlay sound rather easily. Or perhaps they could use PowerPoint to combine print, pictures, and audio clips to convey their point.

This satirical advertising project displays several of Resnick's key features of higher-order thinking. It is most definitely nonalgorithmic in that students do not know exactly what path they will pursue in achieving the final product. Also, there are multiple solutions to accomplishing the task rather than a definitive one (students need to choose from a huge list of products to spoof and the medium through which they will present the ad). Furthermore, since students themselves are responsible for determining what they will satirize and how they will present the project, they "call the shots" as opposed to the teacher.

As you further contemplate the list of characteristics of higher-order thinking, you may ask yourself, "So how does this work with my English classes and reading literature?" Let's assume your class of 11th graders is reading John Steinbeck's Dust Bowl/Depression era classic *The Grapes of Wrath*. As a culminating project, you have asked students to write a paper in which they identify a modern-day social problem that has afflicted a great number of people, just as the Depression did Americans of all sorts, from white-collar workers to laborers. They are to research that problem's origins (causes), what is being done or what has been done to ameliorate the problem (potential solutions), and then generate additional, perhaps utopian, alternative solutions to the problem.

Several of the features Resnick (1987) listed can be recognized as students complete this task. For instance, the problem is complex and yields multiple solutions. Students first need to identify their particular social problem from a slate of many. Will it be homelessness, poverty, AIDS, child abuse, drug addiction, or natural disaster victims, to name a few? Additionally, the problem involves uncertainty. Students will need to consider and research existing ways in which our society copes with the particular issue under consideration. How successful are those measures in addressing the problem? They may also question why a country as resource-rich as the United States is plagued by such a problem in the first place. Finally, students are likely to find the task effortful. They will have to demonstrate that they not only understood the problem and its complexities, but also that they considered multiple avenues for resolving it. The final product should consist of a logically organized paper of perhaps 5–10 pages.

For mature eighth graders, John Green's *Looking for Alaska* (2006) is an excellent vehicle for evoking higher-order thinking. The story centers on Miles, who leaves his Florida home to attend a boarding school in Alabama. While at the school, Miles befriends a group of outcasts, especially a bold, young feminist named Alaska. Ultimately, the reader learns that Alaska dies in a car crash, and the reader is led to believe she committed suicide. After completing this novel, students might research teen suicide, including warning signs and prevention tips. Based on their findings, they could develop brochures for the school, available through the nurse's office and counseling center, which offer services for teens contemplating suicide. Or, students could research coping with death, and help establish a support group at school for those who have lost a loved one.

In this second example, as was the case in the first one, higher-order thinking skills are prominently featured. We offer these scenarios to demonstrate just two of the myriad topics involving higher-order thinking that can be introduced and practiced in an English classroom. Most of the curriculum, unit plans, and lesson plans you develop can be adapted to focus student thinking on higher-order concerns.

# A Taxonomy for Higher-Order Questions

Having established the common characteristics of higher-order thinking and suggesting some approaches to prompting such thinking, we now move to another approach for fostering it—higher-order questioning. While Resnick (1987) helps us understand the features that constitute higher-order thinking, she does not describe specific types of questions that promote it. For guidance in how to do that, we turn to *A Taxonomy for Learning, Teaching, and Assessing* (Anderson & Krathwohl, 2001), which is an updated and expanded version of Benjamin Bloom's seminal text, *Taxonomy of Educational Objectives* (1956). The first type of question listed is not a part of Bloom's taxonomy, although it is frequently used to check for understanding. Questions two through six are from Anderson's and Krathwohl's taxonomy, while the final question represents their ideas combined with others (Galda & Graves, 2007; Graves et al., 2007):

- *Literal comprehension:* recalling direct information from a specific text
- *Understanding:* constructing meaning from instructional messages, including oral, written, and graphic communications
- *Applying:* carrying out or using a procedure in a given situation
- *Analyzing:* breaking material into its constituent parts and determining how the parts relate to one another and to an overall structure or purpose
- *Evaluating:* making judgments based on criteria and standards
- *Creating:* putting elements together to form a coherent or functional whole, reorganizing elements into a new pattern or structure
- *Being metacognitive:* being aware of one's own comprehension and able and willing to repair comprehension breakdowns when they occur

It is not necessary that each type of question be asked with every text read; as we discussed in Chapter 2, some reading you ask students to do should be for entertainment. Furthermore, we do not advocate that you use a specific ratio of higher-order questions (such as analyzing and evaluating) to lower-order questions (such as literal comprehension). When using higher-order questions, you often need to ask lower-order questions in order to ensure that students simply understand the general idea of the text. In fact, you will most likely ask many more lower-order questions than higher-order ones. Over the course of time, we recommend asking all types of questions with some degree of frequency. Thus, we believe that this framework should be at the forefront of your planning as you ask students questions related to their reading. Literal comprehension questions are the easiest ones to generate—and consequently the easiest ones for students to answer— but asking easy questions at the exclusion of more complex ones is likely to result in what we described in Chapter 3 as inert knowledge (Perkins, 1992).

To illustrate the form each level of question might take, we first offer examples for Shirley Jackson's "The Lottery," a text with which most of you are familiar and one that is frequently taught in high school, followed by examples from Philip Pullman's science fiction thriller *The Golden Compass*, which centers on a teenage girl's attempt to save her peers and herself from certain death at the hands of the Oblation Board and could fit well in an eighth-grade classroom.

*Questions on* "The Lottery"

- *Literal comprehension:* Who presides over the drawing for the lottery?
- *Understanding:* Why do the villagers continue holding the lottery?
- *Applying:* Identify a contemporary tradition in society that you consider dangerous or foolish. What steps can be taken to abolish it?
- *Analyzing:* Why does the author repeatedly describe everyday events, such as doing the dishes and stacking wood, as the lottery is about to take place?
- *Evaluating:* If you were in Mr. Hutchinson's place, what would you have done upon learning your family was selected in the lottery?
- *Creating:* Assuming that rituals and traditions are important and necessary practices in society, what might the villagers have replaced the lottery with in order to preserve the significance of a ritual but with less harmful consequences?
- *Being metacognitive:* Did you find any parts of the story confusing as you read? If so, what did you do to help clarify your confusion? Are there other steps you might also have taken?

*Questions on* The Golden Compass

- *Literal comprehension:* What is the name of the college where Lyra is raised?
- *Understanding:* Why does Lyra run away from Mrs. Coulter's house?
- *Applying:* The lust for power is a frequent idea mentioned in the book. Where can you find examples of lust for power in today's society?
- *Analyzing:* What specific examples can you identify that show Lyra maturing from childhood to adulthood over the course of the novel?
- *Evaluating:* In your estimation, did Lyra react appropriately when finding out her uncle was actually her father?
- *Creating:* Since *The Golden Compass* is the first book in a trilogy, its ending leads into the next text. If it weren't part of a trilogy, how would you rewrite the ending to bring the story to a close?
- *Being metacognitive:* As you encounter new ideas in your reading that don't quite make sense, or a new character is introduced but you don't quite see where this person fits into the larger story, stop reading and ask yourself, "At what point did I begin to lose sense of the story?" Go back to where you lost your understanding, retrace the story up to that point, then reread the section that was confusing in an effort to comprehend what has occurred.

We want to emphasize that when generating higher-order questions, it is not important that you label each one according to the taxonomy and relate that information to your students; rather, what is important is that you strive to ask numerous kinds of questions requiring various sorts of complex thinking.

## Sternberg's and Spear-Swerling's Triarchic Theory of Intelligence

Take a moment to think of a short list of people whom you consider particularly smart, clever, and perceptive. Now list what characteristics and abilities they possess that leads you to label them as such. Chances are your list includes something to do with their analytic abilities, which is certainly a hallmark of intelligence, though as we discuss below, intelligence entails much more than that. Sternberg's and Spear-

Swerling's triarchic theory of intelligence (1996) posits that in addition to analytic intelligence, there exists creative intelligence and practical intelligence. Unfortunately, they note, schoolwork mostly focuses on analysis while neglecting the other two forms of intelligence. In this section, we will discuss ways to tap into all three ways of thinking.

To illustrate how intelligence is manifested in various ways, Sternberg and Spear-Swerling relate the following story:

> Two boys were walking in a forest. The first boy was considered very smart; he received excellent grades in school, his test scores were high, and he possessed all the necessary credentials to succeed in higher education. The other boy was quite different. His grades were poor, and he did not do well on tests. In general, he was regarded as crafty and street smart. As they continued walking, they encountered a large, hungry grizzly bear. The first boy, calculating that the bear would overtake them in 17.3 seconds, began to panic. He looked over to his companion, who was calmly removing his hiking boots and putting on running shoes. The first boy said, "You must be crazy. There is no way we are going to outrun that grizzly bear!" The second boy replies, "That's true. But all I have to do is outrun you!" (pp. 5–6)

The point of the anecdote is obvious: Intelligence is not limited to "book smarts." The first boy excelled in terms of thinking and responding analytically, a skill privileged in academic settings. The second boy, meanwhile, relied on creative and practical thinking to cope with the dilemma. According to Sternberg and Spear-Swerling, "To be intelligent is to think well in one or more of three different ways: analytical, creative, and practical. One of the missing elements of our system of education is that typically only one of these ways is valued in tests and in the classroom. Yet no one way is any better than either of the others, and, ironically, the style of intelligence that schools most readily recognize as smart may well be less useful than the others to many students in their adult lives." Below, we describe characteristics of each type of intelligence, followed by ways to tap into each through various questions.

In Table 6.1, we list characteristics of students preferring analytic, creative, and practical thinking. It is unlikely that each student in your classroom will use only one of these types of thinking; more likely than not, each person will use all three, though one type of intelligence probably will be dominant.

Analytical thinkers, as the table suggests, tend to excel in school largely because our instructional patterns coincide with their way of

TABLE 6.1. Characteristics of Students Preferring Analytic, Creative, and Practical Thinking

| Analytic | Creative | Practical |
|---|---|---|
| High grades | Moderate to lower grades | Moderate to low grades |
| High test scores | Moderate test scores | Moderate to low test scores |
| Likes school | Feels confined by school | Feels bored by school |
| Liked by teachers | Often viewed as a pain by teachers | Often viewed as disconnected by teachers |
| "Fits" into school | Doesn't fit well into school | Doesn't fit well into school |
| Follows directions | Doesn't like to follow directions | Likes to know what use task and directions serve |
| Sees flaws in ideas | Likes to come up with own ideas | Likes to apply ideas in a pragmatic fashion |
| Natural "critic" | Natural "ideas" person | Natural common sense |
| Often prefers to be given directions | Likes to direct self | Likes to find self in practical settings |

*Note.* From Sternberg and Spear-Swerling (1996). Copyright 1996 by the American Psychological Association. Reprinted by permission.

processing information and their general disposition. An analytic student is usually very attentive in the classroom, displaying a pleasant disposition and willingness to be told how to proceed. Such a student will likely do very well on multiple-choice test items. One of the primary problems faced by those who are dominant analytical thinkers is that they sometimes struggle to generate their own ideas. They are excellent at recalling and analyzing others' ideas, but when pressed to generate their own, they tend to struggle. An analytic thinker is likely to readily identify the elements of fiction in a story, but when asked to write a story using the same elements, he may struggle with the task.

If you accept the notion that one of the primary functions of school is to prepare students for life in the world of employment, then you can begin to see the complications that arise from struggling to come up with unique ideas to solve a problem. For example, Sternberg and Spear-Swerling describe studies they conducted in which they interviewed business executives who hired highly ranking business school graduates, only to discover that their academic success failed to translate to real-world application. As teachers, we ought to be cognizant of overemphasizing analytical skills, making sure students get opportunities to use creative and practical thinking.

In contrast to analytic thinkers, creative thinkers tend to be independent and "free-spirited," qualities that are often at odds with how schools operate. Linear models of learning—for instance, students must perform step 1, followed by steps 2 and 3—are often the norm in schools, and such practices work against a creative thinker. As Table 6.1 indicates, creative thinkers' true intelligence may not be measured by the types of assessments typically used in school. Our society tends to place great value on standardized test scores, which are used for course placement, admission to colleges and universities, and as an indication of what one should or should not do for a vocation. Another mismatch sometimes occurs in classes where the teacher talks a lot because creative thinkers tend to find lectures boring; they would rather be exposed to a new concept, and then think of a variety of ways to apply it.

Finally, we have practical thinkers, who do not necessarily perform well in academic settings, but thrive in social and pragmatic environments. Practical thinkers tend to understand the importance of interpersonal communication, including the tacit messages conveyed through nonverbal communication. It might be said that practical thinkers possess contextual intelligence. An example of contextual intelligence is found in a study in which women shoppers easily computed in their heads the better value between two products but could not solve a similar problem using the same operations using paper and pencil (Sternberg & Spear-Swerling, 1996). Virtually every teacher has heard a student ask, "Why are we doing this? How does this apply to the real world?" Such questions are often extremely valid, and the more we can do to address these queries when planning instructional activities, the better off our students will be.

We do not believe that any one form of intelligence should be valued over the others. Rather, we strongly urge you to create learning opportunities for students that cut across the three types of intelligence. To be sure, we want our students to display high levels of competence in analytical thinking, if for no other reason, it is what schools privilege. In fact, given society's reliance on standardized tests, ranging from college admissions examinations to civil service assessments, we need to help students develop the necessary analytical skills that will enable them to succeed on such examinations. However, we also know that book smarts alone do not guarantee success in the arts, business, or industry, which is why we need to nurture creative thinking. Additionally, we all must rely on practical intelligence when negotiating everyday life. Sternberg and Spear-Swerling suggest we do our best to help students determine what they are good at, what they are not good at, and what they can do with their strengths while at the same time overcoming their weaknesses. As teachers, our role is to deliver balanced instruction that gives time to each of the three intelligences.

Implementing a balanced approach consistent with the triarchic theory of intelligence does not mean you need to rework your entire curriculum. To give you an understanding of how you might tap into Sternberg's different ways of knowing and learning, we offer below two sets of questions illustrating the three types of thinking.

The first set of questions is designed for eighth graders and focuses on Nikki Grimes's multiple-perspective text *Bronx Masquerade*. Relatively short and accessible to most eighth-grade readers, *Bronx Masquerade* tells the story of Mr. Ward's urban English students, many of whom are turned off to school until he initiates open-mic Friday. His students study Harlem Renaissance poets Monday through Thursday; then on Fridays Mr. Ward allows them to perform original poetry, which is often centered on the realities and feelings teenagers must negotiate.

*Questions on* Bronx Masquerade

- *Analytical thinking:* Tell students that *Bronx Masquerade* is told from the perspective of multiple, alternating narrators. Ask students, "Why does the author, Nikki Grimes, tell this story from the viewpoint of numerous kids in the class, as opposed to say just one person, such as Mr. Ward? What does this allow you, the reader, to understand?"
- *Creative thinking:* Briefly explain that at the conclusion of the book, Mr. Ward gives each student a poetry anthology that includes all the original poetry from the class. Ask students, "If you were to create an anthology, what poems would you place in it? Why? Also, what would you title the collection?"
- *Practical thinking:* Remind students that the poems written by Mr. Ward's class are very personal, reflecting the concerns each individual has. Ask students, "If you were to develop a magazine for readers your own age, what might the contents include? What issues and concerns would you be certain to address? Be sure to explain your choices."

The second set of questions, intended for 11th- or 12th-grade high school students, concerns Michael Dorris's text *The Broken Cord*, an account of the author's adoption of a boy named Adam, who was born with fetal alcohol syndrome (FAS). While devastatingly sad in its outcome for both the author and his son, the book strongly conveys messages regarding the power of love and devotion, as well as a caveat about the dangers of alcohol abuse by pregnant women.

### Questions on The Broken Cord

- *Analytical thinking:* Begin by having students chronicle Dorris's key emotions regarding his hopes and fears for Adam from the time the author adopts him to the book's conclusion. Ask your class, "What patterns, if any, do you notice? What primary message do you think the author wants his readers to take away from this book?"
- *Creative thinking:* In an attempt to have students empathize with the author, you want them to "step into the shoes" of Michael Dorris. To accomplish such perspective taking, ask students, "If you were in the author's position as a parent to Adam, how might you have coped with some of his problems? Identify three incidents in the book that you found powerful or that upset you, and describe what you might have done if you were in Dorris's shoes."
- *Practical thinking:* Review with students the fact that FAS is a very serious, yet preventable disease that is highlighted in *The Broken Cord*. Ask students, "If you were hired to help prevent this disease, what are some courses of action you would take to raise awareness of FAS?"

Within these two sets of questions, you undoubtedly noticed the possibilities for responding are rather open-ended, a fact that places the onus of deep, complex thinking on students. We have found that students typically rise to the occasion when they are given the responsibility to perform tasks that are complex yet manageable, relevant to their lives, and approachable from a variety of vantage points. Additionally, some overlap exists between the seven types of questions listed in the previous section and the questions that align with Sternberg's triarchic theory of intelligence, but we recommend you keep both in mind as you ask students questions and develop assessments of their learning.

# Media Literacy

Media literacy encompasses a wide range of disciplines and modalities, including film, television, radio, magazines, newspapers, and websites, to name the principle elements. As Beach (2007) notes, teachers of media literacy face a dilemma in having to justify instructional time spent on it because media literacy is often viewed as "peripheral to 'teaching the basics.'" As a result, few states have made media literacy a significant part of their curricula, which is problematic in light of how pervasive the media are in our lives. It is common to see large numbers of students flipping open their cell phones after the last bell of the day to send their friends text messages, or placing ear buds in to listen to music they have downloaded to MP3 players. But young people use today's technology in a variety of ways, usually far surpassing their parents' and teachers' limited applications. Alarmingly, one study determined that teens spent an average of 26 hours and 48 minutes per month engaged in some form of online browsing (Bausch & Han, 2006). When factoring in other forms of electronic media such as television, film, and text messaging, the time spent increases significantly. Given students' tendency to interact so frequently with media, it is vital that we prepare them to treat the media with the same sort of critical perspectives that we require of them when responding to written text.

According to Jenkins (2006), one of the primary reasons students spend significant time interacting with media technologies is that they are able to create content of their own choosing without concern for adult oversight. Jenkins refers to this engagement as "participatory culture," which he defines as "a culture with relatively low barriers to artistic expression and civic engagement, strong support for creating and sharing one's creations, and some type of informal mentorship whereby what is known by the most experienced is passed along to novices." In addition, students participating in such cultures believe their efforts matter, and they sense social connections with other users. In fact, one study concluded that more than 50% of all teens created their own media content, and roughly one third of teens who use the Internet shared their media creations with others (Lenhardt & Madden, 2005). Given the astounding number of adolescent media participants, we as teachers ought to be asking ourselves, "In what ways can we use media literacy in the classroom to foster learning and critical thinking?"

We have selected two branches of media literacy—film analysis and the world wide web—that are gaining prominence in some English classrooms to demonstrate the intersection of higher-order thinking and critical analysis. We begin with film analysis.

## Film and Higher-Order Thinking

In many classrooms, printed texts are the primary medium used for learning. With a current interest aimed at media literacy, we find ourselves in a position to help students understand that "texts" encompass more than short stories and novels. For years teachers have used films in conjunction with teaching a piece of literature—think Shakespeare's *Romeo and Juliet* coupled with either Franco Zeffirelli's (1968) version or, more recently, Baz Luhrmann's (1996) version—but more often than not, little has been done with promoting higher-order thinking in relation to viewing films. Instead of treating film as an artistic representation on par with literature, it is too often dismissed as a passive time filler.

According to Golden (2001), "Kids tend to be visually oriented, able to point out every significant image in a 3-minute MTV music video, but when it comes to doing the same with a written text, they stare at it as if they are reading German. Nonetheless, we know, or strongly suspect, that the skills they use to decode the visual image are the same skills they use for a written text." For example, to practice exploring metaphors in film, you can show the opening minutes of Robert Zemeckis's *Forest Gump* (1994), which follows a feather being taken along by gusts of wind. Stop the film, and ask students to write down the meanings and associations they have of the image. After students list several ideas, have them predict how the metaphor of a feather might surface throughout the film.

Golden (2001) further notes that we often err in using a film version of a text after reading it. He suggests reversing that order by using film clips to practice the analytical skills we want our students to possess, and once they have adequately demonstrated their ability to do so, turn to the written word. His argument is based on the idea that students are more interested in and adept at looking at visual imagery, so once they gain a certain comfort level with film, it will more easily transfer to print. This is a good point, but it would probably be unwise to always use film versions before their printed counterparts.

When teaching literature, you undoubtedly want students to move beyond mere plot comprehension; you help them clue in to such matters as a good writer's nuanced use of literary techniques that contribute to a story's overall purpose. To do so, you need students to understand some common literary terms: *protagonist, antagonist, rising action, climax, denouement, theme, symbol,* and *metaphor,* among others. And so it is with film analysis. When we teach students to think critically about a film's composition, they begin to see how particular shots, lighting techniques, and sound contribute to the cumulative structure of a movie. Below we list a few basic film terms described by Beach (2007) and provide examples of how to teach them while at the same time promoting higher-order thinking. We recognize the time limitations faced by teachers, so we have included segments that highlight the techniques under consideration rather than entire films.

## Long Shot

A long shot is one taken from a distance, yet the audience can view the entire body of a character. In Lurie's film *The Contender* (2000), Joan Allen plays Senator Laine Hanson, who is tapped to replace the recently deceased vice president of the United States. Prior to the confirmation hearings, a congressman releases allegedly compromising photographs of Senator Hanson from her college days, which, the audience is led to believe, will put an end to her high political ambitions. After the photographs are made known to key politicians, Laine Hanson is seen jogging through a military cemetery, wearing a white running suit (approximately 54 minutes into the film). The long shot occurs at the end of her run, when she is resting in the midst of a sea of white gravestones. Senator Hanson simply blends in with the dead, a none-too-subtle metaphor. When showing this and similar clips to students, ask them how this scene contributes to the larger themes in the film.

## Close-Up Shot

A close-up shot often fills the screen with only a face or an object for the purpose of dramatizing nonverbal reactions or signaling the symbolic importance of an object. Most films contain this shot, some for comic effect and others for dramatic effect. In Daldry's film *The Hours* (2002), the latter use of a close up is used. In this film, Nicole Kidman portrays Virginia Woolf, who was working on her novel *Mrs. Dalloway*. Approximately 48 minutes in, Virginia has helped a young girl provide a funeral for a dead bird; the girl's mother arrives, ushering the child away, and leaving Virginia with the bird. After placing a few roses next to the bird, Virginia lays her head next to the bird, and the camera closes in on the bird's head, then it turns to a tight shot of Virginia. At this point, you could ask students what the juxtaposition of images might foreshadow.

## Low-Angle Shot

If filmmakers want to place the audience looking up at a person or object, they use a low-angle shot, often for the purpose of associating power with the person or object. A very powerful low-angle shot occurs in Kapur's *Elizabeth* (1998), when the title character, played by Cate Blanchett, determinedly overcomes numerous difficulties—personal as well as political—and commits to ruling England, which she does for 40 years. As Elizabeth presents herself to the court, revealing a striking new appearance, she ascends the thrown, and as she does so, the camera angle is low, thus giving her the appearance of full authority and power. To give students a stark contrast, show the scene 5 minutes prior to the one just described, when Elizabeth is seated beneath a statue of the Virgin Mary, as she faces a life-altering decision about her future. Ask students how the different camera angles convey very different internal thoughts Elizabeth has regarding her capacity to rule England.

## High-Angle Shot

In contrast, a high-angle shot looks down on the person or object places the audience in a dominant position over that person or object. Often, high-angle shots convey a shrinking sense of efficacy, either real or perceived. In Hallström's *Chocolat* (2000), Vianne Rocher, portrayed by Juliette Binoche, moves to a small, tranquil village in France and establishes a chocolate shop. The village's morality enforcer, Comte Paul de Reynaud, played by Alfred Molina, makes life difficult for Vianne, and roughly 33 minutes into the film, he threatens her with banishment, just as his forebear, Auguste Reynaud, did in driving out the radicals years before. Exasperated and angry, Vianne storms out of his office into the village square, where she stands beneath the statue of Auguste Reynaud. As Vianne unleashes her anger at the statue, the camera is positioned to look down upon Vianne, suggesting she has run across a seemingly unstoppable force; she is powerless against the Reynaud legacy. Ask students to compare the camera's position when focused on Vianne with the camera angle when focused seconds earlier on Comte

Paul de Reynaud. Or, later in the film, when the two reconcile their differences at the town's annual celebration, ask what camera angle is used in framing them. What does the camera angle at the point of reconciliation suggest about Vianne's acceptance into her newly adopted village?

In addition to teaching these visual terms and concepts, Golden (2001) recommends teaching students two terms pertaining to a film's sound:

## Diegetic Sound

This is any sound that a character in the movie can hear, such as a car crash or a gunshot. Darth Vader, the villainous icon of Lucas's *Star Wars* (1977), played by David Prowse [voice of James Earl Jones] is accompanied by ominous heavy breathing that can be heard by the characters within the action. Ask students, "What would be the result if such breathing came from Luke Skywalker?"

## Nondiegetic Sound

This is any sound that is intended for the audience only, such as the music in most horror films. Perhaps the most famous nondiegetic sound in a film occurs in Hitchcock's *Psycho* (1960), when Marion Crane, portrayed by Janet Leigh, is showering. Just as Norman Bates, played by Anthony Perkins, tears the shower curtain aside to begin stabbing Marion, the audience hears a repeated chorus of high-pitched, screeching music. As Norman stabs Marion, the music stops, and the camera focuses on the bloodied water swirling down the drain. The characters in the film do not hear the dramatic music; it is intended to underscore the fact that something terribly horrifying is occurring. You could place students in small groups and have them identify nondiegetic sound in other films. They should block the film's image so only the sound is heard. Students then ask their peers, "What do you think this sound foreshadows or accompanies in the film? What does it suggest about the action?"

As we discuss in greater detail in Chapter 7, terms such as these represent new concepts and not simply new terms. Merely giving students a list of terms with the exhortation to learn their meanings will be insufficient. A much more meaningful way to learn and understand these terms involves using film clips that express the technique you want them to internalize. You might even design a short film project that involves students using the techniques described earlier. Such application of concepts and techniques, if done correctly, demonstrates that students have internalized this new knowledge. Students learning these terms and concepts can begin to view films in more critically engaging ways. As they gain confidence and adeptness at critical viewing, they may very well transfer their critical viewing skills to reading tasks, as Golden (2001) suggests.

The New Media Consortium (2005) defined 21st-century literacy as "the set of abilities and skills where aural, visual, and digital literacy overlap. These include the ability to understand the power of images and sounds, to recognize and use that power, to manipulate and transform digital media, to distribute them pervasively, and to easily adapt them to new forms." The short film project described above allows students to be creative while at the same time it serves to give them practice with the sorts of higher-order thinking skills we have discussed throughout this chapter; furthermore, the process of developing a short film is the sort of 21st-century literacy practice students will do well to know.

Once your students possess a working knowledge of some film concepts terminology, you can teach them how to pose questions about films, or any kind of text for that matter. Golden (2001) recommends teaching students to ask questions at three distinct levels: Level one questions focus on factual information. Typically, level one questions can be answered "with a word, phrase, or detail from the text." Level two questions focus on the interpretation of facts or suggestions from the film to gain a deeper insight about the text. Finally, we have level three questions, which seek to unearth some aspect the director/writer is attempting to make regarding the "real world." Below we illustrate how these levels of questions might be used to foster higher-order thinking.

Let's say you are teaching a lengthy unit focused on class in an 11th-grade classroom. The central book of the unit is F. Scott Fitzgerald's *The Great Gatsby*. To provide another perspective on class using a different medium, you show James Cameron's blockbuster film *Titanic* (1997).

> Level One Question (*Gatsby*): How does Gatsby explain his acquisition of wealth?
>
> Level One Question (*Titanic*): Why does Rose's mother insist that Rose marry Cal?

Level Two Question (*Gatsby*): Why is Nick fascinated with Gatsby's lifestyle?

Level Two Question (*Titanic*): Why does the elderly Rose throw her elaborate jewel into the ocean's depths?

Level Three Question (*Gatsby*): What connection, if any, is there between money and happiness in American society?

Level Three Question (*Titanic*): Are social and class distinctions as prevalent today as they are in the film?

In addition to teaching students how to develop their own questions, we believe it is often useful for teachers to pose questions of this nature to students. We also hope you detected some similarities between the leveled questions described by Golden and the taxonomy of higher-order questions discussed earlier. Each system affords you the opportunity to probe your students' understanding of whatever text you are studying be it a traditional text, film, or nonprint source. We urge you to incorporate as many of these ways of knowing and understanding as possible in an attempt to help students think in powerful ways.

## Evaluating Websites and Higher-Order Thinking

Arguably, no other technological innovation has made such a significant impact on teaching—or perhaps, the lives of almost all of us and virtually all of our students—in such a short time as the World Wide Web. According to a survey by Lenhart, Madden, and Hitlin (2005), 87% of U.S. students ages 12–17 use the Internet; 76% get news online; 43% have made a purchase online; and almost half, 45%, own a cell phone. More and more teachers are incorporating some form of digital technology in the classroom, the most common being web-based research, blogging, and website production. Undoubtedly, students ought to learn how to evaluate critically the sites they visit.

If you were about to begin a unit on Elie Wiesel's (2006) memoir *Night* with a 10th-grade class, one activity you may want your students to engage in is web-based research focused on the Holocaust. Should students seek to know more about a term such as *Kristallnacht*, a quick Google search returns well over 600,000 hits, which is a problematic result because students will have a hard time figuring out where to begin reading and what sites are most helpful. Most students who do similar searches click on the first site of the search results, taking that site's information without exploring other possibilities. Thornburg (2003) calls such behavior the "incremental cost of ignorance." To demonstrate the problems students can encounter when using search engines to conduct research, Thornburg searched for sites related to an archery term, the *long bow*. Using Google, he typed in the phrase *long bow*, and the results yielded 546,000 hits. Of those hits, 42% related to archery; 23% related to proper names; 13% were miscellaneous; 12% focused on the bow of a ship; 5% related to bow ties; and 4% related to decorative or hair bows. It is not difficult to see why uncritical web searches often result in questionable, superficial, or just plain wrong-headed student work. Consequently, Thornburg argues that teachers need to impart three basic skills to students: finding information or data, determining its relevance, and determining its accuracy. Below, we discuss how to do this.

As we just noted, providing students with the necessary reasoning skills to evaluate electronic media is essential in today's classroom. Toward that end, the University of California at Berkeley library system (*www.lib.berkeley.edu/TeachingLib/Guides/Internet/Evaluate.html*) provides a list of five questions for students to contemplate when viewing websites:

1. *What can the Uniform Resource Locator (URL) tell you?* For example, websites typically conclude with the indicators *.com, .org, .gov, .edu*, or *.net*. By possessing an understanding of what each suffix represents, students can enter any site with a basic sense of what to expect. For example, *.com* sites are commercial in nature, which indicates some sort of product is being made available. Additionally, a URL usually contains the name of the sponsoring institution or person. If a student is researching African mythology, for instance, he will likely find more reliable information on the homepage of an African Studies department of a well-known university than, say, *bobshomepage.net*. Certainly, some personal websites contain thoughtful, reliable information, but such sites often lack authentication from others.

To help students hone their evaluative skills, provide them with a list of five topics related to a language arts unit you study, such as The Beat Generation. A sampling of the topics falling under this unit may include Allen Ginsberg's *Howl and Other Poems*, a collection of poetry that is highly political and controversial; Jack Kerouac's *On the Road*, a freewheeling travelogue that has become synonymous with the Beat movement; William Burroughs's *Naked Lunch*, a story chronicling a man's addiction to opiates; Tom Wolfe's *The Electric Kool-Aid Acid Test*, a nonfiction account of Ken Kesey and friends traveling the country in a bus; and Ken Kesey's *One Flew Over the Cuckoo's Nest*, the story of a man's trials and tribulations inside a mental institution. Next, students should be instructed to find a credible website for each of the five topics and a corresponding "suspect" site for each topic. By asking students to find a good and a poor source, you can gain a powerful sense of how well they understand the procedural task of evaluating URLs.

2. *Who wrote the page? Is he, she, or the authoring institution a qualified authority?* As we all know, any person with rudimentary computer skills can create and maintain a website, thereby resulting in a proliferation of webpages devoted to almost any conceivable topic. Students should be taught to look for credentials of authors and institutions. Once at a homepage, tell students to seek out a section titled "About Us," "Philosophy," or "Who Am I." Also, ask students to identify the author's credentials on the subject. Is the information presented extremist or highly exaggerated? If so, it may very well be questionable.

As you begin teaching a 10th-grade composition class how to find sources for a research paper on a contemporary social issue, you might have them locate what they consider a highly regarded site and a questionable site, similar to what we recommended in the previous step where they found good examples and poor examples. Ask students to justify their choices with information they found on the webpage. For instance, a student interested in researching affirmative action might find the U.S. Department of Labor site as highly credible, while several personal websites may be extremist and racist in nature.

3. *Is the webpage current and timely?* This question is particularly germane to news sites. If students are studying contemporary ethical issues, for instance, and one person gleans all of his information on stem cell research from a site that has not been updated since 1999, the likelihood of his search meshing with the current state of the debate is slim. Urge students to use sites that are frequently updated with the latest information and findings. This is not as critical if their topics are historical, but often, the more recent the updates, the more useful the information.

4. *What do others say about the site?* Finding out what other webpages link to the site students are interested in can be very revealing. To find out this information, paste the URL of the site under consideration into *alexa.com*'s search box, and you will find how often the site is viewed, personal reviews, sites that link to it, and contact/ownership information for the domain name. Students might also look up the page in a reputable directory—such as Librarians' Internet Index (*lii.org*), or Infomine (*infomine.ucr.edu*)—that evaluates sites' contents. Inclusion in

a directory such as this provides an evaluator with a strong sense of the webpage's credibility. Finally, students might Google the author or the authoring agency to read what others have to say. Should students find numerous comments and reviews that question an author's or site's credibility, that source should probably be avoided.

5. *Does it all add up?* Having followed the steps outlined above, students need to step back and consider all that they have uncovered in their quest for reliable web-based information. Their goal is to gain a keen understanding of why the website was created (intentionality); they ought to know if the site is ironic or satiric (e.g., *TheOnion.com* is not a legitimate news source); and they ought to feel as secure in using a particular web source as they would a hard-copy library source.

All of these criteria for evaluating websites require students to apply higher-order thinking skills. You will want to teach students how to go about doing so, which we strongly recommend you do through explicit modeling. Telling students to be aware of bias in information is one thing, but showing them how to detect it is quite another. In addition, it is important to recognize that working with higher-order thinking skills demands a significant time commitment, both from you as the one organizing your instruction to account for it, as well as your students to demonstrate it. Some excellent additional information about critically evaluating websites is available through the Cornell University library (*www.library.cornell.edu/olinuris/ref/research/webeval. html#eval*).

## Concluding Remarks

The purpose of teaching higher-order thinking is straightforward. We strongly suspect no teacher reading this book will argue against doing so. That said, we acknowledge the difficulty and effort required to teach students to use the skills we have described in this chapter. However, we believe the hard work you put into such instruction will pay off in multiple ways for students, including fostering their ability to think independently when encountering new information, increasing their capacity to distinguish plausible information from implausible information, and enhancing their propensity to view texts of all kinds with a highly critical eye.

We began this chapter by characterizing what constitutes higher-order thinking, and followed that by describing a taxonomy of higher-order questioning. Then, we discussed Sternberg's and Spear-Swerling's triarchic theory of intelligence, which urges us to reexamine how we conceive of intelligent behavior and what we can do to privilege multiple ways of knowing in our classrooms. The chapter concludes with an examination of media literacy, with particular emphasis on film analysis and website evaluation, both of which demand students' higher-order thinking.

While we do not believe that you should develop an extensive list of higher-order questions for each and every text you teach, we do urge you to incorporate the ideas mentioned in this chapter frequently. In many instances, some higher-order questions are beneficial in promoting student thought. From a teacher's viewpoint, higher-order questioning does not always equate to difficult and time consuming.

We recommend that you frequently ask lower-order questions—literal questions—to ensure that students possess basic plot understanding. For example, if you focus whole-class discussions on applying and evaluation questions, most of which seem to produce infrequent responses, perhaps it means you are overlooking students' ability to understand a story's plot. By beginning your instruction with literal comprehension questions, you will gain a sense of what students know and do not know and be able to adjust your instruction accordingly. Doing so will help students understand their reading material—be it traditional print texts or some form of electronic media—more deeply. And perhaps most important of all, such instruction will help equip today's students for future literacy challenges.

## LITERATURE/FILMS CITED

Burroughs, William. (1992). *Naked lunch*. New York: Grove Weidenfeld.

Cameron, James. (Director). (1997). *Titanic* [Film]. United States: Paramount Pictures.

Daldry, Stephen. (Director). (2002). *The hours* [Film]. United States: Paramount Pictures.

Dorris, Michael. (1990). *The broken cord*. New York: Harper Perennial.

Fitzgerald, F. Scott. (1925/1995). *The great Gatsby*. New York: Scribner.

Ginsberg, Allen. (1996). *Howl and other poems*. San Francisco: City Lights Books.

Green, John. (2006). *Looking for Alaska*. New York: Puffin Books.

Grimes, Nikki. (2003). *Bronx masquerade*. New York: Puffin Books.

Hallström, Lasse. (Director). (2000). *Chocolat* [Film]. United States: Miramax Films.

Hemingway, Ernest. (1952). *The old man and the sea*. New York: Charles Scribner's Sons.

Hitchcock, Alfred. (Director). (1960). *Psycho* [Film]. United States: Paramount Pictures.

Jackson, Shirley. (1948). The lottery. In *The lottery* (pp. 291–302). New York: Farrar, Straus & Giroux.

Kapur, Shekhar. (Director). (1998). *Elizabeth* [Film]. United States: Gramercy Pictures.

Kerouac, Jack. (1999). *On the road*. New York: Penguin.

Kesey, Ken. (1963). *One flew over the cuckoo's nest*. New York: Signet.

Lucas, George. (Director). (1977). *Star wars* [Film]. United States: Twentieth Century Fox Films.

Luhrmann, Baz. (Director). (1996). *Romeo and Juliet* [Film]. United States: Twentieth Century Fox Films.

Lurie, Rod. (Director). (2000). *The contender* [Film]. United States: Dreamworks Pictures.

Pullman, Philip. (1995). *The golden compass*. New York: Yearling.

Shakespeare, W. (1996). The tragedy of Romeo and Juliet. In *The Riverside Shakespeare* (pp. 1101–1145). New York: Houghton Mifflin.

Steinbeck, John. (1939/2006). *The grapes of wrath*. New York: Penguin.

Walker, Alice. (1986). Without commercials. *In Horses make a landscape more beautiful* (pp. 55–58). San Diego, CA: Harcourt Brace Jovanovich.

Wiesel, Elie. (2006). *Night* (M. Wiesel, Trans.). New York: Hill and Wang.

Wolfe, Tom. (1999). *The electric kool-aid acid test*. New York: Bantam.

Zeffirelli, Franco. (Director). (1968). *Romeo and Juliet* [Film]. UK/Italy: B.H.E. Film-Verona Production-Dino De Laurentis Cinematografica S.P.A Productions.

Zemekis, Robert. (Director). (1994). *Forrest Gump* [Film]. United States: Paramount Pictures.

# CHAPTER 7

# Vocabulary Instruction in English Classes

Consider the power that a name gives a child. Now this is a
*table* and that a *chair*.... Having a name for something means
that one has some degree of control.... As children get more
words, they get more control over their environment....
Language and reading both act as the tools of thought to
bring representation to a new level and to allow the formation
of new relationships and organizations.... To expand a child's
vocabulary is to teach that child to think about the world.
  —STEVEN AND KATHERINE STAHL, vocabulary scholars

Stahl and Stahl wrote this eloquent testimonial to the importance of
vocabulary with elementary school children in mind, but their senti-
ments apply equally well to secondary students. Unlike phonology
and syntax, vocabulary continues to develop throughout the secondary
grades and beyond. Having a name for something gives students a tremendous advantage. As students' vocabularies grow, so do their abilities to think about their world, to exercise some control over it, and of
course to communicate their thoughts to others. Fortunately, in recent
years research, theory, and common sense have combined to both make
us aware of the tremendous importance of vocabulary in and out of
school and give us a broad array of tools to help students develop rich
and powerful vocabularies.

In this chapter, we describe a comprehensive vocabulary program for assisting each and every student in building the vocabulary
she needs to be a successful learner. Of course, all teachers share the
responsibility for building students' vocabularies, but English teachers,
we believe, have both a greater obligation and more resources for doing
so. Here we describe how to do so. The most effective vocabulary pro-

gram is multifaceted and includes at least four elements: providing rich and varied language experiences, teaching individual words, teaching word-learning strategies, and fostering word consciousness. The plan described here relies primarily on the work of one of us (Graves, 2006, 2000) but also draws from the work of Baumann and Kame'enui (2004); Blachowicz, Fisher, Ogle, and Watts-Taffe (2006); Nagy (2006); and Stahl and Nagy (2006), who have described very similar plans. In the remainder of this chapter, we first discuss the importance of vocabulary and the task students face in mastering English vocabulary. We then describe each of the four parts of the program.

# The Importance of Vocabulary

The findings of over 100 years of vocabulary research provide overwhelming evidence of the importance of vocabulary:

- Vocabulary knowledge is one of the best indicators of verbal ability.
- Vocabulary knowledge in kindergarten and first grade is a significant predictor of reading comprehension in the middle and secondary grades.
- Vocabulary difficulty strongly influences the readability of text. In fact, vocabulary is far and away the most significant factor influencing text difficulty.
- Teaching vocabulary can improve reading comprehension for both native English speakers and ELLs. (Graves, 2006, 2007)

# Some Vocabulary Facts

One could of course write a book about vocabulary instruction, and many people have done just that. Here, however, we briefly discuss four facts that strongly influence the vocabulary program we recommend.

## The Vocabulary Learning Task Is Huge

The vocabulary learning task is enormous! Estimates of vocabulary size vary considerably, but a conservative estimate based on the work of Anderson and Nagy (1992); Anglin (1993); Miller and Wakefield (1993); Nagy and Anderson (1984); Nagy and Herman (1987); and White, Graves, and Slater (1990) is this: The books and other reading materials used in school include over 180,000 different words. The average child enters school with a very small reading vocabulary and a listening vocabulary of perhaps 10,000 words. Once in school, however, a student's vocabulary is likely to soar at a rate of 3,000–4,000 words a year, leading to a reading vocabulary of something like 25,000 words by the time she is in eighth grade, and a reading vocabulary of something like 50,000 words by the end of high school. In order to accomplish this prodigious feat, students learn something like 10 words a day—every day of the week, on the weekends, and throughout the summer. Obviously, we cannot teach them anywhere near 10 words a day. This is why a multifaceted program that provides students with various opportunities and methods of learning words on their own as well as vocabulary instruction that we provide is so important.

## Some Students Face Debilitating Vocabulary Deficits

Many children of poverty enter school with vocabularies about half the size of those of their middle-class counterparts and fall further behind each year (Hart & Risley, 2003). A similar situation exists for many ELLs. Consider this: Assume that average students come to school with vocabularies of about 10,000 words, while linguistically less advantaged students come to school with vocabularies of about 5,000 words. Assume further that the vocabularies of the average students grow at the rate of about 3,500 words, while those of the linguistically less advantaged students grow at half that rate, which is what they have done in the past. By the end of 12th grade, students with larger vocabularies will know something like 52,000 words, while those with smaller vocabularies will know something like 27,000 words. This is a huge and debilitating deficit. Students who are repeatedly stumbling over words will get little meaning from what they read, as well as very little pleasure and satisfaction from reading. Moreover, reducing these differences in vocabulary is something that schools are presently doing little about (Biemiller & Boote, 2006). Thus, in addition to assisting all students in developing their vocabularies as fully as possible, we face the challenge of helping students with smaller vocabularies catch up with their classmates.

### *There Are Various Levels of Word Knowledge*

It is not simply a matter of knowing a word or not knowing it. We know words to various degrees. Here is a continuum Beck, McKeown, and Kucan (2002, p. 10) have suggested:

- No knowledge.
- General sense, such as knowing *mendacious* has a negative connotation.
- Narrow, context-bound knowledge, such as knowing that a *radiant* bride is a beautifully smiling happy one, but unable to describe an individual in a different context as radiant.
- Having knowledge of a word but not being able to recall it readily enough to apply it in appropriate situations.
- Rich, decontextualized knowledge of a word's meaning, its relationship to other words, and its extension to metaphorical uses, such as understanding what someone is doing when they are devouring a book.

### *Different Words Present Different Learning Tasks*

Word-learning tasks differ depending on such matters as how much students already know about the words to be taught, how well you want them to learn the words, and what you want them to be able to do with the words afterwards. Here are several word-learning tasks that are particularly important in secondary English classes.

#### *Learning to Read Words That Are Already in Their Oral Vocabularies*

Most students can read all of the words in their oral vocabularies by the time they get to secondary school, and therefore we do not need to teach them to read words in their oral vocabularies. However, less skilled readers and ELLs may still need assistance in this area.

#### *Learning New Words Representing Known Concepts*

This is the task students face with the majority of new words they encounter. For example, the word *ensemble* meaning "a group of musicians" would be an unknown word for many eighth graders. But the concept of a group of musicians who perform together is a familiar one and easily taught. All students continue to learn words of this sort throughout their years in school. This is also a major word-learning task for ELLs, who, of course, have a number of concepts for which they do not yet have English words.

### Learning New Words Representing New Concepts

Another word-learning task students face, and a very demanding one, is learning to read words that are in neither their oral nor their reading vocabularies and for which they do not have an available concept. Learning the full meanings of such words as *theme, metaphor,* and *fascist* will require most secondary students to develop new concepts. All students continue to learn words of this sort throughout their years in school.

### Learning New Meanings for Known Words

Still another word-learning task students face is learning new meanings for words that they already know with one meaning. Many words have multiple meanings, and thus students frequently encounter words that look familiar but are used with a meaning different from the one they know. A seventh grader, for example, would almost certainly know the word *capital* meaning "a city that is the seat of government" as in "St. Paul is the capital of Minnesota," but many seventh graders will not know *capital* meaning "material wealth in the form of money or property" as in "This particular budget could be used only for capital expenses."

Having described these facts about vocabulary, we now turn to describing the four-part program we recommend—providing rich and varied language experiences, teaching individual words, teaching word-learning strategies, and fostering word consciousness.

# Providing Rich
# and Varied Language Experiences

With something like 50,000 words to be learned, it is clear that we cannot directly teach students anywhere near all the words they need to learn. Most words are learned incidentally—as students are reading, talking, and writing. Thus, to promote vocabulary growth and for the myriad other reasons we became English teachers, our goal is to fill the classroom with rich reading, discussion, and writing experiences.

## Reading

In promoting students' incidental word learning through reading, considerations include giving some attention to vocabulary as you choose literature for classroom study, recognizing the importance of wide reading, helping students select books that will promote vocabulary growth, and facilitating and encouraging their reading widely. Most words are learned from context, and the richest context for building vocabulary is books. Books, as Stahl and Stahl (2003) point out, are "where the words are." Testimony to that fact is shown in Figure 7.1. As can be seen, even children's books contain about one-third more rare words than prime-time adult TV shows and nearly twice as many rare words as adult conversational speech. Of course, short stories and poetry also include rich vocabulary. If we want to help students increase their vocabularies, we need to get them to read more (Anderson, Wilson, & Fielding, 1988; Elley, 1996; Kim & White, in press). Some of this reading, of course, will come as part of the literature study that the class as a whole does. What is important with the reading the class as a whole does is that you call some attention to the vocabulary in the selections. This doesn't mean that you always need to teach vocabu-

| Source | Rare words |
|---|---|
| I. Printed texts | per 1,000 |
| Abstracts of scientific articles | 128.0 |
| Newspapers | 68.3 |
| Popular magazines | 65.7 |
| Adult books | 52.7 |
| Children's books | 30.9 |
| | |
| II. Television texts | |
| Prime-time adult shows | 22.7 |
| Prime-time children's shows | 20.2 |
| | |
| III. Adult speech | |
| Expert witness testimony | 28.4 |
| College graduates talk to friends/spouses | 17.3 |

**FIGURE 7.1.** Frequency of rare words in various sources.

lary, although you will undoubtedly want to teach some words for some of the selections the class reads. For other selections and other words, however, it will be appropriate to merely call students' attention to some of the skillful diction of the author. For example, if your middle school class is reading Laurie Anderson's *Speak,* you might point to a passage such as "I rummage in the bin again and find a half-melted palm tree from a Lego set" and note how fitting the word *rummage* is, why it is superior to *look through* or *search.* Or if your senior high class is reading *Hamlet* you might want to talk a bit about the extensive vocabulary Shakespeare employed and note his skillful use of words such as *beguile, brazen,* and *jaded.* Note that your goal here is not so much to teach these words—many students will know them—as to demonstrate your interest in words and lead students to become similarly interested in them, something we will talk more about in the word consciousness section of this chapter.

In addition to a strong and varied literature program for the class as a whole, we recommend some sort of in-class independent reading program, particularly if your classes include students who are not avid readers. Of course, anything you can do to help students pay some attention to the vocabulary used in material they read will be useful. This can be very simple, for example, merely asking students to record the 10 most interesting words they found in their reading.

In addition to reading in class, students need to read out of class. There simply is not that much class time available. To really build their vocabularies, students need to read a lot outside of school. Unfortunately, both our informal conversations with teachers and students and empirical evidence indicate that all too many students do very little reading outside of school. For example, in their study of how students spend their time out of school, Anderson and his colleagues (1988) found that 50% of students read from books less than 4 minutes a day and 30% of them read from books less than 2 minutes a day. Similarly, data gathered as part of the NAEP (Donahue, Daane, & Jin, 2005) show that about one-fourth of the students questioned reported reading no books outside of school in the previous month. These students, the ones who read no books outside of school or read books outside of school for only a few minutes a day, are almost certainly those most in need of larger vocabularies.

The starting point for encouraging wide reading is getting good books into students' hands. A classroom library—a library with books that you know well, books appropriate for the various levels of readers in your classroom, and books that include appropriately challenging vocabulary—is a terrific asset. As Figure 7.1 shows, newspapers and magazines are also valuable parts of the classroom library and are likely to contain the sort of challenging words students need to learn. While nothing can replace the immediacy and convenience of a classroom library, school and community libraries are other important sources of books.

But just having books available is not enough. Something must be done to entice students to read the books. Many possibilities exist here. You can read parts of a book in class and encourage students to read the rest of it at home. You can give book talks that preview and advertise books the same way movie previews advertise upcoming films. You can encourage students to share the books they read with each other. You can become familiar with individual student's interests and with individual books and thus recommend particular books to particular students. Still another option is to start an out-of-class book club, something Appleman explains just how to do in *Reading for Themselves* (2006). As Appleman notes, such clubs can indeed "transform adolescents into lifelong readers."

### Discussion

Students of all abilities—and ELLs as well as native English speakers—need to engage frequently in authentic discussions, give-and-take conversations in which they get the opportunity to thoughtfully discuss significant ideas. The key to having discussions that will prompt students to use more sophisticated vocabulary is to give them meaty and somewhat academic topics to talk about. As shown in Figure 7.1, casual conversations, even casual conversations among college graduates, do not include a lot of sophisticated vocabulary. If students are going to use sophisticated words, they need to discuss sophisticated ideas. This means talking about academic topics that students have some familiarity with—topics they are reading about, investigating in the library and on the Internet, and probably writing about. Such discussions might focus on the enduring themes of great literature—adversity, courage, responsibility, hardship, race, war, death, and the like. Or they might focus on sophisticated literary topics such as the motivations that prompt a character's action. One good source of meaty discussion topics is the teaching for understanding literature we describe in Chapter 3, for example, Wiggins and McTighe's *Understanding by Design* (2005) or Wiske's *Teaching for Understanding* (1998). These authors describe thematic units that focus on important topics, garner students' interest, engage them, scaffold their efforts, and help them build long-lasting and useful information; and in so doing they provide students with some real grist for discussion.

## Writing

The keys to promoting students' independent word learning through writing are similar to those for discussion. Students need to write about topics that they care about and that are at least somewhat sophisticated. They also need to write with a purpose and for an audience. This is the case because it is only when you are writing with a real purpose and for an audience that you have identified and care about that you are likely to think deeply about the words you use in your writing (Spandel, 2001). Here, for example, are some questions about their word choices you might pose to students to prompt them to critically examine their diction:

- Does this word fully capture my meaning?
- Is this word the very best word to say just what I want to say?
- Is this word precise enough?
- Is this word appropriately formal or informal?
- Will the people to whom I am writing understand this word?
- Will they find this word appropriately formal or informal as the situation demands?
- Is this word a word my reader is likely to find interesting and appealing?
- Have I used this word too frequently; should I perhaps use a synonym?

The goal is to get students to realize that the words they use in their writing are very important, that the words they use will affect both the clarity of what they write and the reaction their writing receives from others, and that they should choose words wisely, honing their word choices as one of the last steps in editing their writing.

# Teaching Individual Words

One thing to keep in mind as you consider teaching individual words is that you need to teach the most important words. Here are four questions we have found useful in identifying important vocabulary:

1. *Is understanding the word important to understanding the selection in which it appears?* If the answer is "yes," the word is a good candidate for instruction. If the answer is, "no," then other words are probably more important to teach.

2. *Are students able to use their context or structural-analysis skills to discover the word's meaning?* If they can use these skills, then they should be allowed to practice them. Doing so will both help them hone these skills and reduce the number of words you need to teach.

3. *Can working with this word be useful in furthering students' context, structural analysis, or dictionary skills?* If the answer here is, "yes," then your working with the word can serve two purposes: It can aid students in learning the word and it can help them acquire a strategy they can use in learning other words. You might, for example, decide to teach the word *regenerate* because students need to master the prefix *re-*.

4. *How useful is this word outside of the reading selection currently being taught?* The more frequently a word appears in material students read, the more important it is for them to know the word. Additionally, the more frequent a word is, the greater the chances that students will retain the word once you teach it.

Note that these four guidelines are not independent. In fact, the answer to one question may suggest that a word should be taught, while the answer to another suggests that it should not. Ultimately, you will need to use your best judgment about which words to teach based on the demands of the reading selection and the needs of your students.

Another thing to keep in mind as you consider teaching individual words is that you get just about what you pay for. Activities that take more time and mental effort, activities that force students to think, and activities that focus on meaning will produce stronger results. Activities that involve both definitional information and contextual information are stronger than activities that involve only one of these. And, as in virtually all learning, active teaching and active learning are generally called for.

A third thing to keep in mind as you consider teaching individual words is that different sorts of instruction are appropriate for the various word-learning tasks we described. In the remainder of this section of the chapter, we discuss some approaches appropriate for these various tasks.

## Teaching Words in Students' Oral Vocabularies

The main thing to remember about teaching words that students already have in their oral vocabularies is that doing so is a relatively simple task and doesn't take a lot of time. Students already know the meaning of these words; they just need to recognize the words when they see them in print. This simple, three-step process will help them do that:

1. Show students the word.
2. Pronounce the word for them.
3. Have them rehearse this association myriad times.

That's it, and while students will need to read the word many times before they will rapidly and automatically recognize it, there is no need to spend a lot of time on initial instruction with this type of word.

## Teaching Words Representing Known Concepts

Here we suggest several methods. Some, you will notice, are stronger than others, but come at the cost of increased time.

### Talking about Words

This approach, suggested by Stahl and Nagy (2006) is the thinnest method we will suggest. It doesn't take much of your time or your students' time, and it does not create rich and lasting word knowledge. But with so many words to teach, it is sometimes all you will have time for and it does serve to get students started on the long road to acquiring rich and deep meanings.

- Identify a potentially unknown and at least somewhat important word in text students are reading.
- Read the sentence in which the word occurs aloud or have a student read it.
- Provide a simple definition or explanation of the word's meaning.

#### Propensity

The politician had an unfortunate *propensity* to give long-winded speeches. *Propensity* simply means tendency.

## Providing Glossaries

This approach requires some out-of-class preparation on your part, but does not take much in-class time.

- Create a glossary of the important words likely to be unknown in a selection the class is reading. List the words in the order in which they come up in the selection and include the page numbers on which they occur.
- Be sure to use simple and straightforward definitions.
- Typically limit a glossary for a short story to something like 10 words and one for a novel to something like 30 words.
- Give students the glossary and encourage them to use it as necessary. You might want to invite them to add words of their own choosing to the glossary and to discuss some of their words after reading.

## The Definition Plus Rich Context Procedure

This method is stronger than either of the previous two. It is also more time-consuming. While it does not require much out-of-class time, it does require a fair amount of in-class time.

- Give students a straightforward definition for the word.
- Give them the word in a rich context.
- Discuss the definition, the context, and some other contexts in which the word might be used.

### Irradiate

To treat something or someone with radiation. It's becoming increasingly common to *irradiate* meat and some other foods to kill potentially harmful bacteria.

## The Context-Relationship Procedure

This method requires quite a bit of out-of-class preparation. However, presenting words in this way takes only about 1 minute per word of class time, and we have repeatedly found that students remember words taught in this fashion.

- Create a brief paragraph that uses the target word three or four times and in doing so gives the meaning of the word.

- Follow the paragraph with a multiple-choice item that checks students' understanding of the word.
- Show the paragraph (probably on an overhead or LCD), read it aloud, and read the multiple-choice options.
- Pause to give students a moment to answer the multiple-choice item, give them the correct answer, and discuss the word and any questions they have.

### Rationale

The *rationale* for my wanting to expose students to a variety of words and their meanings is partially that this will help them become better thinkers who are able to express their ideas more clearly. My *rationale* also includes my belief that words themselves are fascinating objects of study. My *rationale* for doing something means my fundamental reasons for doing it.

*Rationale* means

\_\_\_\_ A. a deliberate error.

\_\_\_\_ B. the basis for doing something.

\_\_\_\_ C. a main idea for an essay.

## Teaching Words Representing New Concepts

It is worth emphasizing that teaching new concepts is a very different matter from simply teaching new labels for known concepts. Here you are teaching a new and potentially challenging idea. Doing so effectively takes a good deal of time and effort on your part and on students' part.

### Semantic Mapping

The first approach to teaching words representing new concepts we will describe, semantic mapping (Heimlich & Pittleman, 1986), actually serves multiple functions. In addition to teaching new concepts, it is useful for improving comprehension of the selections in which the target word appears and for clarifying and extending the meanings of known words. With this method, the teacher puts a word representing a central concept on the overhead, LCD, or board; asks students to work in groups listing as many words related to the central concept as they can; writes students' words on the overhead, LCD, or board grouped in broad categories; has students name the categories and perhaps suggest additional ones; and discusses with students the central concept, the other words, the categories, and their interrelationships. Figure 7.2 shows a semantic map for the concept *prose.*

### Four-Square Vocabulary Instruction

The four-square method, originally developed by Eeds and Cockrun (1985) and recently updated by Stahl and Nagy (2006), begins with students dividing a sheet of paper into four squares. Next, the teacher has students write the target concept in the top left square and gives an oral definition of the concept. After that, the teacher solicits examples of the concept, which are written in the top right square, and nonexamples of the concept, which are written in the bottom right square. Finally, students define the concept and write their agreed-upon definition in the bottom left square. Figure 7.3 shows a completed four-square sheet for the concept *rising action.* Like semantic mapping, four squares draws on students' collective knowledge and is therefore a good tool for reviewing.

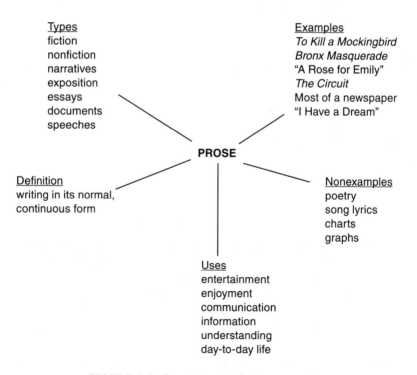

**FIGURE 7.2.** Semantic map for the concept *prose.*

| Target concept | Examples |
|---|---|
| rising action | when Santiago is fighting the marlin in *The Old Man and the Sea* |
| | when Frank questions his morality and determines to go to America and make a success of himself in *Angela's Ashes* |
| | when Shug teaches Celie about love, sexuality, and God in *The Color Purple* |
| **Students' agreed-upon definition** | **Non-examples** |
| It's the part in a novel, short story, or other narrative when the action is building and the story is moving toward the climax but the climax hasn't yet happened. | when Santiago arrives back at the harbor with just the skeleton of his fish |
| | when the priest absolves Frank of his sins, allowing him to leave for America with a clear conscience |
| | when Celie inherits her family's home and goes to live there |

**FIGURE 7.3.** Completed four-square sheet for the concept *rising action.*

## Learning New Meanings for Known Words

Teaching new meanings for known words is generally a simple and straightforward process. Here is one approach:

- *Acknowledge the known meaning.* "I'm sure you all know the meaning of *remove* as 'take away' in sentences like 'Try to *remove* all of the old varnish before refinishing the table.'"
- *Give the new meaning.* "But you may not know the meaning of *remove* as 'step' in sentences like 'She was one remove from bursting into tears.'"
- *Note the similarities between the meanings (if any).* There does seem to be some similarity in meaning that includes the concept of *away,* in one case 'take away' and in the other case 'a step away.'"

## Additional Methods of Teaching Individual Words

The methods of teaching individual words we have just described are those we have found particularly useful and will serve you well in many situations. Still, there are many other techniques available. Beck et al. (2002), Graves (2006), and Stahl and Nagy (2006) are excellent sources of additional techniques.

# Teaching Word-Learning Strategies

No matter how many words you teach directly, students are still going to have to learn most words on their own. Thus, being sure that students have strategies for doing so is extremely important. Notice that we use the phrase "being sure that students have strategies" rather than the phrase "teaching strategies." We do so because by the time they get to the middle and secondary grades most students will have already been taught word-learning strategies. This doesn't mean that older students don't need to practice the word-learning strategies they already know, be reminded to use them as they are reading, and review them from time to time. It also does not mean there are no students who need initial instruction on word-learning strategies; some students definitely need initial instruction. Still, in most middle and secondary classrooms, teaching word-learning strategies is not your primary responsibility. For this reason, we have kept this section of the chapter brief. In what follows, we first describe a general procedure for both teaching and reviewing word-learning strategies and then discuss what needs to be learned about each of three strategies: using context, using word parts, and using the dictionary. Detailed procedures for teaching these and other important strategies are given in Graves (2006).

## A Powerful Procedure for Teaching Strategies

Two approaches to teaching strategies—direct explanation (Duke & Pearson, 2002) and transactional strategies instruction (Pressley, 2006) are widely recommended and supported by substantial research. Here we recommend a combination of those two, which we term "balanced strategies instruction" (Graves & Sales, 2006). A typical balanced strategies instruction lesson used to initially teach a strategy might last from several days to several weeks, while a review lesson might last only a period or so. Here are the basic components of balanced strategies instruction and some suggestions for using the approach.

- *Make motivation a prime concern.* Stress how learning and using the strategy will help students with their reading and learning in school and outside of school.
- *Use prominent visual displays.* Before teaching the strategy, as you are teaching it, and after you have taught it, use posters and the like to create interest in the upcoming instruction, highlight major features of the strategy, and remind students to continue to use it after the initial instruction.
- *Follow the direct explanation model for the initial instruction.*
  - Provide an explicit description of the strategy and when and how it should be used.
  - Model your use of the strategy.
  - Have students model their use of the strategy, with your providing support as necessary.
  - Give students plenty of practice using the strategy, initially providing them with a lot of support and then gradually by giving them more and more responsibility for using the strategy.
  - Have students independently use the strategy. (Duke & Pearson, 2002)
- *Provide substantial and long-term follow-up after the initial instruction.* Prompt students to use the strategy, review it periodically, and do everything possible to make it something that students internalize and use over time.

### Using Context

Using context to infer the meanings of unknown words is clearly the most important word-learning strategy. Most words are learned from context as students are reading, and to a lesser extent listening and discussing. If we can improve students' ability to infer word meanings even a small amount, we can help them substantially build their vocabularies. That said, it needs to be acknowledged that helping students to improve their ability to use context is no mean task. For students who are not already adept at using context, only substantial initial instruction and equally substantial review and follow-up is likely to produce meaningful results.

What students need to learn about context clues is that context only occasionally reveals the full meaning of a word, that context often reveals part of a word's meaning, and that inferring a word's meaning from context is often a fairly complex endeavor. What students need to be able to do to use context is recognize when they have come to an unknown word, decide whether it is important to attempt to determine its meaning, and then have some sort of fairly detailed strategy they can use. Such a strategy typically consists of (1) rereading the sentence in which the unknown word occurs, (2) reading the sentence that follows it looking for clues, (3) rereading the sentence that precedes the one with the unknown word and that with the unknown word looking for clues, (4) determining a potential meaning or turning to some other person or the dictionary for the meaning, or (5) deciding to do without the meaning for the present time. This may sound simple, but a substantial body of research has shown that it is not (Graves, 2006).

### Using Word Parts

While using context is the most important word-learning strategy, using word parts is a close second. About half of the "new words" that students meet in their reading are related to familiar words (Anglin, 1993). Once students can break words into parts, they can use their knowledge of word parts to attempt to deduce their meanings—if of course they understand word parts and how they function. The three types of word parts to consider are prefixes, suffixes, and non-English roots.

#### Prefixes

Prefixes are the most powerful elements to teach because there is a small number of prefixes that are used in a large number of words, prefixes are used at the beginning of words and are consistently spelled so they are easy to recognize, and attaching the meaning of the prefix (e.g., *pre-*) to the meaning of the root word (e.g., *dawn*) to get the meaning of the unknown word (e.g., *predawn*) is generally a straightforward process. Figure 7.4 lists the 20 most frequent prefixes.

Students need to know the meanings of these prefixes and how to combine those meanings with the meanings of root words to infer the meanings of unknown words. What students need to be able to do to use prefixes is recognize that the unknown word has a prefix and a root, access the meanings of the prefix and the root, and combine those two meanings to arrive at the meaning of the unknown word.

| Prefix | Number of words with the prefix | Suffix | Number of words with the suffix |
|---|---|---|---|
| un- | 782 | -s, -es | 673 |
| re- | 401 | -ed | 435 |
| in-, im-, ir-, il- ("not") | 313 | -ing | 303 |
| dis- | 216 | -ly | 144 |
| en-, em- | 132 | -er, -or (agentive) | 95 |
| non- | 126 | -ion, -tion, -ation, -ition | 76 |
| in-, im- ("in or into") | 105 | -ible, -able | 33 |
| over- ("too much") | 98 | -al, -ial | 30 |
| mis- | 83 | -y | 27 |
| sub- | 80 | -ness | 26 |
| pre- | 79 | -ity, -ty | 23 |
| inter- | 77 | -ment | 21 |
| fore- | 76 | -ic | 18 |
| de- | 71 | -ous, -eous, -ious | 18 |
| trans- | 47 | -en | 15 |
| super- | 43 | -er (comparative) | 15 |
| semi- | 39 | -ive, -ative, -itive | 15 |
| anti- | 33 | -ful | 14 |
| mid- | 33 | -less | 14 |
| under- | 25 | -est | 12 |
| All others | 100 | | 160 |
| TOTALS | 2,959 | | 2,167 |

**FIGURE 7.4.** Twenty most frequent prefixes and suffixes. Adapted from White, Sowell, and Yanagihara (1989). Reprinted with permission of the International Reading Association.

## Suffixes

Suffixes represent a more complex situation than do prefixes and present a different learning task for native English speakers than for ELLs. Inflectional suffixes, the most common type, have grammatical meanings (e.g., -ed indicating the past tense) which are difficult to explain. Native English speakers already have a tacit understanding of their function and attempts to teach their meanings may cause confusion. Many ELLs, on the other hand, do need to be taught their meanings. Derivational suffixes, most of which are less common, have abstract meanings (e.g., -ence indicating the state of being), and these too are often difficult to explain. Figure 7.4 also contains a list of the 20 most frequent suffixes.

We recommend teaching the grammatical meanings/functions of inflectional suffixes to ELLs if they don't know them. We recommend teaching the meanings of derivational suffixes only if you identify a number of words that your students are likely to come across that include those suffixes; otherwise, teaching them probably requires more time and effort than it is worth. What students need to know about and be able to do with suffixes is similar to what they need to know about and be able to do with prefixes.

### Non-English Roots

Non-English roots (e.g., *anthro* meaning "man" and appearing in such words as *anthropology, misanthrope,* and *philanthropy*) represent a very different teaching and learning situation than do prefixes or suffixes. There are a large number of non-English roots. Individual roots are not used in nearly the number of words common prefixes or suffixes are used in, they are often variously spelled and thus difficult to identify, and the relationship between the original meaning of the root and the current meaning of the English word in which it is used is often vague. Unfortunately, we know of no valid list of the most important roots to teach; there are just too many of them. Similar to what we suggested in teaching derivational suffixes, we recommend systematic instruction on only non-English roots that you find occurring in a number of words in the materials your students read. Again, what students need to know about and be able to do with non-English roots is similar to what they need to know about and be able to do with prefixes.

## Using the Dictionary

Teaching students to efficiently and effectively use the dictionary is a much smaller task than is teaching the use of context clues or word parts. Nevertheless, many students are not very effective dictionary users and this will not do for a tool that they will use throughout their schooling and as adults.

The starting point in helping students become effective and efficient dictionary users is getting them the right level of dictionaries. Every classroom should have multiple copies of at least one dictionary at students' grade level, at least one below their grade level, and at least one above their grade level. Additionally, every classroom with ELLs—and this means most classrooms in the United States today—should have a dictionary specifically designed for ELLs and a dictionary of idioms. We recommend the *Collins COBUILD New Student Dictionary* (2005) and the *Longman American Idioms Dictionary* (1999). What students need to know and be able to do to effectively use dictionaries is to realize that many words have more than one meaning, check all the definitions the dictionary gives for a word, not just one definition, and decide which definition makes sense in the passage in which they found the word. It is also worth alerting students to the fact that dictionary definitions are all too often rather opaque and that the dictionary works best when you already have some sense of a word's meaning and want to verify or check your understanding.

## Fostering Word Consciousness

The term *word consciousness* refers to an awareness of and interest in words and their meanings (Graves & Watts-Taffe, 2002). Word consciousness integrates metacognition about words, motivation to learn words, and deep and lasting interest in words (Anderson & Nagy, 1992). The student who is word conscious knows a lot of words, and she knows them well. Equally important, she is interested in words and gains enjoyment and satisfaction from using them well and from seeing or hearing them used well by others. She finds words intriguing, recognizes adroit word usage when she encounters it, uses words skillfully herself, is on the lookout for new and precise words, and is responsive to the nuances of word meanings. She is also well aware of the power of words and realizes that they can be used to foster clarity and understanding or to obscure and obfuscate matters. Students who are word conscious simplify our task as teachers because they learn a lot of words on their own.

There are myriad ways of developing and nurturing such positive attitudes. Here are some of them suggested by one of us and our colleague Susan Watts-Taffe (Graves & Watts-Taffe, 2002; Graves, 2006):

- Creating a word-rich environment
- Recognizing and promoting adept diction
- Promoting word play
- Involving students in original investigations

Here we discuss each of these in turn. As you will see, there are some time-consuming word consciousness activities, but for the most part fostering word consciousness does not take a lot of your time or your students' time.

## Creating a Word-Rich Environment

The starting point in fostering word consciousness it to literally fill your classroom with words. Fill the room with books and other material on many topics and many reading levels, and be sure many of these books contain some new words for all students. As you know, secondary classrooms typically include students with a very broad range of reading levels and of course an equally wide range of interests, so making a range of books available is crucial. The same classroom, for example, might include books specifically written for teens like Robert Cormier's *The Chocolate War* and S.E. Hinton's *The Outsiders,* traditional titles like *The Old Man and the Sea* and *The Grapes of Wrath,* books illuminating various cultures such as Michael Dorris's *A Yellow Raft in Blue Water* and Linda Crew's *Children of the River,* and books that contemporary adults read such as Khaled Hosseini's *The Kite Runner* and Lance Armstrong's *It's Not about the Bike.* The books we make available should also represent various genre including poetry, nonfiction, autobiography and memoir, fantasy, historical fiction, mystery and thrillers, and the like. Anita Silvey's *500 Great Books for Teens* (2006) contains a rich set of possibilities, conveniently arranged and annotated.

Read to students from books that include some new vocabulary. Yes, we are talking about reading to middle school and high school students. Readers of all ages—including the two of us—love to be read to. Just look on the reserve shelves of your local library and see how many of the reserved materials are tapes or CDs.

Include lots of discussion of meaty topics that invite sophisticated words. As we noted earlier in this chapter, the teaching for understanding literature, which we discuss in Chapter 3, is rich with suggestions for meaty discussion topics.

Make the classroom a safe place that invites and rewards experimentation with words. In word-rich classrooms, students are expected to experiment with language and in so doing occasionally misuse words. This needs to be accepted by both you and the students.

## Recognizing and Promoting Adept Diction

Make it a point to use some sophisticated vocabulary, and sometimes comment on your word choices. Tell a noisy class yourself that you think the *cacophony* should probably cease. Tell a student that the *hyperbole* in her essay works well. Or suggest that *conjecture* is appropriate in some places and not in others. Sometimes you will want to comment on the sophisticated words you are using, but at other times we suggest you just use them and see what happens.

Point out adept word choices in material students are reading, listening to, or viewing. Comment on the sophisticated vocabulary of *The Grapes of Wrath*, for example, *dissipate, bemused, prodigal, beseech, relinquish,* and *wizened*. Note how Zora Neale Hurston's *Their Eyes Were Watching God* is rich in Southern and Black dialect features: Final consonants are frequently dropped as when *you* becomes *yuh*; vowel shifts occur as when *get* becomes *git*; and double negatives are used as in "Nobody don't know."

Compliment students on their adept word choices in their discussions and writing. Both the seventh grader who comments that the *thunderous* noise of the planes taking off ruined any chance she had for sleep and the 12th grader who observes that the new principal has a somewhat *rakish demeanor* deserve a bit of credit for their adept use of words.

### Promoting Word Play

Not all work with words need be or even should be work. There is plenty of room for playing with words, and of course many people spend a good deal of time playing with words—doing crossword puzzles and playing commercial games like Scrabble, Balderdash, Boggle, and Taboo. There is also plenty of room for playing homemade games like hangman and dictionary. And there is room for word play books, books like Richard Lederer's *Pun and Games* for middle school students and *Get Thee to a Punnery* for high school students. Of course, we are not suggesting that you fill the days with games, but on Fridays, after tests, or as placeholder activities they have a definite place.

### Involving Students in Original Investigations

Still another approach to getting students excited about words is to give them opportunities for original investigations. Because students are surrounded by words, vocabulary makes an excellent topic for investigation. Some possibilities include:

- The use of slang versus more formal vocabulary.
- The vocabulary of different groups: short-order cooks, movie people, hucksters on TV.
- The vocabulary that is appropriate in different settings: school, home, church, the cafeteria.
- How vocabulary changes over time.

As one example of this last activity, you might want to look at "Slinging Slang from the Flappers to the Rappers" (*alphadictionary.com/articles/generation_test.html*). This interactive site lets you explore the slang current at various times. There, for example, students will learn that over the years *get out* has been alternately phrased as *beat it, scram, take a powder, blow, split, boggie, book,* and *navigate.*

The most ambitious investigation we have seen was done by Scott Rasmussen and Derek Oosterman (1999), two seniors at Minnetonka High School in Minnesota. Scott's and Derek's project was designed to investigate procedures for teaching vocabulary, and their ambitious goal was to "determine the best means of vocabulary acquisition in high school students." They began with a review of the literature and from that developed a number of hypotheses and tests of those hypotheses. In one of several studies they did, classes were presented words in ways involving more and stronger sensory clues. One class, the control, took the test with no clues. Another saw the words. A third heard them. And a fourth both saw them and heard them. The results indicated that the more senses led to better word learning, with the four groups described above receiving scores of 42%, 77%, 74%, and 86%, respectively.

The point, of course, is not so much what Scott and Derek learned about vocabulary instruction as the extent to which the experience is likely to leave them with a heightened awareness of words. One of us has corresponded with Scott about his work, and he reports that he now pays more attention to words than he used to. "Before the study," he wrote, "I never gave vocabulary much thought.... In regular conversations and school classes now, I am increasingly cognizant of how words can influence perception and meaning."

## Concluding Remarks

So there you have it, a multifaceted approach to assisting students in building substantial and powerful vocabularies—providing rich and varied language experiences, teaching individual words, teaching word-learning strategies, and fostering word consciousness. In these concluding remarks, we want to address a straightforward yet challenging question: How much time should be spent on vocabulary? If you teach in a typical situation, you have somewhat less than 5 hours a week to deal with literature, writing, language, and the many vital other parts of the English curriculum. You certainly cannot and should not spend an inordinate amount of time on vocabulary. For students with average and above average vocabularies, we suspect that about half an hour a week, divided in the following way, will be sufficient.

As an English teacher, you already engage in rich and varied language experiences—reading, writing, and discussion—much of the time. But the vast majority of what you do is not done primarily to teach vocabulary, and we do not think most of it should be tallied as time spent on vocabulary. The few extra things you do to focus more directly on words should not take more than 5 minutes a week.

Teaching individual words is something we recommend you do some of every week, not just for the sake of teaching words but to repeatedly remind students of the importance of vocabulary. Something like 15 minutes a week should be enough time to spend on individual words.

Initially teaching word-learning strategies takes a good deal of time, but you won't be teaching the strategies to average and above average students, you will be reviewing them. A period or a part of a period here and there is all you should need. Averaged over the whole of a year, providing reviews might amount to 5 minutes a week.

Finally, fostering word consciousness takes almost no time, with much of your effort there coming in little asides, as when you compliment a student for a particularly adept word she has used in an essay. An average of 5 minutes a week should be sufficient to nurture students toward really caring about words.

Unfortunately, for students whose vocabularies are considerably smaller and less powerful than those of their peers, we cannot be nearly as definite nor suggest that the job can be done in some relatively small amount of time. If students who are well behind are to catch up with their peers, they will need to spend a good deal of time reading, discussing, and writing, learning individual words, learning and practicing word-learning strategies, and becoming increasingly interested in words. There is no way to calculate just how much time this will take and it will take very different amounts of time in different classrooms, but it will definitely take much more than half an hour a week.

## LITERATURE CITED

Anderson, Laurie. (1999). *Speak.* New York: Puffin Books.

Armstrong, Lance. (2000). *It's not about the bike.* New York: Putnam.

*Collins COBUILD new student's dictionary* (3rd ed.). (2005). Glasglow, Scotland: HarperCollins.

Cormier, Robert. (1994). *The chocolate war.* New York: Pantheon.

Crew, Linda. (1989). *Children of the river.* New York: Delacorte.

Dorris, Michael. (1987). *A yellow raft in blue water.* New York: Holt.

Hemingway, Ernest. (1952). *The old man and the sea.* New York: Scribner.

Hinton, Susan Eloise. (1967). *The outsiders.* New York: Viking Press.

Hosseini, Khaled. (2003). *The kite runner.* New York: Riverhead.

Hurston, Zora Neale. (1990). *Their eyes were watching God.* New York: Perennial Library.

Lederer, Richard. (1988). *Get thee to a punnery.* New York: Dell.

Lederer, Richard. (1996). *Pun and games.* Chicago: Chicago Review Press.

*Longman American idioms dictionary.* (1999). Edinburgh Gate, UK: Pearson Education.

McCourt, Frank. (1996). *Angela's ashes.* New York: Scribners.

Rasmussen, S., & Oosterman, D. (1999). *Lexical procurement (vocabulary).* Unpublished manuscript.

Shakespeare, William. (1985). *Hamlet, prince of Denmark.* Cambridge, UK: Cambridge University Press.

Steinbeck, John. (1939). *The grapes of wrath.* New York: Viking Press.

Walker, Alice. (1982). *The color purple.* New York: Simon & Schuster.

# CHAPTER 8

# Comprehension in Context

Many teachers, and certainly the vast public, believe that by the time students are in high school, they do not need to be taught to read. If they can't read, the argument goes, then they should be retained or placed in a remedial situation until they've mastered reading. Thus, often the only "reading teachers" in secondary education are Title I teachers and special education teachers. For years, English teachers have taken the stance that if students can't "keep up with the reading," they should get help. But we believe all English teachers should be reading teachers since students continue to be at different stages of reading development, even in high school and college.

KATHLEEN AND JAMES STRICKLAND, literacy specialists

Throughout this book, we have discussed a number of approaches to fostering comprehension in English classrooms. As Strickland and Strickland point out, we must help students, even secondary students, become better thinkers and readers regardless of their existing abilities.

In this chapter, we illustrate how many of our approaches to fostering comprehension can be used in concert to enhance students' understanding, appreciation, and learning as they engage in a month-long unit on American Indian perspectives on life in the United States. The unit would work well in a 9th- or 10th-grade class. It is based on the teaching for understanding model we described in Chapter 3 and includes two SREs as described in Chapter 2. Embedded within the unit and the SREs are experiences with response to literature, comprehension strategies, higher-order thinking, and vocabulary, the topics of Chapters 4–7. The principal readings for the unit are Louise Erdrich's "The Red Convertible" and John Neihardt's *Black Elk Speaks*. In what follows, we first describe the goals of the unit and the types of assessment we will use. Next, we describe the unit itself. This consists of an introduction to the unit, two SREs that comprise much of the unit, and the unit-culminating activities. Finally, we discuss how the various approaches and activities from Chapters 2 through 7 are used in the unit.

## Goals and Assessments for a Teaching for Understanding Unit on American Indian Perspectives on Life in the United States

Using the backward design process described in Chapter 3, planning a teaching for understanding unit begins with determining goals. We developed these following goals for the unit:

- Students will read fiction and nonfiction selections that focus on American Indians, making comparisons across genres and contexts.
- Students will identify contemporary and historical issues affecting American Indians.
- Students will respond to the texts orally in whole-class discussions and through writing (formally and informally) to analyze elements of the authors' craft.
- Students will discern the differences between literal meanings and figurative/symbolic meanings.

In addition to addressing the specific goals just listed, this unit addresses some of the standards established by the NCTE/IRA (1996):

- Students read a wide range of print and nonprint texts to build an understanding of texts, of themselves, and of the cultures of the United States and the world; to acquire new information; to respond to the needs and demands of society and the workplace; and for personal fulfillment. Among these texts are fiction and nonfiction and classic and contemporary works.
- Students apply a wide range of strategies to comprehend, interpret, evaluate, and appreciate texts. They draw on their prior experience, their interactions with other readers and writers, their knowledge of word meaning and of other texts, their word identification strategies, and their understanding of textual features.
- Students apply knowledge of language structure, language conventions (e.g., spelling and punctuation), media techniques, figurative language, and genre to create, critique, and discuss print and nonprint texts.

- Students develop an understanding of and respect for diversity in language use, patterns, and dialects across cultures, ethnic groups, geographic regions, and social roles.

Taken together, the goals and standards employed in this unit help us frame the purpose for engaging students in these texts. Moreover, they allow us to set forth what constitutes enduring knowledge in this unit: Students will read revealing texts to gain insight about issues American Indians have faced in the past and continue to face in the present. Upon completion of the unit, students should understand that American Indians have a long and proud history, although that history has often been threatened by actions of the dominant culture.

Once we determine the overall goals for the unit, it is necessary to consider how we will assess what students have learned. We have chosen to include informal assessments as well as formal assessments. For this unit, we offer the following forms of evidence and understanding performances, each of which is described in greater detail in the unit itself:

- Frequent discussion focused on the previous day's reading
- Responses to story maps and graphic organizers
- Journal writing in response to the reading
- Vocabulary instruction
- Group presentation
- Reading comprehension quiz
- Culminating activity—a formal paper connecting the two primary texts to outside sources

## American Indian Perspectives on Life in the United States

As noted earlier, our teaching for understanding unit consists of introductory activities, two SREs, and culminating activities.

### Introductory Activities

DAY 1

To bring students' existing knowledge on the topic of American Indians to the forefront, begin the unit by having them free-write for about 10 minutes on the following prompt: "What do you know about American Indians, past and present, be it through popular culture, classes you have taken, books you have read, or any other venue?" Encourage students not to censor themselves; the point of free writing is to put on paper as many ideas and thoughts as possible without stopping.

Upon completing the free-write, students share their responses in a whole-class discussion. In order to see the range of students' thoughts, list their answers on the board, making sure not to comment on anything they say until the list is finished. The idea here is to gain a sense of what they know and the accuracy of their knowledge so that you can determine what information you might need to preteach. For instance, one student might say that the federal government gave Indians huge tracts of land where they could fully sustain themselves. This is partially true, but it is by no means the full story. In such a case you would want to explain how treaties were often reneged on, or that the land tribes were offered was not always in the most desirable locales.

If it is warranted, you may also need to spend time in this discussion addressing stereotypes, should students raise such issues. Popular culture is replete with images of the "savage" Indian whose only language is an anglicized grunt. Someone might bring forth the topic of how poorly maintained reservations are, or how American Indians are all alcoholics. While there may be some truth to certain conceptions—many American Indians do suffer from alcoholism—it is important to uncover the story behind the stereotypes.

As the discussion draws to a close, tell students that they are about to begin a unit on American Indian perspectives of life in the United States. Let them know they will be reading a contemporary work of fiction set during the end of the Vietnam War and a longer work of nonfiction focused on a significant Indian leader who lived in the late 1800s. Finally, ask students to copy in their notebooks the list generated on the board for use in an activity at the close of the unit.

### SRE for "The Red Convertible"

"The Red Convertible" is a widely anthologized chapter from Louise Erdrich's first novel *Love Medicine*, which was published in 1984. The narrator, Lyman Lamartine, is the second-born son of an at times unlucky family living on a reservation in northern North Dakota. Lyman and his brother Henry, whom Lyman idolizes and desperately loves, purchase a red convertible and take to the open road before Henry reports for a tour of duty in the Vietnam War.

This SRE, modeled on one developed by Swanson (2003) and taken with permission from *www.onlinereadingresources.com*, is designed to help students develop their critical thinking skills as they carefully examine the effects of foreshadowing, symbols, and expressive language within a tightly constructed text. The SRE also fosters students' metacognition, as it pushes them to reread and reconstruct the foreshadowing that affected their first reading of the text. Students will analyze several of the symbols in the text, and reflect on expressive language that caught their attention as they read.

The specific objectives for this SRE are for students to:

- Understand how fiction deals with and comments upon reality.
- Appreciate the importance of rereading for increased comprehension.
- See how foreshadowing can be tightly woven into a piece of literature.
- Pick out particularly expressive language and comment on the effects that language has on readers.
- Understand the use of symbols.

In addition to the overall teaching for understanding standards this unit seeks to meet and the objectives above, this SRE strives to foster the following higher-order thinking skills:

- *Understanding:* Constructing meaning from instructional messages, including oral, written, and graphic communications.
- *Analyzing:* Breaking material into its constituent parts and determining how the parts relate to one another and to an overall structure or purpose.
- *Being metacognitive:* Being aware of one's own comprehension and being able and willing to repair comprehension breakdowns when they occur.

*Detailed List of Activities*

DAY 2

*Prereading Activities*

- *Activating background knowledge, 5–10 minutes.* Ask students to point out North Dakota; Winnipeg, Manitoba; and Alaska on a map of North America. The action of this story takes place mostly in North Dakota, close to the Canadian border, but the main character, Lyman Lamartine, and his brother Henry travel to Winnipeg and then to Alaska, so students need to visualize the expansive area those travels cover as well as the time necessary to drive that distance.

In order to fully understand Henry Lamartine's character, students need to know what posttraumatic stress disorder (PTSD) is and that, after the soldiers arrived home from Vietnam, the number of them suffering from this condition provoked its classification as a psychological disorder. PTSD is not new (it was called *shell shock* during World War I), but it is important for students to understand that soldiers felt, among other things, quite disconnected from their lives once they returned home from fighting. The U.S. Department of Veterans Affairs has reached out to treat soldiers, as treatment has helped to reintegrate veterans into society. The character Henry is not treated, and he suffers tremendously when he returns home to North Dakota.

• *Author background, 5 minutes.* Provide information on Louise Erdrich, including her other publications and her collaboration with her husband Michael Dorris, now deceased.

### During-Reading Activities

• *Reading to students, 5 minutes.* Pass out copies of the story and begin reading aloud to the students.

• *Silent reading and first story map, 20 minutes.* Students should continue to read the story and complete the story map as they read. The story map (Beck & McKeown, 1981) shown in Figure 8.1 will assist students in keeping track of the most important details of the story as well as their thoughts about the story as they read.

• *Graphic organizer—expressive language, 5–10 minutes.* Just before students leave for the day, they should spend some time reflecting on the expressive language that Erdrich uses in this story. Have students complete as much of the graphic organizer (Alvermann, 1991) on expressive language shown in Figure 8.2 as they can.

### DAY 3

#### During-Reading Activities

• *Complete silent reading and story map, 35 minutes.* Students should complete reading the story and filling out their answers to the story map.

• *Story map—focus on foreshadowing, 15 minutes.* After they have finished reading the story, students should complete the second story map, which is shown in Figure 8.3, which asks them to reflect on sections of foreshadowing.

- When the story opens, the narrator Lyman Lamartine introduces himself, his brother, and his home to the reader. He immediately says that he was the first person on his reservation to drive a convertible. Why is it important to note his statement, "of course it was red"?
- How does Lyman make his money?
- Reflect on this short passage about the car: "There it was, parked, large as life. Really as *if* it was alive. I thought of the word *repose*, because the car wasn't simply stopped, parked, or whatever. That car reposed, calm and gleaming ... " List words and phrases from this passage that indicate that the car *is* alive. Why does Erdrich describe the car this way? What is the effect of this passage on the reader?
- After Lyman and Henry leave Alaska, think about this section of the story. What aspects of this part of the story seem otherworldly, odd, or unreal?
- After Henry leaves for Vietnam, Lyman says, "I wrote him back several times, even though I didn't know if those letters would get through. I kept him informed all about the car. Most of the time I had it up on blocks in the yard or half taken apart, because that long trip did a hard job on it under the hood.... In those years [when Henry was gone] I'd put his car into almost perfect shape. I always thought of it as his car while he was gone, even though when he left he said, 'Now it's yours,' and threw me his key. 'Thanks for the extra key,' I'd said. 'I'll put it up in your drawer just in case I need it.' He laughed." During those 3 years that Henry was in the war, what is the convertible coming to represent for Lyman?
- What does it mean when Erdrich writes that Henry "was eating his own blood mixed in with the food"? What has just happened with Henry?
- What does Lyman say that indicates a reason for his smashing up the red convertible?
- What does Henry then do with the car?
- What happens between Lyman and Henry the night that they witness the flooding?

**FIGURE 8.1.** First story map for "The Red Convertible."

*Postreading Activity*

- *Graphic organizer—expressive language; finish for homework.*

DAY 4

*Postreading Activities*

- *Discussion of story maps, 20–25 minutes.* Discuss with students their answers to the first story map, designed primarily to assist them in understanding the events of the story.
- Discuss with students their answers to the second story map on foreshadowing. Ideally, students will see, upon reflection and reread-

ing, that they understand more clearly how Erdrich leads readers relentlessly toward an understanding that Henry could no longer function in his life at home in North Dakota, even though he loved his family, especially his brother Lyman.

• *Discussion of graphic organizer—expressive language, 20–25 minutes.* If students are not used to tracking their appreciation of expressive language, they may have found this graphic organizer difficult to complete. This type of work with literature is difficult for students whose metacognitive skills are under-developed or who have just not

**Directions:** After the first day of reading the story and after you have finished reading the story, find at least three examples of well-written text and expressive or figurative language that captured your interest and helped you see or understand something in a new way. Write about what that phrasing says to you. Lastly, draw a conclusion about Erdrich's use of language in this story.

| Quotation from the story | Your reflection on that quotation |
|---|---|
| Example: "[In the spring] when everything starts changing, drying up, clearing off, you feel like your whole life is starting." | I feel this same way about spring, that I can start everything over in my life if I want to. It is that feeling that makes winter worth enduring. I'd never expressed this feeling in this way before. When I read this sentence, I realized that Erdrich helped me understand what I feel each spring. |
|  |  |
|  |  |
|  |  |
| **Conclusion:** | |

FIGURE 8.2. Graphic organizer for "The Red Convertible": Expressive language.

- After you have finished reading the story, reflect back on the section that begins, "After that I thought he'd freeze himself to death" and ends with "We started off, east, toward Pembina and the Red River because Henry said he wanted to see the high water." What does Lyman say in this section that tells the reader that Henry has, perhaps, planned to die?
- Now, reread the first paragraph of the story and answer the following four questions:

  1. What does it mean when Lyman says, "He bought out my share"?
  2. What does it mean when Lyman says, "Now Henry owns the whole car"?
  3. Why does Lyman shift to third-person narration for a moment to say, "and his younger brother (that's myself) Lyman walks everywhere he goes"?
  4. Why do you think Lyman does walk everywhere he goes?

- After you have finished looking at these sections of the story again, discuss how the elements of foreshadowing colored your reading of the story. What effects has the foreshadowing had on you as a reader?

**FIGURE 8.3.** Second story map for "The Red Convertible": Focus on foreshadowing.

completed many close readings with an eye toward figurative language.

## DAY 5

### Postreading Activities

- *Graphic organizer—use of symbols, 20–25 minutes.* Have students complete the graphic organizer on the use of symbols shown in Figure 8.4.
- *Discussion of graphic organizer—use of symbols, 20–25 minutes.* Discuss students' answers to the questions about the use of symbols in Erdrich's story.

## DAY 6

### Postreading Activity

- *Writing, 50 minutes.* Students have completed the primary SRE activities for "The Red Convertible." To ensure that students fully grasp the story's significance, have them respond to the following two questions, using any of the story maps and graphic organizers they completed earlier. Students should also be presented with a copy of the story so they can use quotes, should they choose.

**Directions:** Reflect on the story as a whole as you answer these questions about the use of symbols in the story. Be sure to complete both pages.

| To Lyman before Henry leaves | What does the car mean to the brothers? | To Henry before he leaves |
|---|---|---|
| To Lyman after Henry leaves | | To Henry after he returns |
| Before Henry went off to Vietnam, what did he and Lyman mean to each other? | | |
| To Lyman, Henry symbolizes ... | After Henry came back from Vietnam, what do the two brothers symbolize for each other? Think deeply about this, as there are many potential answers. Think about their past, their current lives, and their prospects for the future. | To Henry, Lyman symbolizes ... |

*t*
*(continued)*

**FIGURE 8.4.** Graphic organizer for "The Red Convertible": Use of symbols.

Flooding

The author, Louise Erdrich, often places characters in situations where rivers are flooding. Why do you think that is? What does the flooding say or underscore in any narrative's action?

Reflect on Henry's last words and Lyman's description of how he said them. How are these lines symbolic of Henry's life since returning home from Vietnam?

Henry's Death from Drowning

| From Henry's point of view, why is this death particularly fitting? | What makes this type of death difficult for Lyman? |
| --- | --- |
| | |

Why is it appropriate, also, that the car "dies" in that same current of flooding water?

FIGURE 8.4. (page 2 of 2)

1. To what extent do you think "The Red Convertible" is a story particular to American Indians? That is, in what ways might the story be different if Lyman and Henry were Caucasian or African American? What do you think the author is attempting to say about American Indians' lives in this story? Use specific, concrete examples to support your ideas.

2. What new information or ideas did you learn from reading "The Red Convertible"? Once again, use specific information and try to convey the significance of what you learned.

## *SRE for* Black Elk Speaks

*Black Elk Speaks* is a historical account of an important figure within the American Indian community. The book focuses on Black Elk, who was born in the middle 1800s, a time when numerous events unfolded that would change the course of history for Indians in the United States. John Niehardt, the author, wrote the book in 1932 after hearing oral accounts of Black Elk's legacy. *Black Elk Speaks* is a challenging text that is equal parts historical record, biography, and spiritual treatise.

The following SRE for *Black Elk Speaks* is modeled on one created by Voss (2003) and taken with permission from *www.onlinereadingresources.com*. It functions to provide students with many activities to engage with a non-fiction text that shows the rich history of American Indian life and culture in the United States. Through small-group discussion, vocabulary activities, reciprocal reading, and writing opportunities, students develop a deeper understanding of and appreciation for American Indians' past and present.

At the onset of this teaching for understanding unit, we listed several goals and standards that allowed us to choose the appropriate texts and activities. Additionally, the *Black Elk Speaks* SRE is guided by the following objectives. Students will:

- Study voice and narration for its impact on a text's meaning.
- Learn about some historical and spiritual elements of the Lakota people.
- Discuss and observe one way that history is recorded.
- Develop reading skills, such as vocabulary enrichment, close reading, and symbolic representation helpful for understanding difficult texts.

We also strive in this SRE to focus on the following higher-order thinking skills:

- *Understanding:* Constructing meaning from instructional messages, including oral, written, and graphic communications.
- *Creating:* Putting elements together to form a coherent or functional whole, reorganizing elements into a new pattern or structure.
- *Being metacognitive:* Being aware of one's own comprehension and being able and willing to repair comprehension breakdowns when they occur.

## Detailed List of Activities

DAY 7

### Prereading Activities

- *Relating the reading to students' lives, 20 minutes.* Have students brainstorm in their journals all of the various noises they can recall since waking up this morning. After 1–2 minutes, ask students to volunteer their responses, which you can write on the board. Ask students to listen intently for subtle noises within the classroom such as a clanking radiator, the buzz of computers, or a ticking clock. Next, ask students if the noises they recorded in their journals and noted from the classroom would be evident if they lived in 1880. Most likely, very few of the sounds students listed would be. Have students return to their journal writing, describing how technology has changed their (our) lives. Next, read the following statement, authored by Vine Deloria in the preface to *Black Elk Speaks*, aloud to students: "Reflection is the most difficult of all our activities because we are no longer able to establish priorities from the multitude of sensations that engulf us." Inform students that in the forthcoming text, they will read that reflection is a critical component linked to spirituality.
- *Motivating, 10 minutes.* Put the following events and names on the board and ask students if they can identify any: Crazy Horse, Battle of Little Big Horn, Sitting Bull, Queen Victoria, Buffalo Bill, and Wounded Knee. Students should write down all terms in their journals. Tell students that by the book's end, they should know the significance of each person/event on the list.
- *Preteaching vocabulary, 10 minutes.* Complete the preteaching vocabulary activity shown in Figure 8.5.
- *Suggesting strategies (questioning), 10 minutes.* Inform students of the importance of asking questions while reading. Provide students a

Translating Black Elk's story from his Lakota language to English posed many challenges, largely because some Lakota words simply do not have English counterparts. This text does a good job of footnoting and parenthetically noting words that may pose problems, but know that you can use context to determine words and phrases. Below are five words or phrases and their context. See how well you can do in figuring out the bold words just by using context.

1. The first time I saw a **wasichu**, I was frightened because I had heard so many stories of how they lived in square houses and how they fight.

   A. Bears
   B. Wild turkeys
   C. Soldiers
   D. Buffalo

2. The people seemed to go crazy when they discovered the **yellow metal.**

   A. Butter
   B. Gold
   C. Copper
   D. Plastic

3. The soldiers went away in the **Moon of Falling Leaves.**

   A. January
   B. March
   C. June
   D. November

4. The buffalo herd began to disappear because the **iron road** appeared in their land.

   A. Railroad tracks
   B. Guns
   C. Knives
   D. Bicycles

5. I did not feel well after I ate too much food and drank too much **black medicine.**

   A. Raspberry juice
   B. Coffee
   C. Dirty water
   D. Maple syrup

**FIGURE 8.5.** Preteaching vocabulary: Example from *Black Elk Speaks.*

copy of the six categories of Bloom's taxonomy (1956) and explain each one.

## DAY 8

### During-Reading Activities

- *Reading to students (Chapter 1), 20 minutes.* Chapter one allows students to obtain a feel for the voice of the text. Ask students to take out their Bloom's taxonomy handout from yesterday. While reading, pause when appropriate to ask higher-order questions. You should encourage students to ask higher-order questions, too.
- *Silent reading (Chapter 2), 20 minutes.*

### Postreading

- *Questioning, 20 minutes; finish for homework.* Using the higher-order questioning handout, have students create three to four questions based on Chapter 2. The questions, which are to be recorded in their journals, should cover different levels of the taxonomy.

## DAY 9

### Postreading Activity

- *Questioning (check homework), 10 minutes.* Have students open their journals and quickly check the 3 to 4 questions they generated on Chapter 2. Spend a few minutes discussing the strengths and weaknesses of their work.

### Prereading Activity

- *Providing text-specific knowledge, 10 minutes.* Since Chapter 3 is quite difficult for many students, begin by reading the preview (Graves, Prenn, & Cooke, 1985) for the chapter, which is shown in Figure 8.6. Allow adequate time for students to respond to the opening paragraph of the preview before moving on.

### During-Reading Activity

- *Guided reading (Chapter 3), 20–30 minutes.*

*Postreading Activity*

• *Writing, as homework.* Students should respond in writing to the questions posed at the end of the Preview. Remind students that the chapter is "dream-like" and should not be read as a linear narrative.

DAY 10

*Prereading Activity*

• *Providing text-specific knowledge (Chapters 4–13), 10–15 minutes.* Begin by reading the opening paragraph of the preview for Chap-

---

Recall a vivid dream you have had. What do you know of dreams in general? What might be their purpose? Why do people have them? What are the basic qualities of a dream?

Chapter 3 of *Black Elk Speaks* is a significant chapter in the book. It describes the dream in which Black Elk believes he sees the future. The chapter begins when Black Elk is nine years old. He recalls the time when he fell sick and was forced to rest in his family's tepee. From the opening of the tepee, he can see two men descend from the clouds to visit him. They encourage him to follow, and Black Elk does so, though he no longer feels ill. They travel swiftly through clouds and plains and are visited by a group of beautiful horses that take him to the grandfathers. There are six grandfathers, each representing a different direction or element: North, South, East, West, Sky, and Earth. The grandfathers, who have renamed the boy (Black Elk) Eagle Wing Stretches, present various gifts to him. With these gifts he is asked to walk the black road, where he first encounters a blue man. With the aid of his gifts, he defeats the blue man and continues on his dreamland journey. Eagle Wing Stretches is told to walk over four hills (called ascents), and he is told that each ascent represents a different generation. The first ascent represents his grandfather's generation, the second represents his father's, the third his own, and the fourth ascent refers to a future generation. Each ascent contains pleasant and difficult qualities. After visiting each ascent, Eagle Wing Stretches receives more advice from his grandfathers, and then he returns home to his tepee and awakes.

As you read this chapter, remember that it is a dream, not a story. So read carefully for qualities that make it "dream-like." If you don't understand something, stop and ask yourself, "What am I specifically not getting here?" You may need to reread certain sentences and paragraphs. Keep an eye out for symbols and objects that seem to reoccur. Lastly, try to figure out what the dream predicts.

**FIGURE 8.6.** Preview for Chapter 3 of *Black Elk Speaks*.

ters 4–13, which is shown in Figure 8.7. Allow students time to discuss the prompts.

### During-Reading Activity

- *Silent reading (Chapters 4, 5, and 6), 30 minutes; finish for homework.*

### DAY 11

### Postreading Activity

- *Discussion, 40 minutes.* In groups of four, students discuss differences between their own lifestyles and Black Elk's. Refer students to the discussion on *Black Elk Speaks*: differences in lifestyles overhead shown in Figure 8.8. After 15 minutes or so, return to a whole-class discussion and ask students to volunteer responses.

### Prereading Activity

- *Building background knowledge, 10 minutes.* Show students the building background knowledge for *Black Elk Speaks*—historical time line overhead shown in Figure 8.9.

### During-Reading Activity

- *Silent reading (Chapter 7); for homework.*

### DAY 12

### During-Reading Activity

- *Guided reading (Chapter 8), 40 minutes.* Model for students the four comprehension practices associated with reciprocal teaching (Palinscar & Brown, 1984)—generating questions, summarizing, predicting, and clarifying—while reading the opening few paragraphs of Chapter 8. Next, pair students together, and explain that one person will act as the teacher, reading the text aloud and stopping periodically to question, predict, summarize, or clarify the text. The other partner will act as a student and will attempt to answer questions. After 15 minutes, the partners should switch roles.

Can you recall a point in your life when others began to treat you with adult-like responsibilities? Perhaps you were invited to a function that you were excluded from in the past. Or maybe you were asked to complete a task that previously was the domain of adults.

The next chapters of *Black Elk Speaks* take us through that phase in his life. He begins to see how he is growing up and becoming a more important part of his community. At the same time, he is still not old enough to do certain things, and he is left to wonder when he will have his day. The chapters can be divided into two parts. The first part presents some insight into the customs and traditions of Black Elk's life, including a chapter on courting (dating). The second part presents some of the significant historical events that Black Elk witnessed.

Chapters 4, 5, and 6 take the reader through some events that highlight the society and culture of Black Elk's people. Black Elk travels with the men of his tribe to partake in a bison hunt, his first. Standing Bear, a friend of Black Elk's, interjects at this point to talk about that bison hunt. For him, it was the first time he killed a buffalo, and he recalls it fondly. Black Elk picks up the story by describing some of the games he played with other boys after such hunts. From there, his family moves to the Soldier's Town, Fort Robinson, where he sees his first wasichu, or soldier. He also tells of an incident where a young Indian boy chops down the American flag inside Fort Robinson, and it nearly causes a fight. However, the wise chief Red Cloud steps in and calms the anxieties of both sides. After leaving the fort, Black Elk describes an older man of the tribe who used to tease him. His name was Watanye, and he was full of colorful stories, like the story of High Horse Courting, which tells the tale of a young Lakota warrior who becomes lovesick when he is not allowed to marry the woman he wants. The story relates how the young warrior visits his lover late at night, until the family catches him. Eventually, the warrior goes out and proves his worth to the family, and they allow the union to take place.

Chapters 7–13 describe the rising tensions of the Lakota and other Indian people as General Custer enters the Black Hills. Though the Lakota were promised the land "as long as the grass grows and the water flows," greedy settlers begin to encroach. Skirmishes occur and the U.S. government sends in the military to stabilize the region. Black Elk discusses two important battles he witnessed—the Battle of Rosebud and the Battle of Little Bighorn. In so doing, he introduces readers to Crazy Horse, his cousin.

As you read, take note of who is involved in the various events, observe what they do, and when it takes place.

**FIGURE 8.7.** Preview for chapters 4–13 of *Black Elk Speaks.*

Today you will be asked to discuss the differences between Black Elk's lifestyle and your own. Stay focused on what we know of Black Elk's lifestyle based on what we have read. Do not make assumptions on his lifestyle from what you may have previously learned about American Indian culture.

Below are categories to consider as you discuss the similarities and differences. Examine these categories as a group, and be prepared to share your findings with the class.

* Games and entertainment
* Basic needs: food, shelter, clothing
* Religion, spirituality, faith
* Responsibilities
* Dating
* Views or perceptions of adults and leaders
* Medicine and health

Question: If Black Elk were to visit our school today, what would be the most difficult aspect for him to adjust to? What might be the easiest?

**FIGURE 8.8.** Discussion on *Black Elk Speaks*: Differences in lifestyles [overhead].

* *Guided reading (Who? What? When?), 10 minutes.* Model this technique for students. Ask who is or are the central characters in the chapter, what are the characters doing, and when is the action occurring? Since Chapter 8 contains many names, dates, and events, this activity will help them sort through a great deal of information.
* *Silent reading (Chapter 9); for homework.*

1863: Black Elk is born

1866: Feterman Fight

1868: Red Cloud's Treaty

1872: Black Elk's great vision (Chapter 3)

1874: Mad rush for Black Hills gold

1876: Battle of Rosebud; Battle of Little Big Horn

1877: Death of Crazy Horse

1890: Wounded Knee

**FIGURE 8.9.** Building background knowledge: Historical time line.

DAY 13

*During-Reading Activities*

- *Reading to students (Chapter 10), 20 minutes.*
- *Guided reading (Who? What? When?), 10 minutes.*
- *Silent reading (Chapters 11–13), remaining time; finish for homework.*

DAY 14

*Prereading Activity*

- *Small-group formation (Chapters 14–16), 10 minutes.* Chapters 14–16 are rather complex, so in an effort to construct understanding, students will be placed in groups of four to work together on interpreting meaning. After forming a total of six groups, assign two groups to each chapter, so groups one and two are responsible for Chapter 14, groups three and four are responsible for Chapter 15, and groups five and six are responsible for Chapter 16.

*During-Reading Activity*

- *Group read-aloud, 30–40 minutes.* Have students read aloud their respective chapters, with each reader pausing at or near the end of a page (or at a natural break) so that they can collectively check each other's understanding of the text. Each group continues reading and checking for understanding until they complete the chapter. One group member should be appointed the group recorder.

*Postreading Activity*

- *Determining ideas for presentation, remaining time.* With any time remaining, each group determines the most important elements of the chapter for which it is responsible, in preparation for presenting to the larger group on Day 15.

DAY 15

*Postreading Activities*

- *Small-group presentation organizing, 15 minutes.* Picking up where the class left off on Day 14, students assemble in their groups to determine the most important events, ideas, or elements for presenting to the rest of the class.

• *Presentations, 35 minutes.* Beginning with Chapter 14, groups one and two alternately present key ideas they encountered in their reading. The purpose behind alternating between groups is twofold. First, if the groups have identical elements, then it helps ensure that the most significant aspects of the chapter are covered. Second, if competing or different ideas are offered, the two groups can civilly debate why they included or excluded it. Follow the same pattern for Chapters 15 and 16. If misconceptions or confusion arises, help students clarify their ideas through asking questions.

DAY 16

*Prereading Activity*

• *Motivating (Chapter 17), 20 minutes.* Ask students to share stories of their experiences with doctors, medicine, and health care generally. Next, ask them to imagine overcoming those maladies without today's health care practices and facilities. Instead, they should picture a medicine man, such as Black Elk, who visits patients with herbs, a drum, and a song. Ask students if they would be willing to be treated by such a person. Allow sufficient time for a discussion.

*During-Reading Activity*

• *Silent reading (Chapter 17), 20 minutes; finish for homework.*

DAY 17

*Postreading Activities*

• *Questioning (story map), 10 minutes.* Pass out story map for Chapter 17 shown in Figure 8.10. Students should work in pairs.
• *Discussion, 30 minutes.* Pass out a half sheet of paper to students. Have them write three questions or comments based on the text read thus far. Inform students that these questions will form the basis of the discussion. Collect their questions, and begin discussing them; students should attempt to answer the questions and if they cannot, guide them to the text to help them.

A story map is a list of questions that map the events of a text in chronological order. The final question asks you to extend your knowledge of characters or events beyond the text.

Event 1: Black Elk talks about the important symbol that gives his people power. What is that symbol?

Event 2: What item does Black Elk recall from his visions when he is with his friend One Side?

Event 3: How do Black Elk and One Side know where to look for the herb?

Event 4: What does Cuts-to-Pieces come to tell Black Elk? And why did Cuts-to-Pieces choose Black Elk?

Event 5: What does Black Elk feel as he works his way through the cemetery?

Event 6: What happens to the little boy?

Extension Question: What would be your reaction to Cuts-to-Pieces if he had come to you with this request?

**FIGURE 8.10.** Story map for Chapter 17 of *Black Elk Speaks*.

DAY 18

*Prereading Activity*

• *Building background knowledge, 50 minutes.* The closing, dramatic events of *Black Elk Speaks* center on the Ghost Dance. Provide students the following web addresses:

*php.indiana.edu/~tkavanag/visual5.html*
*www.bgsu.edu/departments/acs/1890s/woundedknee/WKghost.html*
*www.pbs.org/weta/thewest/resources/archives/eight.*

• Using these URLs, students should attempt to uncover as much information as possible. To help keep their web searching focused, provide them with the following guiding questions: Who was Wokova? What was the Ghost Dance, and what did people believe it would do? Why do you think so many people believed in the Ghost Dance? How did U.S. authorities respond to this trend? What happened at Wounded Knee in 1890?

*During-Reading Activity*

- *Independent reading (Chapters 19 and 20), for homework.*

DAY 19

*Prereading Activity*

- *Building background knowledge, 20 minutes.* Students share information they discovered from the previous day's Internet search. Be sure to address the guiding questions.

*During-Reading Activities*

- *Guided reading (Who? What? When?), 10 minutes.*
- *Silent reading (Chapters 21–24), 20 minutes; finish for homework.*

DAY 20

*During-Reading Activity*

- *Reading to students (Chapter 25 and author's postscript), 30 minutes.*

*Postreading Activity*

- *Questioning, 10 minutes.* Have students take out their higher-order questioning sheet and ask questions orally. Again, encourage students to answer their peers' questions.

DAY 21

*Postreading Activity*

- *Discussion, 50 minutes.* Inform students that for the next 2 days, they will discuss the most important ideas in the text. Specifically, they will concentrate on history, reflection and silence, personal agency, interconnectedness, visions, and spirituality.
- Place students in groups of four and assign each group a theme to discuss from the discussion for *Black Elk Speaks* themes shown in Figure 8.11. Students will present their group findings to the whole class, and the group presentation overhead in Figure 8.12 contains the guidelines they need to follow.

Give each group one of the thematic groupings to discuss (e.g., History).

**History**
- What is it?
- What are your personal views of history?
- Do you think American teenagers today have a good sense of "personal history"?
- Try to think of at least one issue related to history's importance.

**Reflection and Silence**
- Is personal reflection important to an individual's well-being?
- How much time per day do you think people spend in reflection?
- How often during the day do you think people spend in silence?
- Make some predictions comparing the reflection and silence of a Lakota medicine man with that of a current-day high school student.

Other themes include **Personal Impact, Connection,** and **Visions and Psychic Powers.**

**FIGURE 8.11.** Discussion on *Black Elk Speaks* themes handout (abbreviated examples).

DAY 22

*Postreading Activity*

- *Discussion presentations, 40 minutes.*

DAY 23

*Postreading Activities*

- Final quiz (Figure 8.13), 30 minutes.
- *Connecting and extending, 20 minutes.* Discuss with students any similarities they see between the two texts in this teaching for

**Group Presentation Expectations**

Organization
- Presentation has an introduction that sets up the topic and format of your materials.
- Members know when to speak versus making it up as they go.

All member participate equally.

Details of the presentation are specific, as is supporting evidence.

Proper use of a visual aid (poster, PowerPoint slides, handout, etc.).

**FIGURE 8.12.** Discussion on *Black Elk Speaks* themes: Group presentation [overhead].

**Matching Vocabulary**

1. Moon of Frost in the Tepee     a. January
2. Greasy Grass                          b. Railroad tracks
3. Paha Sapa                             c. Little Big Horn
4. Yellow Metal                          d. Gold
5. Iron Road                             e. Black Hills

**Matching**

6. Black Elk                 a. The man who claimed to be the Messiah
7. General Custer            b. Long Hair
8. Wovoka                    c. Took Black Elk across the Great Water
9. Buffalo Bill              d. Queen Victoria
10. Grandmother England      e. Dreamed Ghost Shirts to be given to people

**True/False**

11. Black Elk communicated his great vision to the people as soon as he had it.

12. The Ghost Dance was designed to keep the ghosts of dead relatives away.

13. Crazy Horse died in the Battle of Little Bighorn.

14. The Battle of One Hundred Slain was won by the Lakota.

15. Black Elk is left behind in England because he gets separated and lost from the group.

**Multiple Choice**

16. Black Elk saw Wounded Knee as the death of what?
    a. a dream      b. hatred      c. anger      d. dance.

17. What part of bison was in particular demand with the Wasichus?
    a. tongue      b. hoof      c. horn      d. eyeball

18. Black Elk was afraid his people would starve to death because they could not eat what?
    a. herbs      b. a vision      c. lies      d. dirt

19. Whom does Black Elk meet in London?
    a. Big Foot      b. the queen      c. his brother      d. Black Road

20. What does Black Elk take from the battlefield at Wounded Knee?
    a. a gun      b. his father      c. young babies  d. a scalp

*(continued)*

**FIGURE 8.13.** Final quiz on *Black Elk Speaks*.

**Short Answer (2 points each)**

21. According to Chapter 2, the Lakota were supposed to have rights to the Black Hills for how long?

22. Describe three of the practices and rituals of a bison hunt.

23. Describe Black Elk's role in the battle of Little Bighorn, which appeared in the chapter "The Rubbing Out of Long Hair."

24. Describe one of the visions Black Elk experienced.

**FIGURE 8.13.** *(page 2 of 2)*

understanding unit. Also, ask students to take out the list generated as a class on Day 7 of the unit, which is a compilation of their thinking at the time. Review the list in a discussion, noting how their knowledge base has or has not changed over time.

## Culminating Activity for the Unit

DAY 24

To conclude the unit, students will write an analytic paper focused on one of the choices below. The purpose of this task is to bring together the ideas from the two primary texts of this unit, and at the same time, extend student learning to other aspects of American Indian culture and heritage.

Begin by revisiting some of the ideas students mentioned in the brief discussion at the end of Day 23 regarding any connections between the two primary texts. Reservation life, the authors' use of imagery, and the importance of family are likely ideas they will forward. Explain that their last task for the unit will be to write an analytic paper. Here are the three options from which students select one:

- Select and read two myths from *American Indian Myths and Legends* (Erdoes & Ortiz, 1984). Summarize each myth, noting what its function is. Does it explain how humans came to be? Does it account for how the world was formed? Or perhaps it describes the afterlife. Once you have done that, analyze any connections between the myths and either "The Red Convertible" or *Black Elk Speaks*. For example, if one of the myths you select is "Coyote and the Origin of Death," you could discuss Henry's death in "The Red Convertible" in terms of what the myth says. This paper should be word-processed and roughly three or four double-spaced pages.

- View a film in which American Indians play a substantial role. Pay particular attention to how the Indians are portrayed. Are they depicted as warriors and savages? Are they friendly and loving? How do they live? Where do they live? Does the director, in your estimation, honor or dishonor American Indian people? What evidence do you have to make your claim? What, if any, stereotypes do you notice? You have many titles to choose from, ranging from 1950s Westerns to more contemporary films such as *Dances with Wolves*, *Last of the Mohicans*, and *Smoke Signals*. Finally, what ideas from the "The Red Convertible" and/ or *Black Elk Speaks* are confirmed or denied in the film you reviewed?

Provide specific evidence. This paper should be word-processed and three or four double-spaced pages.

- "The Red Convertible" mostly takes place on a reservation in North Dakota, and *Black Elk Speaks* mentions the Pine Ridge Agency. Using the Internet and other sources available in the school's media center, research a specific American Indian reservation and report on its founding, its inhabitants, and any other information you deem interesting and important. You are encouraged to discuss in your paper both the positive and negative aspects you discover about the reservation. This paper should be word-processed and three to four double-spaced pages.

Much of the work required of students in this culminating project can be completed outside of the regular class schedule. However, as we allude to in Chapter 1, setting aside one day for students to peer review their writing will likely result in more engaging, readable essays.

# Explicating the Facets of Our Comprehension Practices

As noted, our purpose for including this teaching for understanding unit in this concluding chapter is to demonstrate how various approaches discussed in Chapters 2–7 can work in concert to foster secondary students' comprehension of complex texts. Clearly, we did not intend to touch on every aspect presented in this book; rather, we selected a representative number of activities and approaches that underscore the major facets of our book. In the pages to follow, we elaborate on our curriculum design choices and how they correspond to specific chapters.

As we discussed at some length in Chapter 3, teaching for understanding units demand a significant amount of time, must promote essential learning, and should produce knowledge and understandings applicable in a variety of contexts. In the case of this unit, these conditions are met. Overall, this unit spans 24 instructional days, slightly more than 1 month. Because time is such a precious commodity in school, we urge the implementation of units of this length only when you know the learning is central to the discipline and relevant to students' lives. We believe the unit presented in this chapter enables students to view the legacy of American Indians in a new light—namely, that American Indians developed complex, intelligent ways of living long before Europeans landed in North America. Furthermore, students also learn that the difficulties many American Indians experience in contemporary society are rooted in historical events, such as being displaced by Anglo settlers and having their customs and cultural values quashed. Through studying this unit, students can better understand how peoples throughout the world need autonomy and respect from others to flourish.

Within a teaching for understanding framework, we followed the backward design approach (Wiggins & McTighe, 1998) that calls for using goals and standards to drive curriculum decisions, which is Stage 1 of planning. We developed our own goals that are quite specific and supplemented them with select standards for the English language arts established by NCTE and IRA. Next, we proceeded to Stage 2 planning, which focuses on establishing assessments to determine if important ideas and concepts are learned. Prior to describing any instructional activities, we list several items that allow us to evaluate whether students are grasping the material in deep and meaningful ways. Our assessments rely on informal as well as formal evaluation procedures. Finally, we move to Stage 3, the texts and instructional activities we employ to promote essential knowledge.

The primary design structure we use in our teaching for understanding unit is an SRE, which is the focus of Chapter 2. In fact, we use two SREs in this unit, one focused on a work of fiction and one focused on a work of nonfiction. Both SREs we present contain some common features, such as the use of whole-class discussion as a postreading activity and writing as a tool for thinking. Conversely, they also present many differences, with "The Red Convertible" SRE concerned with having students use graphic organizers to discover symbolic meanings while the *Black Elk Speaks* SRE often focuses on asking students to compare Black Elk's life in the late 1800s to adolescents' lives today.

Within both SREs, students are given ample opportunities to respond to literature, the focus of Chapter 4. Although neither SRE was developed with a particular critical lens in mind, elements of different lenses are evident. For example, in the *Black Elk Speaks* story map for Chapter 17, the extension question clearly has a reader-response bent. Additionally, the graphic organizer: use of symbols exercise for "The Red Convertible" is rooted in the tradition of formalist literary analysis. We also include journal writing as a tool to help shape thinking and understanding. And, we describe a culminating activity that is more formal in nature. The final writing assignment provides students with choices, something we believe is important in terms of promoting student engagement. Throughout the unit, we have included both structured (e.g., story maps) and less structured (e.g., expressive language graphic organizer for "The Read Convertible") activities for responding to literature, all of which aid students in coming to deeper understanding and appreciation of what they read.

Chapter 5 elaborates on ways to teach comprehension strategies, a practice that we think happens far too infrequently at the secondary level. This teaching for understanding unit, while not explicitly involved with teaching comprehension strategies, nevertheless does require students to use key strategies. As we note in Chapter 5, one key strategy is asking and answering questions, which occurs regularly in the *Black Elk Speaks* portion of the unit. For example, on Day 7, students are taught Bloom's taxonomy (1956), and for homework they are to develop questions based on it. On Day 12, students participate in reciprocal reading, one component of which requires students to ask and answer questions. Finally, on Day 17, students develop questions that form the foundation for the day's discussion. In addition to asking and answering questions, students engaged in this unit use the strategy of making inferences. In order for a reader of "The Red Convertible" to grasp fully why Henry's life ends in his suicide, readers must infer that fighting in a war extracts a terrible psychological cost on a soldier. Lastly, monitoring comprehension is a strategy that students are asked to use at almost every step of reading, though it is perhaps most evident in the preview for Chapter 3 of *Black Elk Speaks*, when Black Elk describes his dream/vision. Students are instructed to read this chapter, not as literal narrative, but as a "dream-like" sequence; they are reminded to look for recurring symbols and images. Giving students these instructions prior to reading the chapter will remind them to pause throughout to ask, "Do I understand what is happening now? Do I know what I'm reading, and if not, what can I do to make it clearer?"

Teaching higher-order thinking skills also factors into this unit in several ways. Beginning on Day 7 of the *Black Elk Speaks* SRE and revisited several times thereafter, students are required to ask and answer questions using the higher-order questioning taxonomy we discuss in Chapter 6. Depending on the class you are teaching, you could refrain from providing students the Ghost Dance URLs (Day 18) and ask them to find and evaluate websites on their own using the guidelines we enumerate from the University of California—Berkeley library system. Another higher-order thinking skill taught in this unit—which is central to both SREs—is understanding that results from constructing meaning from instructional messages, including oral, written, and graphic communications. The instructional activities developed for this entire unit strongly encourage students to read closely, paying attention to details with the goal of understanding how the parts of a text contribute to its whole.

Vocabulary instruction, the focus of Chapter 7, is particularly important to the *Black Elk Speaks* SRE. Many terms and phrases used in the text are Lakota in origin, and without a clear sense of their meanings, students will struggle to understand Black Elk's story. As we note in Chapter 7, we do not expect you to spend an inordinate amount of time teaching vocabulary, and in this unit we do not. However, we think you will find that brief time spent preteaching vocabulary will enable students to move through the text with significantly more clarity and understanding, which should be a goal we all strive to achieve.

## Concluding Remarks

The teaching for understanding unit we presented in this chapter has allowed us to demonstrate how many of the approaches to fostering comprehension we describe in this book come to fruition in an English classroom. The unit does not of course involve all of the approaches we have suggested since doing so in a single unit is neither feasible nor advisable. Moreover, the unit is not something you are likely to import unchanged into your classroom. Good teaching demands choice, and each day you must make innumerable decisions as you plan activities specifically tailored to your students, classroom, and texts. This chapter and this book as a whole do, however, provide a rationale, a plan, and specific techniques for powerful comprehension instruction that you can adapt to fit your classroom.

We have remarked at various points along the way on the tension between the very limited time available in school and the fact that truly deep and lasting learning requires significant time. There is simply no way around it; good instruction takes time. The approaches we describe throughout this book, if used wisely and adjusted based on your experiences and the strengths and needs of your students, can aid them in becoming adept, critical thinkers who are prepared for democratic citizenship. With a bit of creativity and a large degree of commitment, you will be able to help students better navigate our increasingly literacy-based society.

## LITERATURE/FILMS CITED

Contreras, Fred. (1991). *Black Elk speaks* (Cassette Recording No. RC 922 99856). San Bruno, CA: Audio Literature.

Costner, Kevin. (Director). (1990). *Dances with wolves* [Film]. United States: Tig Productions.

Erdoes, Richard, & Ortiz, Alfonso. (Eds.). (1984). *American Indian myths and legends*. New York: Pantheon.

Erdrich, Louise. (1984). The red convertible. *Love medicine*. New York: Holt, Rinehart & Winston.

Eyre, Chris. (Director). (1998). *Smoke signals* [Film]. United States: Shadow-Catcher Entertainment.

Mann, Michael. (Director). (1992). *Last of the Mohicans* [Film]. United States: Morgan Creek Productions.

Neihardt, John G. (1932). *Black Elk speaks*. Lincoln: University of Nebraska Press.

# References

ACT. (2006). *Reading between the lines: What the ACT reveals about college readiness in reading.* Iowa City, IA: Author.

Adams, M., & Bruce, B. (1982). Background knowledge and reading comprehension. In J. A. Langer & T. M. Smith-Burke (Eds.), *Reader meets author: Bridging the gap* (pp. 2–25). Newark, DE: International Reading Association.

Aebersold, J. A., & Field, M. L. (1997). *From reader to reading teacher: Issues and strategies for second language classrooms.* Cambridge, UK: Cambridge University Press.

Allington, R. L. (2001). *What really matters for struggling readers: Designing research-based programs.* New York: Longman.

Almasi, J. F. (2003). *Teaching strategic processes in reading.* New York: Guilford Press.

Alvermann, D. E. (1991). The discussion web: A graphic aid for learning across the curriculum. *The Reading Teacher, 45,* 92–99.

Alvermann, D. E. (2000). Classroom talk about texts: Is it dear, cheap, or a bargain at any price? In B. M. Taylor, M. F. Graves, & P. van den Broek (Eds.), *Reading for meaning: Fostering comprehension in the middle grades* (pp. 136–151). New York: Teachers College Press.

Alvermann, D. E., Hinchman, K. A., Moore, D. W., Phelps, S. F., & Waff, D. R. (2006). *Reconceptualizing the literacies in adolescents' lives* (2nd ed.). Mahwah, NJ: Erlbaum.

Anderson, L. W., & Krathwohl, D. R. (2001). *A taxonomy for learning, teaching, and assessing: A revision of Bloom's taxonomy of educational objectives.* New York: Longman.

Anderson, R. C., & Nagy, W. E. (1992, Winter). The vocabulary conundrum. *American Educator,* pp. 14–18, 44–47.

Anderson, R. C., Wilson, P. T, & Fielding, L. G. (1988). Growth in reading and how children spend their time outside of school. *Reading Research Quarterly, 23,* 285–303.

Anglin, J. M. (1993). Vocabulary development: A morphological analysis. *Monographs of the Society for Research in Child Development, 58*(Serial No. 238).

Anson, C., & Beach, R. (1995). *Journals in the classroom: Writing to learn.* Norwood, MA: Christopher-Gordon.

Applebee, A. N. (1993). *Literature in the secondary school: Studies of curriculum and instruction in the United States.* Urbana, IL: National Council of Teachers of English.

Appleman, D. (2000). *Critical encounters in high school English: Teaching literary theory to adolescents.* New York: Teachers College Press.

Appleman, D. (2006). *Reading for themselves: How to transform adolescents into lifelong readers through out-of-class book clubs.* Portsmouth, NH: Heinemann.

Aronson, E., Blaney, N., Stephan, C., Sikos, J., & Snapp, M. (1978). *The jigsaw classroom.* Newbury Park, CA: Sage.

Aronson, E., & Patnoe, S. (1997). *The jigsaw classroom* (2nd ed.). New York: HarperCollins.

Atwell, N. (1998). *In the middle: New understandings about writing, reading, and learning* (2nd ed.). Portsmouth, NH: Heinemann.

Baumann, J. F., & Kame'enui, E. J. (Eds.). (2004). *Vocabulary instruction: Research to practice.* New York: Guilford Press.

Bausch, S., & Han, L. (2006). *U.S. teens graduate from choosing im buddy icons to creating elaborate social networking profiles, according to Nielsen/netratings.* Retrieved September 14, 2007, from *www.pbs.org/mediashift/2006/10/media_usagefinding_balance_in.html.*

Beach, R. (2007). *Teachingmedialiteracy.com: A web-linked guide to resources and activities.* New York: Teachers College Press.

Beach, R., Appleman, D., Hynds, S., & Wilhelm, J. (2006). *Teaching literature to adolescents.* Mahwah, NJ: Erlbaum.

Beach, R. W. (1993). *A teacher's guide to reader-response theory.* Urbana, IL: National Council of Teachers of English.

Bean, T. W., Valerio, P. C., & Stevens, L. (1999). Content area literacy instruction. In L. B. Gambrell, L. M. Morrow, S. Newman, & M. Pressley (Eds.), *Best practices in literacy instruction* (pp. 175–192). New York: Guilford Press.

Beck, I. L., & McKeown, M. G. (1981). Developing questions that promote comprehension: The story map. *Language Arts, 58,* 913–918.

Beck, I. L., McKeown, M. G., Hamilton, R., & Kucan, L. (1997). *Questioning the author: An approach for enhancing student engagement with text.* Newark, DE: International Reading Association.

Beck, I. L., McKeown, M. G., & Kucan, L. (2002). *Bringing words to life: Robust vocabulary instruction.* New York: Guilford Press.

Biancarosa, G., & Snow, C. E. (2004). *Reading next—A vision for action and research in middle and high school literacy: A report to the Carnegie Corporation of New York.* Washington, DC: Alliance for Excellent Education.

Biemiller, A., & Boote, C. (2006). An effective method for building meaning vocabulary in primary grades. *Journal of Educational Psychology, 98,* 44–62.

Blachowicz, C. L. Z., Fisher, P. J. L, Ogle, D., & Watts-Taffe, S. (2006). Vocabulary: Questions from the classroom. *Reading Research Quarterly, 41,* 524–539.

Bloom, B. (Ed.). (1956). *Taxonomy of educational objectives.* New York: McKay.

Brophy, J. (1986). Teacher influences on student achievement. *American Psychologist, 41,* 1069–1077.

Brophy, J. (1987). Socializing students' motivation to learn. In M. L. Maehr & D. A. Kleiber (Eds.), *Advances in motivation and achievement: Enhancing motivation* (Vol. 5, pp. 181–210). Greenwich, CT: JAI Press.

Brown, A. L., & Day, J. D. (1983). Macrorules for summarizing text: The development of expertise. *Journal of Verbal Learning and Verbal Behavior, 22,* 1–14.

Burke, J. (2003). *The English teacher's companion: A complete guide to classroom, curriculum, and the profession* (2nd ed.). Portsmouth, NH: Heinemann.

Cazden, C. (1988). *Classroom discourse: The language of teaching and learning.* Portsmouth, NH: Heinemann.

Center for the Humanities. (1970). *Eye of the storm.* New York: ABC News.

Center on Instruction. (2007). *Interventions for adolescent struggling readers: A meta-analysis with implications for practice.* Portsmouth, NH: RMC Research Corporation.

Chambliss, M. J., & Calfee, R. C. (1998). *Textbooks for learning: Nurturing children's minds.* London: Blackwell.

Christenbury, L. (2000). *Making the journey: Being and becoming a teacher of English language arts* (2nd ed.). Portsmouth, NH: Heinemann.

Ciborowski, J. (1992). *Textbooks and the students who can't read them: A guide to teaching content.* Cambridge, MA: Brookline Books.

Clark, K. F., & Graves, M. F. (2005). Scaffolding students' comprehension of text. *The Reading Teacher, 56,* 570–580.

Cooke, C. L. (2002, December). *The effects of scaffolding multicultural short stories on students' comprehension and attitudes.* Paper presented at the 51st annual meeting of the National Reading Conference, Miami, FL.

Cornell University Olin & Uris Libraries. *Evaluating web sites: Criteria and tools.* Retrieved February 10, 2007, from *www.library.cornell.edu/olinuris/ref/ research/webeval.html#eval.*

ADaniels, H. (2002). *Literature circles: Voice and choice in book clubs and reading groups.* Portland, ME: Stenhouse.

Donahue, P. L., Daane, M. C., & Jin, Y. (2005). *The nation's report card: Reading 2003.* Washington, DC: U. S. Department of Education.

Dornan, R. W., Rosen, L. M., & Wilson, M. (2003). *Within and beyond the writing process in the secondary English classroom.* Boston: Allyn & Bacon.

Duke, N. K., & Pearson, P. D. (2002). Effective practices for developing reading comprehension. In S. J. Samuels & A. E. Farstrup (Eds.), *What research has to say about reading instruction* (3rd ed., pp. 203–242). Newark, DE: International Reading Association.

Echevarria, J., Vogt, M., & Short, D. R. (2004). *Making content comprehensible for English language learners: The SIOP model* (2nd ed.). Boston: Allyn & Bacon.

Eddleston, S. (1998). *Whole-class discussions of literature: What students and their teacher say in and about them.* Unpublished doctoral dissertation, University of Minnesota, Minneapolis.

Eddleston, S., & Philippot, R. (2002). Implementing whole-class literature discussions: An overview of the teacher's roles. In J. Holden & J. Schmit (Eds.), *Inquiry and the literary text: Constructing discussions in the English classroom* (pp. 49–59). Urbana, IL: National Council of Teachers of English.

Eeds, M., & Cockrun, W. (1985). Teaching word meanings by expanding schemata vs. dictionary work vs. reading in context. *Journal of Reading, 28,* 492–497.

Elbow, P. (1973). *Writing without teachers.* New York: Oxford University Press.

Elley, W. B. (1996). Using book floods to raise literacy levels in developing countries. In V. Greaney (Ed.), *Promoting reading in developing countries* (pp. 148–162). Newark, DE: International Reading Association.

Elliot, A. J., & Dweck, C. S. (Eds.). (2005). *Handbook of competence and motivation.* New York: Guilford Press.

Fish, S. (1980). *Is there a text in this class?: The authority of interpretive communities.* Cambridge, MA: Harvard University Press.

Fitzgerald, J., & Graves, M. F. (2004). *Scaffolding reading experiences for English-language learners.* Norwood, MA: Christopher-Gordon.

Fitzgerald, J., & Graves, M. F. (2004–2005). Reading supports for all. *Educational Leadership, 62*(4), 68–71.

Fosnot, C. T. (1996). *Constructivism: Theory, perspectives, and practice.* New York: Teachers College Press.

Fountas, I. C., & Pinnell, G. S. (1996). *Guided reading: Good first teaching for all students.* Portsmouth, NH: Heinemann.

Fournier, D. N. E., & Graves, M. F. (2002). Scaffolding adolescents' comprehension of short stories. *Journal of Adolescent and Adult Literacy, 40,* 30–39.

Fulkerson, R. (1979). Four philosophies of composition. *College Composition and Communication, 30,* 343–348.

Galda, L., & Graves, M. F. (2007). *Reading and responding in the middle grades: Approaches for all classrooms.* Boston: Allyn & Bacon.

Galda, L., & Guice, S. (1997). Response-based reading instruction in the elementary grades. In S. A. Stahl & D. A. Hayes (Eds.), *Instructional models in reading* (pp. 311–330). Hillsdale, NJ: Erlbaum.

Gambrell, L. B., & Almasi, J. E. (1996). *Lively discussions! Fostering engaged reading.* Newark, DE: International Reading Association.

Garner, R. (1987). *Metacognition and reading comprehension.* Norwood, NJ: Ablex.

Gaskins, I. W. (2005). *Success with struggling readers: The Benchmark School approach.* New York: Guilford Press.

Gavalek, J. R., Raphael, T. E., Biondo, S. M., & Wang, D. (2000). Integrated literacy instruction. In M. Kamil, P. Mosenthal, P. D. Pearson, & R. Barr (Eds.), *Handbook of reading research* (Vol. 3, pp. 587–607). Mahwah, NJ: Erlbaum.

Gergen, K. J. (1985). The social constructionist movement in modern psychology. *American Psychologist, 40,* 266–275.

Gibbons, P. (2002). *Scaffolding language, scaffolding learning: Teaching second language learners in the mainstream classroom.* Portsmouth, NH: Heinemann.

Golden, J. (2001). *Reading in the dark: Using film as a tool in the English classroom.* Urbana, IL: National Council of Teachers of English.

Good, T., & Brophy, J. (2003). *Looking in classrooms* (9th ed.). Boston: Allyn & Bacon.

Graves, M. F. (2000). A vocabulary program to complement and bolster a middle-grade comprehension program. In B. M. Taylor, M. F. Graves, & P. van den Broek (Eds.), *Reading for meaning: Fostering comprehension in the middle grades* (pp. 116–135). New York: Teachers College Press.

Graves, M. F. (2006). *The vocabulary book.* New York: Teachers College Press, International Reading Association, National Council of Teachers of English.

Graves, M. F. (2007). Conceptual and empirical bases for providing struggling readers with multi-faceted and long-term vocabulary instruction. To appear in B. M. Taylor & J. Ysseldyke (Eds.), *Educational perspectives on struggling readers* (pp. 55–83). New York: Teachers College Press.

Graves, M. F., & Graves, B. B. (2003). *Scaffolding reading experiences: Designs for student success* (2nd ed.). Norwood, MA: Christopher-Gordon.

Graves, M. F., Juel, C., & Graves, B. (2007). *Teaching reading in the 21st century* (4th ed.). Boston: Allyn & Bacon.

Graves, M. F., & Liang, L. A. (2003). On-line resources for fostering understanding and higher-level thinking in senior high school students. In D. L. Schallert, C. M. Fairbanks, J. Worthy, B. Maloch, & J. V. Hoffman (Eds.), *51st yearbook of the National Reading Conference* (pp. 204–215). Oak Creek, WI: National Reading Conference.

Graves, M. F., Prenn, M. C., & Cooke, C. L. (1985). The coming attraction: Previewing short stories to increase comprehension. *Journal of Reading, 28,* 549–598.

Graves, M. F., & Sales, G. (2006). *Digging reading: Teaching reading comprehension strategies.* Minneapolis: Seward.

Graves, M. F., & Watts-Taffe, S. M. (2002). The place of word consciousness in a research-based vocabulary program. In S. J. Samuels & A. E. Farstrup (Eds.), *What research has to say about reading instruction* (3rd ed., pp. 140–165). Newark, DE: International Reading Association.

Hart, B., & Risley, T. R. (2003, Spring). The early catastrophe: The 30 million word gap by age 3. *American Educator, 27*(1), 4–9.

Hayes, D. P., & Ahrens, M. (1988). Vocabulary simplification for children. *Journal of Child Language, 15,* 395–410.

Heimlich, J. E., & Pittelman, S. D. (1986). *Semantic mapping: Classroom applications.* Newark, DE: International Reading Association.

Ippolito, J., Steele, J. L., & Samson, J. F. (2008). Adolescent literacy. *Harvard Educational Review, 78*, 1–280.

Jenkins, H. (2006). *Confronting the challenge of participatory culture: Media education for the 21st century.* Retrieved July 15, 2007, from *www.digitallearning.macfound.org*.

Johnson, D. W., Johnson, R. T., & Holubec, E. J. (1994). *The new circles of learning: Cooperation in the classroom.* Alexandria, VA: Association for Supervision and Curriculum Development.

Kent, T. (1993). *Paralogic rhetoric.* London: Associated University Press.

Kim, J., & White, T. G. (in press). Scaffolding voluntary summer reading for children in grades 3 to 5: An experimental study. *Scientific Studies of Reading.*

Langer, J. (1986). Learning through writing: Study skills in the content areas. *Journal of Reading, 29*, 400–406.

Langer, J., & Applebee, A. N. (1987). *How writing shapes thinking: A study of teaching and learning.* Urbana, IL: National Council of Teachers of English.

Langer, J. A. (2001). Beating the odds: Teaching middle and high school students to read and write well. *American Educational Research Journal, 38*, 837–880.

Lenhart, A., & Madden, M. (2005). *Teen content creators and consumers.* Retrieved June 2, 2007, from *www.pewinternet.org/PPF/r/166/report_display.asp*.

Lenhart, A., Madden, M., & Hitlin, P. (2005). *Teens and technology: Youth are leading the transition to a fully wired and mobile nation.* Retrieved February 12, 2007, from *www.pewinternet.org/PPF/r/162/report_display.asp*.

Liang, L. A. (2004). *Using scaffolding to foster middle school students' comprehension and response to short stories.* Unpublished doctoral dissertation, University of Minnesota, Minneapolis.

Liang, L. A., Peterson, C., & Graves, M. F. (2005). Investigating two approaches to fostering children's comprehension of literature. *Reading Psychology, 26*, 387–400.

Manguel, A. (1996). *A history of reading.* New York: Penguin.

Marshall, J. D., Smagorinsky, P., & Smith, M. W. (1995). *The language of interpretation: Patterns of discourse in discussions of literature.* Urbana, IL: National Council of Teachers of English.

Marzano, R. J. (2004). *Building background knowledge for academic achievement.* Alexandria, VA: Association for Supervision and Curriculum Development.

McTighe, J., Seif, E., & Wiggins, G. (2004). You can teach for meaning. *Educational Leadership, 62*(1), 26–30.

Miller, G. A., & Wakefield, P. C. (1993). Commentary on Anglin's analysis of vocabulary growth. In J. M. Anglin, Vocabulary development: A morphological analysis. *Monographs of the Society for Research in Child Development, 59*(10), 167–175.

Milner, J. O., & Milner, L. F. M. (2003). *Bridging English* (3rd ed.). Upper Saddle River, NJ: Pearson Education.

Moore, D. W., Bean, T. H., Birdyshaw, D., & Rycik, J. A. (1999). *Adolescent lit-*

*eracy: A position statement.* Newark, DE: International Reading Association Commission on Adolescent Literacy.

Moore, J. N. (1997). *Interpreting young adult literature: Literary theory in the secondary classroom.* Portsmouth, NH: Heinemann.

Nagy, W. E. (2006). Metalinguistic awareness and the vocabulary-comprehension connection. In R. K. Wagner, A. E. Muse, & K. R. Tannenbaum (Eds.), *Vocabulary acquisition: Implications for reading comprehension* (pp. 27–44). New York: Guilford Press.

Nagy, W. E., & Anderson, R. C. (1984). How many words are there in printed school English? *Reading Research Quarterly, 19,* 304–330.

Nagy, W. E., & Herman, P. A. (1987). Breadth and depth of vocabulary knowledge: Implications for acquisition and instruction. In M. C. McKeown & M. E. Curtis (Eds.), *The nature of vocabulary acquisition* (pp. 19–35). Hillsdale, NJ: Erlbaum.

National Association of State Boards of Education. (2005). *Reading at risk: The report of the NASBE study group on middle and high school literacy.* Alexandria, VA: Author.

National Center for Education Statistics. (2005). *NAEP 2005: Reading: Report card for the nation and the states.* Washington, DC: U.S. Department of Education, Office of Education Research and Improvement.

National Council of Teachers of English and International Reading Association. (1996). *Standards for the English language arts.* Retrieved October 7, 2007, from *www.ncte.org/about/over/standards/110846.htm.*

National Council of Teachers of English Commission on Reading. (2004). *A call to action: What we know about adolescent literacy and ways to support teachers in meeting students' needs.* Urbana, IL: National Council of Teachers of English.

National Reading Panel. (2000). *Report of the National Reading Panel: Teaching children to read* (NIH Report No. 00-4769). Bethesda, MD: National Institute of Child Health and Human Development.

National Research Council. (2004). *Engaging schools: Fostering high school students' motivation to learn.* Washington, DC: The National Academies Press.

Newmann, F. N. (1996). *Authentic achievement: Restructuring schools for intellectual quality.* San Francisco: Jossey-Bass.

Newmann, F. N. (2000). Authentic intellectual work: What and why? *Research/ Practice, 8*(1), 15–20.

New Media Consortium. (2005). *A global imperative: The report of the 21st century literacy summit.* Retrieved November 8, 2007, from *www.nmc.org/pdf/ Global_Imperative.pdf.*

Ogle, D. (1986). K–W–L: A teaching model that develops active reading of expository text. *The Reading Teacher, 39,* 564–570.

Opitz, M. F., & Rasinski, T. (1998). *Goodbye round robin.* Portsmouth, NH: Heinemann.

Organisation of Economic Co-operation and Development. (2004). *Learning for tomorrow's world: First results from PISA 2003.* Paris: Author.

Palincsar, A. S., & Brown, A. L. (1984). Reciprocal teaching of comprehension and monitoring activities. *Cognition and Instruction, 1*(2), 117–175.

Pearson, P. D. (2005, November). *Assessing reading comprehension and vocabulary development.* Paper presented at Minnesota Center for Reading Research, St. Paul, MN.

Pearson, P. D., & Gallagher, M. (1983). The instruction of reading comprehension. *Contemporary Educational Psychology, 8,* 317–344.

Pearson, P. D., Roehler, L. R., Dole, J. A., & Duffy, G. G. (1992). Developing expertise in reading comprehension. In S. J. Samuels & A. E. Farstrup (Eds.), *What research has to say about reading instruction* (2nd ed., pp. 145–199). Newark, DE: International Reading Association.

Perie, M., Grigg, W., & Donahue, P. (2006). *The nation's report card: Reading 2005.* Washington, DC: U.S. Department of Education.

Perkins, D. (2004). Knowledge alive. *Educational Leadership, 62*(1), 14–18.

Perkins, D. H. (1986). *Knowledge as design.* Hillsdale, NJ: Erlbaum.

Perkins, D. H. (1992). *Smart schools: From training memories to educating minds.* New York: The Free Press.

Phelps, S. (2005). *Ten years of research on adolescent literacy, 1994–2004: A review.* Naperville, IL: Learning Point Associates.

Pirie, B. (1997). *Reshaping high school English.* Urbana, IL: National Council of Teachers of English.

Prawat, R. S. (1989). Teaching for understanding: Three key attributes. *Teaching and Teacher Education, 5,* 315–328.

Pressley, M. (2000). What should comprehension instruction be the instruction of? In M. Kamil, P. Mosenthal, P. D. Pearson, & R. Barr (Eds.), *Handbook of reading research* (Vol. 3, 545–561). Mahwah, NJ: Erlbaum.

Pressley, M. (2006). *Reading instruction that works: The case for balanced teaching* (3rd ed.). New York: Guilford Press.

RAND Reading Study Group. (2002). *Reading for understanding: Toward an R&D program in reading comprehension.* Santa Monica, CA: RAND Education.

Ranson, J. C. (1941). *The new criticism.* Norfolk, CT: New Direction.

Readence, J. E., Moore, D. W., & Rickelman, R. J. (2000). *Prereading activities for content area reading and learning* (3rd ed.). Newark, DE: International Reading Association.

Resnick, L. B. (1987). *Education and learning to think.* Washington, DC: New Academy Press.

Richards, I. A. (1929). *Practical criticism.* New York: Harcourt Brace.

Richardson, J. S. (2000). *Read it aloud: Using literature in the secondary content classroom.* Newark, DE: International Reading Association.

Romano, T. (2000). *Blending genre, altering style: Writing multigenre papers.* Portsmouth, NH: Heinemann.

Rosenblatt, L. (1938/1995). *Literature as exploration* (5th ed.). New York: Modern Language Association.

Rosenblatt, L. M. (1978). *The reader, the text, the poem: The transactional theory of the literary work.* Carbondale: Southern Illinois University.

Rothenberg, S. S., & Watts, S. M. (1997). Students with learning difficulties meet Shakespeare: Using a scaffolded reading experience. *Journal of Adolescent and Adult Literacy, 40,* 532–539.

Rumelhart, D. E. (1977). Toward an interactive model of reading. In S. Dornic (Ed.), *Attention and performance* (Vol. 6, pp. 573–603). Hillsdale, NJ: Erlbaum.

Rumelhart, D. E. (1980). Schemata: The building blocks of cognition. In R. J. Spiro, B. C. Bruce, & W. F. Brewer (Eds.), *Theoretical issues in reading comprehension* (pp. 33–58). Hillsdale, NJ: Erlbaum.

Schoenbach, R., Greenleaf, C., Cziko, C., & Hurwitz, L. (1999). *Reading for understanding: A guide to improving reading in middle and high school classes.* San Francisco: Jossey-Bass.

Scriven, M., & Paul, R. (n.d.). A working definition of critical thinking. Retrieved August 6, 2007, from *lonestar.texas.net/~mseifert/crit2.html.*

Silvey, A. (2006). *500 great books for teens.* Boston: Houghton-Mifflin.

Slavin, R. E. (1987). *Cooperative learning: Student teams* (2nd ed.). Washington, DC: National Education Association.

Smith, F. (1990). *To think.* New York: Teachers College Press.

Spandel, V. (2001). *Creating writers through 6-trait writing assessment and instruction* (3rd ed.). New York: Longman.

Spandel, V. (2004). *Creating writers through 6-trait assessment and instruction* (4th ed.). Boston: Allyn & Bacon.

Stahl, S. A., & Nagy, W. E. (2006). *Teaching word meanings.* Mahwah, NJ: Erlbaum.

Stahl, S. A., & Stahl, K. D. (2004). Word wizards all!: Teaching word meanings in preschool and primary education. In J. F. Baumann & E. B. Kame'enui (Eds.). *Vocabulary instruction: Research to practice* (pp. 59–78). New York: Guilford Press.

Stanovich, K. E. (1994). Constructivism in reading education. *The Journal of Special Education, 28,* 259–274.

Sternberg, R. J., & Spear-Swerling, L. (1996). *Teaching for thinking.* Washington, DC: American Psychological Association.

Strickland, K., & Strickland, J. (2002). *Engaged in learning: Teaching English, 6–12.* Portsmouth, NH: Heinemann.

Swanson, A. (2003). Scaffolded reading experience for fostering higher-order reading and comprehension skills with "the red convertible" from *love medicine* by Louise Erdrich. Retrieved September 16, 2007, from *www.sewardinc.com/olrr/search/results.asp.*

Thornburg, D. (2003). *Building critical thinking skills for online research.* Retrieved February 13, 2007, from *teacherline.pbs.org/teacherline/resources/thornburg/thornburg0803.cfm.*

Tierney, R. J., & Readence, J. E. (2005). *Reading strategies and practices: A compendium* (6th ed.). Boston: Allyn & Bacon.

Tomlinson, C. A. (2003). *Fulfilling the promise of the differentiated classroom: Strategies and tools for responsive teaching.* Alexandria, VA: Association for Supervision and Curriculum Development.

Tomlinson, C. A., & Strickland, C. A. (2005). *Differentiation in practice: A resource guide for differentiating curriculum, grades 9–12.* Alexandria, VA: Association for Supervision and Curriculum Development.

Tyson, L. (1999). *Critical theory today: A user-friendly guide.* New York: Garland.

University of California—Berkeley Library. *Evaluating web pages: Techniques to apply and questions to ask.* Retrieved July 31, 2007, from *www.lib.berkeley.edu/ TeachingLib/Guides/Internet/Evaluate.html.*

Voss, S. (2003). Scaffolded reading experience for fostering higher-order reading and comprehension skills with *Black Elk* speaks by John Neihardt. Retrieved October 8, 2007, from *www.sewardinc.com/olrr/search/results.asp.*

Vygotsky, L. S. (1978). *Mind in society: The development of higher psychological processes.* Cambridge, MA: Harvard University Press.

Whimby, A. (1975). *Intelligence can be taught.* New York: Dutton.

White, T. G., Graves, M. F., & Slater, W. H. (1990). Growth of reading vocabulary in diverse elementary schools: Decoding and word meaning. *Journal of Educational Psychology, 82,* 281–290.

White, T. G., Sowell, J., & Yanagihara, A. (1989). Teaching elementary students to use word-part clues. *The Reading Teacher, 42,* 302–308.

Wiggins, G., & McTighe, J. (1998). *Understanding by design.* Alexandria, VA: Association for Supervision and Curriculum Development.

Wilhelm, J. (2002). *Action strategies for deepening comprehension.* New York: Scholastic.

Wiske, M. S. (1998). *Teaching for understanding: Linking research with practice.* San Francisco: Jossey-Bass.

Wittrock, M. C. (1974). Learning as a generative process. *Educational Psychologist, 11,* 87–95.

Wittrock, M. C. (1991). Generative teaching of comprehension. *The Elementary School Journal, 92,* 169–184.

Wood, D. J., Bruner, J. S., & Ross, G. (1976). The role of tutoring in problem solving. *Journal of Child Psychology and Psychiatry, 17*(2), 89–100.

Wood, K. D., Lapp, D., & Flood, J. (1992). *Guiding readers through text: A review of study guides.* Newark, DE: International Reading Association.

Yopp, R. H., & Yopp, H. K. (1992). *Literature-based reading activities.* Boston: Allyn & Bacon.

# Index

Page numbers in italics indicate figures or tables.